Creative Labour

What is it like to work in the media? Are media jobs more 'creative' than those in other sectors? To answer these questions, this book explores the creative industries, using a combination of original research and a synthesis of existing studies.

Through its close analysis of key issues – such as tensions between commerce and creativity, the conditions and experiences of workers, alienation, autonomy, self-realisation, emotional and affective labour, self-exploitation, and how possible it might be to produce 'good work' – *Creative Labour* makes a major contribution to our understanding of the media, of work, and of social and cultural change. In addition, the book undertakes an extensive exploration of the creative industries, spanning numerous sectors including television, music and journalism.

This book provides a comprehensive and accessible account of life in the creative industries in the twenty-first century. It is a major piece of research and a valuable study aid for both undergraduate and postgraduate students of subjects including business and management studies, sociology of work, sociology of culture, and media and communications.

David Hesmondhalgh is Head of the Institute of Communications Studies at the University of Leeds, where he is Professor of Media and Music Industries, and Director of the Media Industries Research Centre (MIRC). His publications include *The Cultural Industries* (2nd edition, 2007).

Sarah Baker is Lecturer in Cultural Sociology at Griffith University, Australia. She has previously held research fellowships at The Open University and University of Leeds, UK, and the University of South Australia. She is the author of numerous refereed journal articles and book chapters.

Culture, Economy and the Social

A new series from CRESC – the ESRC Centre for Research on Socio-cultural Change

The *Culture, Economy and the Social* series is committed to innovative contemporary, comparative and historical work on the relations between social, cultural and economic change. It publishes empirically based research that is theoretically informed, that critically examines the ways in which social, cultural and economic change is framed and made visible, and that is attentive to perspectives that tend to be ignored or side-lined by grand theorising or epochal accounts of social change. The series addresses the diverse manifestations of contemporary capitalism, and considers the various ways in which the 'social', 'the cultural' and 'the economic' are apprehended as tangible sites of value and practice. It is explicitly comparative, publishing books that work across disciplinary perspectives, cross-culturally, or across different historical periods.

The series is actively engaged in the analysis of the different theoretical traditions that have contributed to the development of the 'cultural turn' with a view to clarifying where these approaches converge and where they diverge on a particular issue. It is equally concerned to explore the new critical agendas emerging from current critiques of the cultural turn: those associated with the descriptive turn for example. Our commitment to interdisciplinarity thus aims at enriching theoretical and methodological discussion, building awareness of the common ground that has emerged in the past decade, and thinking through what is at stake in those approaches that resist integration to a common analytical model.

Series titles include:
The Media and Social Theory (2008)
Edited by David Hesmondhalgh and Jason Toynbee

Culture Class Distinction (2009)
Tony Bennett, Mike Savage, Elizabeth Bortolaia Silva, Alan Warde,
Modesto Gayo-Cal and David Wright

Material Powers (2010)
Edited by Tony Bennett and Patrick Joyce

The Social after Gabriel Tarde (2010)
Debates and assessments
Edited by Matei Candea

Cultural Analysis and Bourdieu's Legacy (2010)
Edited by Elizabeth Silva and Alan Warde

Milk, Modernity and the Making of the Human (2010)
Richie Nimmo

Creative Labour (2010)
Media work in three cultural industries
David Hesmondhalgh and Sarah Baker

Inventive Methods (forthcoming)
The happening of the social
Edited by Celia Lury and Nina Wakeford

Rio de Janeiro (forthcoming)
Urban life through the eyes of the city
Beatriz Jaguaribe

E·S·R·C
ECONOMIC
& SOCIAL
RESEARCH
COUNCIL

CRESC
Centre for Research on
Socio-Cultural Change

Creative Labour

Media work in three cultural industries

David Hesmondhalgh and
Sarah Baker

Routledge
Taylor & Francis Group

LONDON AND NEW YORK

First published 2011
by Routledge
2 Park Square, Milton Park, Abingdon, Oxon OX14 4RN

Simultaneously published in the USA and Canada
by Routledge
711 Third Avenue, New York, NY 10017

Routledge is an imprint of the Taylor & Francis Group, an Informa business

First issued in paperback 2011

Typeset in Times New Roman by Glyph International Ltd.

British Library Cataloguing in Publication Data
A catalogue record for this book is available from the British Library

Library of Congress Cataloging in Publication Data
Hesmondhalgh, David, 1963–
Creative labour : media work in three cultural industries / by David
Hesmondhalgh and Sarah Baker.
    p. cm.
Includes bibliographical references.
1. Cultural industries–Social aspects. 2. Mass media–Employees.
3. Creativity. 4. Labor–Social aspects. I. Baker, Sarah, 1977– II. Title.
HD9999.C9472H47 2010
331.7'9–dc22   2010010442

ISBN10: 0-415-57260-6 (hbk)
ISBN10: 0-415-67773-4 (pbk)
ISBN10: 0-203-85588-4 (ebk)

ISBN13: 978-0-415-57260-6 (hbk)
ISBN13: 978-0-415-67773-8 (pbk)
ISBN13: 978-0-203-85588-1 (ebk)

Contents

Acknowledgements

This research was funded by the UK Arts and Humanities Research Council (AHRC) under a research grant (number 112075) awarded to David Hesmondhalgh, from January 2006 to January 2008. The completion of the writing of the book was made possible by research leave given by the Institute of Communications Studies at the University of Leeds, and a research leave award from the AHRC, both in 2009. Some of the project was carried out at the Open University, some at the University of Leeds. Thanks to those who work at the AHRC, and various university administrative staff, for making such research grants possible.

Material from Chapters 5 and 7 have appeared elsewhere, respectively:

- Hesmondhalgh, D. and Baker, S. (2010) ' "A very complicated version of freedom": conditions and experiences of creative labour in three cultural industries', *Poetics*, vol. 38, no. 1: 4–20.
- Hesmondhalgh, D. and Baker, S. (2008) 'Creative work and emotional labour in the television industry', *Theory, Culture and Society*, vol. 25, no. 7–8: 97–118.

We are grateful to the editors of the journals for permission to use this material.

We would like to thank the following for their comments on ideas, proposals and issues that eventually shaped this book, and for other contributions: Mark Banks, Ros Gill, Peter Golding, Helen Kennedy, Vicki Mayer, Justin O'Connor, Andy Pratt, Matt Stahl and Anna Zoellner. Thanks especially to Des Freedman, Teresa Gowan and Jason Toynbee for their invaluable comments on drafts of some chapters. The book also benefited enormously from comments made by audience members at conferences and seminars where we presented our ideas, and from discussions with undergraduate and postgraduate students in classes at the University of Leeds.

Thanks too to Tony Bennett for his support for the project, from its inception at the Open University, to the publication of this book as part of the CRESC series, and to Stephen Coleman, Gary Rawnsley and Graham Roberts for helping to enable study leave at Leeds.

We are very grateful to all the people who agreed to be interviewed or observed for this book, and to the independent television company that allowed Sarah to work on its talent show for a few months in 2007. Thanks also to various friends, and friends of friends, who helped set up initial contacts, especially Angela Vermond, who got us started.

And of course our thanks to the families and friends that sustain us during our work. The irony of working very hard on a project about the problems of creative work has not escaped us. Please forgive us if we don't name all the people who kept us going through the years of researching and writing this book. But Dave would like to mention new Yorkshire mates who made the Big Move North conducted in the middle of this research so much easier than it might otherwise have been, including Duncan Cooper, Simon East, Kev Grant and Steve Parker. Thanks to creative workers Joolz and Kersh and possible future creative workers Rosa Hesmondhalgh and Joe Hesmondhalgh for their inspiring examples, to Mum and Dad for their unwavering love, and Helen Steward for her graceful and intelligent commitment to quality of life, at work and everywhere else.

Sarah would like to thank the research fellows of CRESC for their support and friendship during her time at the Open University, especially David Wright for being such a wonderful office-buddy. And to good mates Melissa Chapman and Charles Holloway who always made her feel like she wasn't so far from home.

Dave would like to dedicate this book to the memory of Gary Conway (1961–2009). Gary was a painter and decorator who lived in Oxford all his life. He liked his job well enough, and he did it excellently. He loved knowledge and learning, and he loved life. That life was cruelly taken away from him by a brain tumour. He will never be forgotten by the many people who loved him.

David Hesmondhalgh, Ilkley, Yorkshire
Sarah Baker, Gold Coast, Queensland
February 2010

1 Introduction
Can creative labour be good work?

1.1 Good and bad work in the cultural industries

It is often wisely said that there's more to life than work. But work takes up huge amounts of people's time and energy. It has the capacity to absorb and enrich us, and it can be experienced as futile or degrading. The quality of working life matters, and so does the relationship of work to well-being.

For many people nowadays, the degree to which their job offers the chance for them to be creative is an important feature of its quality. People can of course be creative in any kind of work but some types of employment are commonly thought to offer greater possibilities for creativity than others. Because of the special association of creativity with 'art', amongst them are occupations that are primarily aesthetic and expressive, perhaps most obviously in 'the arts' (painting, sculpture and literature and so on) but more prominently in the television, film, music and publishing businesses, in the various institutions known as 'the media'. A term commonly used for this mixture of commercial and publicly subsidised enterprises is the *cultural industries*.

The research *problem* this book explores is, put simply, to what extent is it possible to do good work in the cultural industries? We explore this problem by drawing upon research we ourselves conducted in three major cultural industries: television, magazine journalism and music.[1] The research *question* we sought to answer emphasises the quality of subjective experience. What kinds of experiences do jobs and occupations in the cultural industries offer their workers?[2]

As we shall see, the nature of work in the cultural industries is an issue that has rightly concerned a growing corpus of researchers of creative labour, especially those influenced by cultural studies. Strangely though this body of research has paid at most only sporadic attention to thinking about labour more generally, be it the long history of reflection on this vital domain of

---

1 See the Acknowledgements for more details of the length and funding of this research, and Sections 1.5 and 1.6 below for the research design and methods.
2 On the difference between research problems and research questions, see Alford (1998).

human activity (Tilgher 1931) or academic research fields such as the sociology of work, social and political theory, or organisation, business and management studies. Conversely, with some exceptions, these academic research fields have not examined the cultural industries much.[3] Given the seeming special desirability of work in the cultural industries, these fields of research, and policy-makers and activists, might benefit from analysis of this specific area of employment. The book aims to bring these areas of analysis into mutual dialogue as a way of advancing our understanding of creative work, and of the difficult concepts of *good and bad work*. Because our focus is cultural industries, that requires special attention to the concept of culture and why it might be the object of utopian aspirations for the work we do.[4] We hope then that this is more than just a study of work in the cultural industries. We have aimed to produce a study of jobs that are considered particularly desirable in the times in which we live.

This chapter explains our approach and methods, clarifies definitions, and lays out what follows in the rest of the book. First though, we explain why we think the issue of creative labour in the cultural industries is a pressing one. We do so by explaining some of the political, economic and cultural circumstances surrounding the rise of what has been called a *doctrine of creativity* in recent years. Part of our purpose is to acknowledge that the terms 'creativity' and 'creative' have been abused and over-used. It will become clear that we nevertheless feel that they still refer to issues of great importance concerning the potential value of culture in people's lives. To sceptics, we would also say that to point to the motherhood-and-apple-pie banality of many uses of the term 'creativity' is nothing new. As the great Welsh writer Raymond Williams put it many years ago, 'No word carries a more consistently positive reference than "creative"' (1965/1961: 19). But Williams continued his sentence: 'and obviously we should be glad of this, when we think of the values it seeks to express and the activities it offers to describe'. Those activities include the making of products that entertain, inform and even enlighten us, and the values potentially bound up in the term include the idea that, when done well, such products might enrich our lives and make the world a better place to be. This is not romanticism or mysticism; nor is it elitism. Our interest in the work behind cultural production is motivated by the same commitment to equality, social justice, well-being, and the democratisation of creativity that motivated Williams.

---

3 We consider some of the exceptions in Chapter 3. A recent contribution from organisation, business and management studies is an edited collection by McKinlay and Smith (2009), which was published a few months after we signed the contract to write this book, and which, we discovered to our alarm a few weeks before we completed this manuscript, bears a very similar title to ours! It has useful contributions on employment issues, but is less concerned with creativity and culture than our perspective (again, see Chapter 3).

4 We also intend this as a push in the direction of developing what Michael Denning has called 'a labor theory of culture' (Denning 2004: 90–6).

1.2 Creativity as doctrine

To create is simply to bring something into being. 'Produce' has a similar meaning but 'create' has strong implications of newness, invention, innovation, making something afresh. Originally applied to divine intervention, the word 'creative' became increasingly attached to art, thought and learning from the nineteenth century. The recent fetishisation of creativity in policy and academia draws on the prestige attached to these spheres in sections of nearly all societies and civilisations.[5]

How did the concept of creativity come to be the object of such reverence? Psychologists showed great interest in the term from the mid twentieth century.[6] But it has been the attention of two groups in particular that has been decisive in making creativity a key word of the last three decades (1980 to 2010). One group consisted of management analysts, seeking in psychological theories the secrets of innovation and motivation as sources of competitive advantage. In the late 1950s, human relations management took up the ideas of humanist psychotherapists (McGregor 1960). By the 1980s, the booming academic fields of organisation, business and management studies were increasingly seeking in the concept of creativity a way of combining pursuit of the bottom line with a higher purpose.[7] The other group was economists. Economic theories of endogenous growth, central to much governmental economic planning over the last twenty years (Aghion et al. 1998), assign a central role to idea generation, creativity and knowledge, and see human creativity as the 'ultimate inexhaustible source of growth' (Menger 2006: 801).[8]

Economic and management thinking had a direct impact on policy in the 1990s. In an era where government increasingly took many of its cues from business fashion, think tanks were soon portraying creativity as a key source of prosperity in the post-industrial city (Landry and Bianchini 1995) – a line of thinking eventually turned into zealous advocacy by some (Florida 2002). By the 2000s, in the words of Philip Schlesinger (2007: 378), creativity had become not merely a discourse but a *doctrine* for policy-makers, 'an object of unceasing advocacy by its proponents'. While in business and management studies creativity may now be a little beyond its fashionable peak, its effects in public policy continue to resonate. It is not unusual these days to hear of a

---

5 We discuss the ambivalent social status of art and knowledge as part of our discussion of the specificity of creative labour in Chapter 3.5.
6 The term gained some social-scientific credibility from the interest shown in it by cognitive psychologists such as Guilford (1950) and psychotherapists such as Maslow (1987/1954) and Rogers (1954). Koestler (1964) and others popularised the concept.
7 Writers who have had a strong influence on the dissemination of creativity as a key idea in organisations and management include Teresa Amabile (e.g., 1996) and Tom Peters (e.g., 1997). See Prichard (2002) for a critique of discourses of creative management.
8 Such theories have many of their roots in Schumpeterian ideas of how capitalist creative destruction is founded on entrepreneurial innovation (see Schumpeter 1994/1943).

shift to innovation from creativity in policy discourse, but most of the same issues still apply.

The term 'cultural industries' had been widely used from the 1960s onwards, by sociologists and progressive policy-makers. But in the wake of economics and management's celebration of creativity, policy-makers in the 1990s began to prefer the formulation *creative industries* and new definitions that included such heterogeneous activities as architecture and antiques, designer fashion and film (DCMS 1998). Software was also included, and this allowed the sector to be presented as an area of special growth.[9] For many politicians, 'culture' was a confusing word, redolent of vague and abstract theories. In the UK context for example it carried a continental European flavour that was often considered too pungent for British tastes. Creativity was a blander term: few would wish to take a strong stance against it.

Creative industries initiatives are in many respects versions of employment and education policies that have long aimed to replace the steadily declining role of manufacturing in national economies, under names such as 'the information society' and 'the knowledge economy' (see Garnham 2005). This is apparent in this extract from a 1997 article by the then British Prime Minister Tony Blair, who was justifying his government's strategy of directing significant resources towards the development of creative industries:

> Britain was once the workshop of the world ... It was defined by ship-building, mining and heavy industry ... Once again Britain can claim to be leading the way. We can say with pride that we are the 'design work-shop of the world' – leading a creative revolution.
>
> (quoted in Blair et al. 2001: 170)

The focus on creativity is by no means just a parochial British matter. In the People's Republic of China, creative industries policy is now incorporated into the five-year plans of various cities, including Beijing, Shanghai and Nanjing (Ross 2009: 53). As Andrew Ross (2009: 43) points out, there are material influences behind the international spread of creative industries policies, in particular their relationship with the increasing importance of intellectual property, and with urban property markets, through dynamics of 'regeneration' and gentrification. Also, compared with other policy areas, such policies could be implemented cheaply, and easily marketed as benign interventions.

---

9 See Garnham (2005), Hesmondhalgh (2007: 11–25, 2008), O'Connor (2007) and Throsby (2008) for discussions of the development of the terms 'cultural industries' and 'creative industries', including varying definitions. Putting aside the many difficulties of classification and measurement, the size of the cultural industries – the main employers of creative labour as we define it here – is growing steadily, though more slowly than many of the more excitable commentators on this topic would have us believe (see Hesmondhalgh 2007: 177–84).

These policies have explicitly aimed to increase the number of jobs centred on symbol making in modern economies. Crucially, these creative jobs have been presented by policy-makers and other commentators as desirable not only because of their economic benefits, but also because they supposedly offer greater fulfilment and self-actualisation than other kinds of work. This extract from a publication called *Your Creative Future*, issued by the Department of Media, Culture and Sport, the Design Council and the Arts Council of England, offers a particularly wide-eyed version of such thinking:

> Just imagine how good it feels to wake up every morning and really look forward to work. Imagine how good it feels to use your creativity, your skills, your talent to produce a film [...] or to edit a magazine [...] Are you there? Does it feel good?
>
> (cited in Nixon and Crewe 2004: 129)

Recently, there has been a shift in creative industries policies, now rebranded under names such as 'creative economy' (Howkins 2001). In the UK at least, these recent initiatives are increasingly driven by a narrowly focused skills and employability agenda, which pays little attention to negative aspects of creative labour markets (see Banks and Hesmondhalgh 2009).

Academics too have continued to celebrate creative work, and not only in management and economics. In his influential and widely read 2002 book on *The Rise of the Creative Class*, the geographer Richard Florida discusses why young people do not want to go into skilled craft jobs but instead want to work in creative jobs. Florida has a very broad definition of creative work, and the example he gives is working in a hair salon:

> Sure, the pay isn't as good, but the environment is more stimulating. It's more flexible; it's clean; you're scheduled to meet your clients and then left alone with them, instead of grinding away to meet quotas and schedules with bosses looking over your shoulder. You get to work with interesting people and you're always learning new things, the latest styles. You get to add your own touches and make creative decisions, because every customer is a new challenge, and you're the one in charge. When you do good work, you see the results right away: People look good; they're happy. If you are really talented, you can open your own salon. Maybe even become a hairdresser to the rich and famous.
>
> (Florida 2002: 86)

In this passage, Florida concisely invokes a number of desirable features of work: flexibility, safety, autonomy, intrinsic interest, skill, the blending of conception and execution, recognition. This is an unlikely picture of working in most salons. He is not being ironic here, and while he appears to be paraphrasing the reasons given by young people about why they would prefer the hair salon to secure work in 'machine shops', he does very little in his book to distance himself from this beatific notion of creative work.[10]

1.3 The critical backlash, the debate and our own approach

There has been a backlash against such celebrations and simplifications of creative labour in government policy and academia. Pierre-Michel Menger, the leading sociologist of artistic labour markets, has discussed the role of artistic workers within such discourses as those outlined above. According to myth, says Menger (2006: 801), 'artists supply the golden legend of creation, that of a subversive, anti-conformist, inspired behaviour, rebelling against social conventions and commercial utilitarianism'. Surveying a formidable body of statistical and qualitative evidence, Menger goes on to point out that in fact artistic work can be seen as characterised by conditions highly compliant with the demands of modern capitalism: 'extreme flexibility, autonomy, tolerance of inequality, innovative forms of teamwork' (ibid.).

Much of the backlash has come from cultural studies. Andrew Ross has done more than any other writer to develop a critical analysis of creative and artistic labour, including information technology work. In an early contribution, he claimed that

> the traditional profile of the artist as unattached and adaptable to circumstance is surely now coming into its own as the ideal definition of the knowledge worker: comfortable in an ever-changing environment that demands creative shifts in communication with different kinds of clients and partners; attitudinally geared towards production that requires long, and often unsocial hours; and accustomed, in the sundry exercise of their mental labour, to a contingent rather than a fixed, routine of self-application.
>
> (Ross 2000: 11)

A number of other critical analysts have also sought to show that the jobs offered by cultural and creative industries, and by different but related sectors such as information technology, are marked by high levels of insecurity, casualisation and long working hours. A key basis of the critique has been 'self-exploitation', whereby workers become so enamoured with their jobs that they push themselves to the limits of their physical and emotional endurance.

---

10 Accounts such as Florida's chime with analyses of transformations in work by some social theorists, even if the latter are less celebratory. Zygmunt Bauman (2000), for example, sees work as a key form of what he calls 'liquid modernity' embodying new uncertainties, whereas in 'solid' modernity work supposedly gave shape to the future and replaced chaos and control with order. For Ulrich Beck (2000), 'individualization' compels people to make themselves the centre of their own planning of their life, and work is especially important in this. Such accounts are stimulating, but risk overstating transformation.

We discuss some of the most notable contributions to such recent critical analysis in this book, especially in Chapter 3, but a flavour of their approach is indicated by this quotation from one pioneering researcher:

> The willingness of individuals to work in television production is partly to be explained by the tantalizing possibilities thereby for securing social recognition and acclaim, that is self-affirmation and public esteem, and partly by the possibilities for self-actualization and creativity (be it aesthetic or commercially entrepreneurial). For the workers, television production is simultaneously a source of potential rewards, both material and existential, and a source of definite exploitation.
>
> (Ursell 2000: 819)

According to such views, recognition, self-realisation and creativity become the basis for exploitation. This paradox has been at the core of recent critiques of creative labour.

There is, then, substantial disagreement on the quality of work offered by the contemporary cultural or creative industries. Our aim is to intervene in these debates by examining what kinds of jobs and occupations are really on offer. There is only very limited statistical evidence available concerning work in the cultural industries, mainly drawn on research on artistic labour markets (which are only a sub-set of the cultural industries, as we explained above). We refer to these data where relevant in this book. But our own training and backgrounds are not in social surveys. Our approach emphasises both theory-building and a qualitative, empirical concern with subjective experience.

We have sought to advance knowledge and understanding of creative work in a number of ways. First, we have interviewed and observed creative workers across a number of cultural industries and genres, whereas most previous studies have been confined to one particular cultural or related industry. Second, we have focused on workers' reports of their subjective experience of the quality of their working lives, and our observations of their work, but we contextualise these 'subjective' data by looking at the economic, political, organisational and cultural dimensions that shape and refract these experiences. While there is no space to offer a systemic account of structural causality, we draw on other work that would contribute to such an account, including our own previous research (for example, Hesmondhalgh 2007). Third, we seek to clarify the normative dimensions of creative labour. Put simply, in our view, neither the celebrants of creative labour nor the critical pessimists have been sufficiently clear about what constitutes good work and bad work, and this has inhibited debate and understanding about the meaning of contemporary creative labour. Some of the celebrations of creative labour are deeply complacent about the conditions of such work and the reality of the labour markets involved. Yet even the best critical accounts have not found time to scrutinise the normative implications of their critiques. There is wide agreement that creative labour is marked by many positive characteristics. Yet these features are ultimately understood to be the basis of alienation and self-exploitation. This is particularly so in the work of writers influenced by neo-Foucauldian governmentality theory. The result is a lack of political clarity about what forms better creative work would take, about what transformations and reforms are being implicitly argued for.[11] We hope that our book will contribute to the development of these debates.

In order to achieve the three main objectives just outlined, we develop our own approach, drawing on aspects of Marxism, post-structuralism and liberal political thought. We take from various Marxisms a concern with inequality, and the occlusion of exploitative divisions of labour. We borrow from post-structuralism an attention to the complex politics of subjectivity, including the limits of certain notions of personhood. From liberal political thought, we draw an interest in questions of freedom, autonomy and self-realisation. We specify our positions with regard to these different perspectives in Chapters 2 and 3.

Our approach is innovatively eclectic in another way. As indicated briefly at the beginning of this chapter, we make use of, and hope to make some contribution to, a number of different analytical fields that are very rarely in mutual dialogue. One is media, communication and cultural studies, which are where the cultural industries have been most studied and theorised. The second is the sociology of work, and a third the related fields of organisational, business and management studies. Naturally enough, sociology and management studies have had a huge amount to say about work, occupations and careers, and yet only a few of the recent contributions to debates about creative labour in media and cultural studies have made use of them. Equally though, researchers working in sociology and in business, management and organisational studies have usually paid little attention to the cultural industries. Even where this has not been the case, they have tended to ignore the relevant theories and research of media, communication and cultural studies.[12] A fourth field we make use of is social and political theory, including classical theories, but also more recent philosophical contributions concerning justice and 'meaningful' or good work.

---

11 In this respect and others, Mark Banks's *The Politics of Cultural Work* (2007) was a major and welcome intervention. This is the most important existing synthesis of research on work in the cultural and information technology industries. Our research seeks to build on Banks's by further developing his attention to normative criteria, and by drawing more fully on primary qualitative research across a range of cultural industries.

12 To criticise research and conceptualisation carried out in media, communication and cultural studies would be perfectly reasonable; but to ignore pretty much all the considerable range of contributions from these fields, as some sociologists and management analysts have done when analysing cultural industries, and without explanation, seems inadequate.

1.4 Definitions and boundaries

This book is a study of work and occupations in the cultural industries. Even though all labour is potentially creative, we use the term 'creative labour' throughout this book to refer to those jobs, centred on the activity of symbol-making, which are to be found in large numbers in the cultural industries. Such work exists in other sectors, but only in the cultural industries is the primary aim of businesses to make profit from such activity, and this raises important issues about tensions and contradictions between economics and culture, creativity and commerce.[13]

Our term 'creative labour' is really a compressed version of 'creative work in the cultural industries', the original title of our research project. Occasionally, we will use that longer formulation to avoid ambiguity.[14] We avoid the term 'artistic labour' partly because of the problematic connotations of conservative traditionalism that have sometimes been attached to the concept of art, and also because the cultural industries involve other kind of symbol-making, centred less on what might be called art and more on the kinds of interpretive knowledge that are at the core of activities such as journalism.[15] We have also resisted the temptation to lump workers in the cultural industries in with the very broad and amorphous category of 'knowledge workers', for reasons explained in Section 3.4.

In using the terms 'creative labour' and 'creative workers', we recognise of course that there is a division of labour in cultural production. This can be expressed as involving primary creative personnel such as writers, actors, directors, musicians; craft and technical workers such as camera operators, film editors and sound engineers; creative managers such as television producers, magazine editors and A&R personnel; administrators; executives; and unskilled labour (see Hesmondhalgh 2007: 64–5). We intend the term 'creative labour' to refer to the work of all these groups, as part of an organisational division of labour, while recognising that the input of different groups of workers into 'creative' outputs varies, and that this variety can be the source of important hierarchies and distinctions in cultural production.

---

13 To say that there are tensions and contradictions is not the same thing as adopting a romantic position where creativity and commerce should always be opposed to each other. Some discussions of the cultural industries seem mistakenly to equate any discussion of creativity–commerce tensions with naive romanticism. See Faulkner et al. (2008) for an example.

14 Banks (2007) opts for 'cultural work', which is just as good, and raises just as many problems of boundary and definition. We considered the hybrid 'creative cultural labour' but this felt too unwieldy.

15 This involves the communication of knowledge to audiences, rather than the very general sense of information as data or for more instrumental purposes (such as an accounting spreadsheet). It refers to the work of journalists and photographers rather than to those who code or input data, or those who create code in order to make a piece of software function effectively.

The most socially prominent cultural or creative industries involve *mediated* communication. For this reason, we focus mainly on *industrialised, commercial media work* as examples of creative labour in this book, rather than those forms of artistic labour that are usually carried out with some degree of public support, or even under modern forms of patronage (see Menger 1999). As will become evident, our view is that good work can be found in these commercial industries, and not only in the subsidised public sector.[16] But, influenced by political economy and by critical sociology and social theory, we show that there are systematic blockages and inequalities of access that make such good work available only to a few. Underlying our research is the political principle that work needs to be made better, for more people.

1.5 Research design: selection of industries and cases

The research was carried out in England in 2006 and 2007. We conducted semi-structured interviews with 63 managers and workers across three industries: television, music recording and magazine publishing. In addition, we carried out participant observation in the production of a television programme; Sarah Baker worked for 16 weeks at the level of television researcher, as part of a production team of 12 people in a London independent television production company. These methods were supplemented by textual analysis of key products, and analysis of the trade press associated with each industry. We will begin by discussing our selection of industries and recruitment of interviewees, and contextualising those industries. We then reflect in Section 1.6 on our two main methods, interviewing and participant observation.

The three industries were selected because they represent examples of each of three different 'logics' of cultural production identified in Bernard Miège's seminal account of cultural industries. As we explain further in Chapter 3, Miège's is one of the few analyses of cultural industries that attempts to provide a systematic and historically informed analysis of labour. What is more, his analysis of different logics goes beyond analysis that would treat the cultural industries as an undifferentiated mass, and that which would simply list the different industries contained underneath that umbrella term, without analysing their different organisational, economic, technological and cultural dynamics.

Three 'logics' are pre-eminent in Miège's analysis (1989: 133–59):

- The *publishing* or 'editorial' logic, based on offsetting risk by producing a catalogue of repertoire, whereby inevitable failures are balanced out by

---

16 Here, as elsewhere, the influence of cultural studies on our approach may be apparent, for at its best cultural studies recognises the complexity and ambivalence of commercial cultural production.

occasional hits or successes. This logic or model, according to Miège, is used in books, music and film.[17]

- The *flow* logic, based on a continuous flow of product, and the gaining of audience loyalty, as in radio, television and new media.
- The *written press* logic, involving the regular and loyal consumption of a series of commodities, found in newspapers and magazines.

These logics of cultural production incorporate a number of factors, including organisation, working conditions and characteristics of the market or audiences. In his analysis of the publishing logic, for example (represented in our work by music and in particular by the recording industry), Miège wrote of irregular, sporadic employment in 'talent pools' and small companies, and 'a wide range of remuneration' (1989: 147); whereas the flow logic featured a very varied mix of creative personnel, and 'generally regular salaried employment' (p. 147). Meanwhile for Miège the characteristics of the creative professions in the written press logic were the co-existence of journalists, technicians and 'editorial production by networks of external correspondents, news agencies, etc.' (p. 147). A testing of Miège's model was *not* our main aim, however. Using these categories seemed the most effective way to ensure a spread of examples of creative labour that might encompass a rich variety of different dynamics.[18]

The three industries we selected all have large workforces and substantial revenues. In 2006, the UK television industry employed approximately 55,800 people, with over one-third being freelancers (Skillset 2006). About 102,210 people are employed in music, about half of them in live performance, about 10,000 people in recording, and 3,000 in composing and songwriting (Creative and Cultural Skills 2004). Nevertheless, it can be argued that recording remains central to the meaning of musical labour. Securing a recording contract and releasing successful recordings is usually a goal of popular musicians, at least early on in their careers. The publishing sector overall is reported to employ over 209,000 people, with 20 per cent of these working in the journals and periodicals subsector, including magazines (Skillset 2009).

---

17 In spite of its name, this logic does not refer to the magazine publishing industry (see below). The term 'publishing' was intended to evoke the way in which businesses influenced by this logic seek to issue a wide repertoire or catalogue of products, as in the book publishing industry. Miège (1989: 136) emphasises that 'logic' should not be understood in a deterministic way, and that logics result in contradictory strategies.

18 A number of developments mean that Miège's original discussion requires updating, as Miège himself has recognised in more recent publications. These obviously include the rise of the 'new media' logic that was marginal at the time of Miège's study. We would also note the increasing adoption of the publishing logic in broadcasting, as channels proliferate and viewing habits change. Certainly, the flow logic is no longer associated strongly with regular salaried employment. Our view though is that the idea of different logics still has considerable validity in differentiating cultural industries, even if the meanings of the terms have changed.

All three industries were undergoing change at the time we studied them (2006 to 2008). The recording industry was in the middle of a crisis, as revenues plummeted, even amidst an economic bubble that burst shortly after our research was completed. The digitalisation of music meant that from the early 2000s onwards, consumers became increasingly unwilling to pay high prices for music that could be more and more easily copied from friends, or by using file-sharing technologies over the Internet. Nobody seemed to know quite what was going to happen, as record shops closed down all over the UK, and various new forms of distribution (such as Apple's iTunes store) struggled to establish themselves as rivals.

British television, centred for decades on a limited number of channels and the dominance of two giant public service-oriented broadcasters (BBC and ITV), had been considerably 'deregulated', with significant implications for industrial relations (McKinlay and Quinn 2007). The UK had recently entered the multi-channel age, with the widespread take-up of digital television, and the television industry was anxiously seeking to understand the potential impact of the Internet (YouTube became a widespread phenomenon among Internet users in 2006 and was purchased by Google towards the end of that year, signalling its move into the cultural mainstream). A change in the 'terms of trade' between broadcasters and independent production companies, brought about by the UK media regulator Ofcom in 2004, had confirmed the rise to power of the independents (Faulkner et al. 2008). Magazines too were looking anxiously ahead to a digital future.[19]

Since we conducted our research, the impacts of digitalisation and the Internet have continued to manifest themselves, and the anxieties generated by them have been made much worse by the onset of global economic recession from 2008 onwards. Does this mean that our study has been outdated and invalidated by events since we conducted our research? We don't think so. It is not sufficiently understood that cultural industries are always in the midst of some degree of flux. The factors driving such changes can be economic, technological and socio-cultural, and are usually a mixture of all of these. Economic patterns are always unpredictably cyclical in capitalist systems, and the cultural industries are always in a difficult symbiotic relationship with the consumer electronics and IT sectors, whose products sometimes serve to create new demand for cultural products, and sometimes destroy entire swathes of cultural business. (The music industry, inflated by various factors such as the high price and remarkable popularity of CDs in the 1990s, has at the time of writing been undergoing this process of 'correction' for something like a decade – see Hesmondhalgh 2009.) Furthermore, cultural production and consumption are closely linked to expressions of tastes, which are in turn connected to displays of social power and dynamics of competitive

---

19 Further details of all three industries and the various genres we studied within them are provided in the course of the empirical work in Part Two (Chapters 4 to 9).

individualism (Bourdieu 1984 is the classic study of this). Producers and consumers regularly shift their conceptions of what is interesting, desirable and exciting, as last decade's or last year's style comes to seem jaded, tired, spent. For these various reasons, there will never be some fixed point where the cultural industries are stable.

Having said this, it would also be a mistake to think of cultural industries as always in such a state of permanent flux that there is no stability. Change is often exaggerated at the expense of continuity. At the time of our research, the Internet had been part of general public consciousness for something like 12 to 13 years.[20] Yet compared with the impact of the rapid rise of television in the 1950s on other cultural industries, the effects of the Internet were taking a long time to emerge. Music, with its low requirement for bandwidth compared with audio-visual products, was in the vanguard of change, and was widely perceived as a test case for future transformation in other industries. Yet even in music, where an oligopoly of large corporations and a series of large independents dominated the market as they had for many years, most consumers still regularly bought concrete physical objects such as CDs and DVDs, and musicians generally wanted to be signed to record companies if they wished to gain widespread recognition and fame for their creations. In television, major broadcasters were still at the centre of British cultural experience, as they had been since the early 1960s. The BBC had been the beneficiary of a settlement that secured real-term growth in its public funding from 2000 to 2007, and this was renewed on slightly less generous terms in 2007 for the following six years. Magazines continued to proliferate too, with titles available for seemingly every conceivable niche interest, and sales and advertising relatively healthy for the sector as a whole. All three of our industries, then, displayed evidence of change and continuity and have lessons to tell beyond the specific historical conjuncture we studied.

Our focus is on paid work, on occupations and careers. But in cultural production, the line between paid and unpaid work, between 'professionals' and 'amateurs' is often blurred. Many creative workers spend many years honing their talents as amateurs before gaining entry into the business. It is not unusual for unpaid work to provide the basis of a reputation that allows people to turn professional: such as a fanzine writer, or a musician paying for their own recordings. Aspirant workers develop their skills and portfolios at colleges and schools, either in actual classes in acting, singing, writing, directing, lighting, sound engineering and so on, or in doing more conventional subjects and working with others on a short film or a magazine or forming a band. Some argue that digital technologies, including the Internet, have made it more and more easy for amateurs and semi-professionals to

---

20 If we follow the practice of taking the rise of the World Wide Web and graphical interface browsers in 1993–94, and the massive media coverage in industrial countries that followed, as the beginning of the Internet as a widespread social phenomenon.

disseminate their own work. 'Convergence culture' (Jenkins 2006; Deuze 2007) is one term for this supposedly new media environment, and 'user generated content' was a phrase very widely used at the time we carried out our research. No-one seemed to know quite what it meant: some felt threatened by it, others felt that it was a great way of generating income cheaply. In this respect, it was yet another source of anxiety and insecurity in what have always been highly anxious and insecure forms of work. Even if more and more amateurs are producing content to fill the massive requirements of digital television and sites such as YouTube, and even if music fans occasionally discover a band via the Internet before that band is heard on the radio or television, the fact is that the vast majority of the cultural productions we share in modern societies are still produced by people who are trying to make a living out of that activity.

A further way of ensuring breadth in our sample of interviewees and cases was to concentrate on three genres in each industry: in the television industry on arts and history documentary, drama and 'factual entertainment'; in the recording industry on rap, jazz and rock-pop;[21] and in the magazine industry on the music press, the building and construction trade press and on men's magazines. Cultural industries tend to use genre as a way of attempting to match audiences to texts. Genre terms are based on shared understandings among producers and among audiences, and sometimes across this production–consumption divide. We say 'sometimes' because some genre terms refer to highly recognisable entities, such as rap, or men's magazines, or documentary. But usually there is a great deal of uncertainty and fluidity, and even in highly recognisable genres, definitions constantly change. For example, categories that begin as 'sub-genres' of other categories emerge over time to be major types in their own right.

Genres, then, constantly change in response to the practices of creative workers. Nevertheless they provide some kind of institutionalisation and routinisation in a highly uncertain interpretive production world. Production comes, in effect, to be organised in terms of genres, as Keith Negus (1999) showed in his study of the rap, country and Latin divisions of major US record companies. Interacting with cultural consumption beyond industry organisations, particular sets of values, meanings and behaviours become associated with particular genres. Television documentary workers tend to go about their business in somewhat different ways from people who make 'light entertainment' talent shows for example. So genre is an important dimension of understanding the organisation and experience of creative work in a differentiated way.

In terms of our selection of interviewees within each industry, we sought a mixture that would balance the following dimensions: men and women; older and younger workers; those relatively well established in their industries,

---

21 By this term, we mean those forms of rock music intended for the mass market. See Regev (2002) on the 'pop-rockization' of popular music.

mid-career workers and relative newcomers; people working for larger companies and those working for 'independent' production or working as freelancers; those based in London, the heartland of UK cultural production, and those working outside that city. Of our 63 interviewees, 5 were non-white, reflecting roughly the proportion of non-white employees in these industries (though non-white employees are under-represented at higher levels). In recruiting interviewees we were guided by these principles, but we also made the most of opportunities provided by particular contacts, at times shifting direction and learning, as is appropriate to a qualitative research project.[22]

1.6 Methods: interviews and participant observation

As indicated in Section 1.1, our primary research question is *What kinds of experiences do jobs in the cultural industries offer their workers?* Our approach is qualitative, in that we aim to capture an aspect of social life – creative labour – as it is experienced and interpreted by participants. More precisely, we operate what Rom Harré (1979) calls an 'intensive' rather than an 'extensive' research design. Intensive research does not seek common properties and general patterns of a population (e.g., all creative workers as defined here), as in extensive research; instead, it aims to investigate how processes work in a small number of cases, seeking explanation of the production of certain objects, events and experiences (Sayer 1992: 242–4). So in this particular research project, we were looking for explanations of what might bring about positive and negative experiences of work in the cultural industries. At the same time, as we have shown, we took considerable measures to ensure a degree of representativeness in our interviewees, so that as wide as possible a range of experiences might be made available to us within the limitations determined by our funding.

Intensive interviewing of the kind we conducted for this project was appropriate because it allowed us to consider the accounts of interviewees about their experiences and products, and to listen to some of their accounts of what happens to them, and why they think that things happen in the way that they do. However, there are some well-known potential limitations of interviewing as a method. Interviewers can ask leading questions, and interviewees can be affected in all sorts of other ways by the interview situation. They might, for example, seek to impress the interviewer by making definite statements about issues they are uncertain about. Many of us may tend to change our views about complex phenomena over time, even from one day to the next, and especially so in complex and confusing situations. Interviews are events in which people are asked to reflect in language on processes that they may, for most of the time, take for granted. Indeed, there may well be aspects

---

22 See the Appendix for a list of our interviewees and the pseudonyms used in this study.

of practice and experience which people will simply be unable to account for even when prompted: the unacknowledged conditions, unconscious motivations and unintended consequences of what we do. All these factors point to the problem of whether interview data should be seen as a *resource* for gaining insight into reality beyond, as it were, the accounts people give, or whether it might be better seen instead as a *topic* in its own right, with the focus being just on what people say (see Taylor 2001). Our view is that if enough care is applied to interviews, they can provide relevant knowledge not only about language and the rhetorical strategies people use, but about the phenomena that interviewer and interviewee are seeking to address.

To address the potential pitfalls of interviews, we adopted a number of strategies. One was to keep guidance and direction to a minimum, but also to bring out the value-laden implications of responses (in line with Merton and Kendall's classic guidelines, 1946: 555). Another was to gain as much information as we could about the person being interviewed, and the company they worked for, to help detect equivocations, evasions, unusual frankness and so on. We sought, within each industry-genre combination we studied, to recruit interviewees from the same company, or the same cultural 'world', to increase the chances that we might be able to check interviewees' accounts against each other. And in analysing interviews, using the NVivo7 qualitative data analysis software, we constantly looked for confirmations and challenges of the understandings we had gained from reading previous studies and in conducting earlier research.

We also used participant observation. This is a very time-consuming method, and so, given our limited time and research budget, we were only able to undertake one such observation, over a period of four months, of the making of a television talent show. But participant observation allowed us to gain a number of advantages compared with an interview-only project. It permitted us to trace the experiences of a number of co-workers over a sustained period of time, rather than in a short one to two-hour interview. This meant that these workers could be observed when they were off duty and/or off guard, and as they went through a number of different states and experiences. Trust could be, and was, built up between observer and observed. Participant observation also allowed us to go beyond language and discourse – the primary product of interviews – to observe much more fully other aspects of creative workers' lives and subjectivities, such as their comportment, demeanour, behaviour and attitudes. We discuss the participant observation in more detail in later chapters of this book, especially Chapter 7.

Nevertheless, we do not see the semi-structured intensive interview as an inferior method to participant observation. It allows for a much wider range of contexts and situations to be examined than the in-depth study of a single case. And although it is certainly important not to see interview data as a transparent reflection of reality, we do not think of the interviews as merely performances. By immersing ourselves in the analysis of cultural production, not only in the course of this project but over many years, we hoped to give ourselves a basis for judging when insight was being provided into real events and processes that might throw light on our understanding of creative labour, and on the possibilities of good work. In short, our own deepening knowledge allowed us to apply a reality check to the interviews.

1.7 Outline of the book

In the book, Chapters 2 and 3 form Part One: Theoretical Synthesis, which, along with Chapter 10, is a contribution to theoretical and conceptual debates about creative labour. Part Two: Empirical Study (Chapters 4 to 9) tests the theories and debates developed in Part One by examining our empirical data.

Chapter 2 develops a model of good and bad work. It begins with Marx because of his foundational status as a critic of labour under capitalism. His concept of alienation directs our attention to the fact that many people in modern, capitalist societies experience their work as lacking in meaning and purpose. But Marx was not a sociologist and he was not concerned with analysing the subjective experiences of workers. A sociological analysis of alienation was taken up by late twentieth-century sociologists and we provide a critique of categories developed by Robert Blauner (1964), in order to develop our own normative framework for analysis of the experience of good and bad work (terms we prefer to unalienated and alienated labour). This framework consists of the following elements of good work: decent pay, hours and safety; autonomy; interest and involvement; sociality; esteem and self-esteem; self-realisation; work–life balance; security. Conversely, it outlines features of bad work: poor pay, hours and safety; powerlessness; boredom; isolation; self-doubt and shame; overwork; insecurity and risk. These all relate to the labour *process* but we also include elements relating to *products*, as they bear on experience of work: the quality of products involved and their potential contribution to the well-being of others, including (potentially) the common good.

However, because our study of work is based on the particular case of labour in the cultural industries, in Chapter 3 we turn to the formidable body of research on cultural production. Identifying three major paradigms of analysis (political economy of culture; organisational, business and management studies; and cultural studies) we point out that until recently the labour involved in cultural production has been neglected in all these traditions, and we speculate on why this might be the case. Surveying some major exceptions in political economy, we outline a tension within that paradigm. Some analysts think it is important to recognise the specificity of culture and creativity, as part of an explanatory account of dynamics in the cultural industries, including creative work. Some prefer to stress commonality with other forms of production. Our view is that we need both. But the former is harder to grasp for many analysts, and this can result in reductionist accounts that fail to understand what is distinctive about cultural products – with their ability to influence our understandings of the world more than any other product. For an analysis of the specificity of culture, but one which balances it with an understanding of creativity as *ordinary*, we turn to the historical sociology of Raymond Williams, and his argument that creative workers are involved, more than any other occupations, in *the communication of experience*. This provides a basis for appreciating the particular forms that struggles over working autonomy, as discussed in Chapter 2, might take in cultural production. We differentiate two important variants of autonomy relevant to cultural production: aesthetic autonomy and professional autonomy. We engage with important criticisms of both but we defend a critical conception of them, drawing on Pierre Bourdieu, Andrew Bowie and (again) Raymond Williams. However, it is vital to realise that the partial and relative autonomy of creative workers gives them only a limited amount of power and privilege in class terms. We argue that creative workers tend to cluster in lower-authority, higher-skilled class locations. They are experts and skilled workers with little or no supervisory or managerial power. Having established an understanding of the specificity and ordinariness of creative workers, as a basis for explaining work in the cultural industries, we then return to the evaluative and normative issues raised in Chapter 2 by addressing the recent critiques of creative labour already introduced above. These are mainly influenced by cultural studies and by post-structuralism, and ultimately they see creative autonomy and other features of the specificity of creative labour as controlling or disciplining mechanisms that serve to subordinate creative workers. We acknowledge the importance and partial validity of some of these perspectives, but then turn to other evaluations of creative labour which, in our view, allow us the possibility of holding on to the remaining emancipatory possibilities in creative labour as part of a more balanced assessment.

Throughout Part One, then, we stress that questions of quality of creative work can only be understood within the context of an understanding of the power-laden and contradictory historical dynamics within which creative labour operates. Turning to Part Two, Chapter 4 serves as a meso level chapter, mediating between this macro focus on structural causality and our micro focus on the experiences of workers. It does so by establishing the organisational contexts within which creative labour takes place. It recognises questions of power, and the specificity of creative labour as cultural production, centred on symbol-making. It forefronts the way that tensions between creative autonomy and commercial imperatives are structured into creative labour. The strategy adopted in the first part of the chapter is to outline how 'creative management' (Ryan 1992) operates in the three cultural industries that we studied. Creative management is understood as a means of managing the desires for creative autonomy on the part of some influential workers and audiences that arise from the historical development of art and knowledge outlined in Chapter 3. We also discuss how genre is an important mediator of these creativity–commerce tensions in the context of cultural-industry organisations. In the second part of the chapter, we then examine a number of ways in which creative autonomy is under threat in the cultural industries – a longstanding struggle, but arguably one that might have intensified in a socio-political conjuncture marked by marketisation and neo-liberalism.

In Chapter 5, we begin our explicit assessment of the degree to which creative labour might offer good and bad work in the senses defined in Chapter 2. We begin with inequalities in pay, the result of the huge 'reservoir' of labour available to the cultural industries. We discuss the problem that many workers, especially young ones, are willing to work for free in the cultural industries, and the implications for the class composition of the workforce. We show that the over-supply of aspiring entrants leads to a sense of vulnerability and even disposability among many workers. We go on to examine a number of problems with regard to working hours: the requirement to be 'flexible', the long and sometimes unpaid hours many workers put in, and the need to take on second and third jobs to make ends meet. Related to this, we discuss the anxieties among workers, especially freelancers, about the effectiveness of trade unions, and the possibilities of victimisation for union involvement. Other factors that we examine from our model here are security and esteem. We further discuss the mental and emotional states produced by the uncertainty facing many creative workers, including anxiety, frustration and self-doubt – in forms of work where confidence can be a vital competitive asset. We also recognise however that many workers gain pleasure and satis-faction from the fact that their jobs are considered interesting, unconventional and even glamorous by others, and from the complexity and challenge afforded by their work. We argue that the seemingly genuine and effusive proclamations of enthusiasm for their work on the part of those we inter-viewed makes it difficult to conceive of such satisfactions and rewards purely as some kind of compensation for insecurity. We provide evidence that many workers find their work varied and pleasurably absorbing. What is more, many experience the kinds of working and creative autonomy discussed in Chapter 4 as pleasurable – but this is a pleasure that can easily be compro-mised. All this suggests that worker experiences of creative labour are highly ambivalent.

In Chapter 6, we examine other aspects of the model of good and bad work: self-realisation, sociality and work–life balance. We show that creative labour, at least according to creative workers, offers genuine possibilities for self-realisation. Creative workers find in their occupations ways of fulfilling potential and developing talents that give them a sense of purpose and meaning in their lives. For others the particular challenges of creative work helped build their self-esteem, confidence and sense of recognition by others. Yet there are at least two problems with creative careers. One is that they are 'fragile', difficult to sustain over an entire life, especially for women. Another is that the very lure of self-realisation brings about an over-identification of the self with work. We go on to explore how workers reflect on the sociable and collaborative nature of much creative labour. Many of our interviewees reported high degrees of sociality, friendship and teamwork. Others though, especially freelancers, experienced considerable isolation, while others felt obliged to engage in a kind of forced sociability – or to suffer the career consequences of not networking.

A number of the issues addressed in Chapters 5 and 6 are then examined in Chapter 7, through the lens of participant observation. We begin by returning to theory, and some recent, rather optimistic theorisations of contemporary work, relevant to consideration of the cultural industries, which draw on autonomist Marxist concepts of immaterial and affective labour. Using our ethnography of a television talent show, we question the validity and political utility of these concepts. The ethnography allows us to look in more detail at the organisational and experiential aspects of creative labour in one particular genre, and in the production of one particular text. We draw attention to important issues regarding the specific nature of the end product of the cultural industries, and how this is articulated with the particular forms of precariousness and insecurity faced by creative workers in a particular industry (television) and genre (the talent show). We also provide evidence of some of the pleasures and bonds created in creative labour, lending some support to autonomist assertions. It is the job of television workers to produce television programmes of specific kinds, and we argue that one of the reasons that a programme like *Show Us Your Talent* is interesting is that it involves the power to change people's lives – choices are made about who gets to appear on TV and who doesn't, with drastic consequences for career success. This, we claim, is an instance of the symbolic power accorded to media producers in modern societies. This symbolic power is unevenly distributed, however, residing mainly in the commissioning organisation (in this case, the BBC) and the independent production company. We show that this creates tensions between the two organisations which are then 'passed down' the production hierarchy to junior workers. The working relations produced were felt particularly keenly by workers who, if they were to stay in the UK television industry, needed to remain on good terms with their colleagues. As an important part of this discussion, we argue that Arlie Hochschild's concept of emotional labour, in spite of its problems, is more compelling and useful than the autonomist concepts of immaterial labour and affective labour. This chapter, then, investigates in greater detail the issues of insecurity and anxiety, autonomy, self-realisation and sociality discussed in Chapters 5 and 6. Our participant observation found evidence of sociality and pleasure in work, which we discuss, but more prominently it uncovered levels of anxiety and conflict that were likely to be highly disruptive to people's sense of personal reward and life-progress.

While some consideration of the issue of good and bad work, in the sense of good and bad *products*, runs throughout all the above chapters, Chapters 8 and 9 turn more directly to issues of product and audience. In Chapter 8, we examine how workers discuss the satisfactions and rewards involved in making what they consider to be good products. Discussion of these issues requires an understanding how workers conceive of what quality is. Workers' conceptions of quality, we show, includes not only well-crafted or excellent work, but also work that has a powerful social and cultural impact, and that contributes to the common good. Just as high-quality work can be satisfying and rewarding to workers, involvement in mediocre products can be frustrating and disappointing. And it is as important to understand what constitutes poor quality as what comprises outstanding products. We demonstrate that the contemporary cultural industries provide opportunities for workers to do work that they consider to be of social, cultural and political significance, and/or to be involved in making cultural products that bears the mark of high levels of care and skill. Many of the workers we spoke to were deeply concerned about the aesthetic quality of the goods they produced, and about their ethical implications. But cultural production is by no means protected from the worst aspects of what Marx and others called alienation (and which, in order to cover a greater variety of ills, we are preferring simply to call bad work). We demonstrate that workers can experience deep frustration and disappointment, as a result of careless, meaningless ideas, and the distortion or perceived hijacking of good ones. Some of these problems emanate from the kinds of structural pressure we outlined in Part One and discussed as part of our analysis of organisational forms in Chapter 4.

These positive and negative experiences of the quality of creative work are intensified by the fact that cultural products are highly visible and audible in public, and workers' names are often displayed in association with those products. These questions of visibility, audibility and publicness bring us to how creative workers conceive of their relations with audiences. So Chapter 9 examines how creative workers pay attention to the needs of audiences, try hard to please them, or conversely, ignore them, or even hold them in contempt. Many of the tensions regarding creativity and commerce that we explored in organisational terms in Chapter 4 here appear as ambivalences and anxieties concerning audiences, which in turn has consequences for the way in which workers experience what they do.

Finally, Chapter 10 summarises our assessment of the quality of experiences that we observed and heard in interviews. We differentiate the most important good and bad aspects of creative labour across the three cultural industries we studied. But we move beyond the initial objectives of our study to address a question that has been marginalised both by 'creative industries' discourse and by cultural studies (and more recently critical management studies) critiques. This concerns how positive and emancipatory aspects of labour, including creative work, might be made more prevalent. We discuss the crucial role of trade unions and of networks of creative workers. But we also address questions of 'self-exploitation' and the relationship of good work to notions of a good life. Questions of quality of life, we claim, need to be addressed as part of a discussion of equality, social justice and the social division of labour. So, in the final part of the book, we examine debates in political theory about how the benefits and burdens associated with labour might be spread in modern societies. There are of course no easy solutions. A guaranteed basic income provides one possibility, and we also examine the idea of adjustments to the social division of labour.

Part One
Theoretical synthesis

2 A model of good and bad work

2.1 Marx on work and alienation

Marx provides a searing and powerful critique of work under capitalism, and a basis for thinking about why we might undertake ethical analysis of labour. This affords us a point of entry for a sociological evaluation of contemporary work, but Marx was not a sociologist, and his categories need considerable development for our purposes.

Marx's concept of the fetishism of the commodity, developed in *Capital* (1990/1867: 163ff.), potentially illuminates a vital fact about work in modern capitalist societies: we are surrounded by commodities that are produced by others, but the human experience of that production is usually forgotten or concealed. A fetish is an object which is believed to have magical properties and the core of Marx's idea is that things that are bought and sold in capitalist societies come to be invested with magical powers. For Marx, the advent of economies based on money as opposed to barter dissolves the bonds and relations that make up traditional communities and 'money becomes the real community' (Harvey 1989: 100). Money ends up masking the social relationships between the things in our world. As a result, the conditions of labour and life, 'the sense of joy, anger, or frustration that lie behind the production of commodities, the states of mind of the producers, are all hidden to us as we change one object (money) for another (the commodity)' (ibid.). Production becomes what Marx went on to refer to as a 'hidden abode' (Marx 1990/1867: 279). Marx's suggestion, then, is that we are dependent in capitalism on the work of distant others but for nearly all of the time we are not aware of this fact. Much may have changed in capitalism since Marx's times, but this feature seems to be with us more than ever. Marx was making a kind of serious joke: capitalism fancies itself as modern, but in fact commodities are like 'primitive' fetishes. It is as if they have magically appeared from nowhere. So the fetishism of commodities was a powerful way of drawing attention to the fact that the social division of labour, based on exploitation and inequality, is occluded in modern societies.[1] This element of Marxist thought is valuable in making us aware of how others' experience of labour can be forgotten or concealed. The critical analysis of work attempts to remember or uncover that hidden abode of production.[2]

But how might we understand others' experiences of labour? Marx's own attempt to consider subjective dimensions of work under capitalism appears in his early work via the concept of *alienation* (Marx 1959/1844). It is here that Marx draws attention to the way in which work under capitalism is experienced by workers as lacking in meaning or purpose. The worker, wrote the young Marx,

> does not confirm himself in his work, but denies himself, feels miserable and not happy, does not develop free mental and physical energy, but mortifies his flesh and ruins his mind. Hence, the worker feels himself only when he is not working; when he is working, he does not feel himself. He is at home when he is not working, and not at home when he is working. His labour is, therefore, not voluntary but forced, it is forced labour. It is, therefore, not the satisfaction of a need but a mere means to satisfy needs outside itself. Its alien character is clearly demonstrated by the fact that as soon as no physical or other compulsion exists, it is shunned like the plague.
>
> (Marx 1959/1844: 30)

As well as alienation or estrangement from the process of labour, Marx also discussed the alienation of workers from the products they were involved in making. 'It is true that labour produces marvels for the rich, but it produces privation for the worker. It produces palaces, but hovels for the worker. It produces beauty, but deformity for the worker' (Marx 1959/1844: 30).

Marx also wrote about how this alienated people from their own nature as humans. Instead of making their lives the object of their will and consciousness, a capacity that in Marx's view distinguished humans from other

---

1 We use the term 'social division of labour' in the way that it has come to be used in contemporary social theory (Murphy 1993) rather than the confusing way in which the term is used in Marx's own work (see Sayer 1995: 44–5). The idea of an occluded social division of labour has been developed in important ways by feminists, who indicated how the caring and domestic work of women has sustained societies but has gone unrecognised and unrewarded. A classic account is Pateman (1988). For more recent contributions from political theory and sociology respectively, see Rössler (2007) and Crompton (2008). Other analysts have considered how the social division of labour has taken an increasingly international form, with much poorly paid and hard work done in developing countries (Froebel et al. 1980).

2 Of course the concept of exploitation is central to Marxist understandings of work. We are not Marxists, and the view underlying the analysis here is that exploitation inheres in infringements of autonomy, and in unfair distributions of burdens and benefits – as argued by Cohen (1995). In other words, exploitation is unjust. Understanding the notion of exploitation in relation to creative work in the cultural industries requires an examination of the class position of creative workers – see Chapter 3.

creatures, capitalist relations turned work into a means only for existence. We leave aside here the issue of whether Marx's remarks on workers' alienation from their species being are 'essentialist' or not, coherent or otherwise. Our purpose here is confined to suggesting that Marx usefully pointed to ethical problems surrounding our reliance on the labour of exploited others, and that he provides at least a starting point for thinking about problems concerning workers' relations to their work, as process and as product.[3]

2.2 A sociological concept of alienation

The manuscripts in which the above passages occur, usually known as the *Economic and Philosophical Manuscripts*, were not published in Marx's lifetime. They were eventually published in Russian in 1932, and became widely available in other languages only in the late 1950s. Classical Marxism in fact had relatively little to say about the subjective experience of labour.[4] But by the 1950s, a crisis in work was raging in the capitalist world.[5] Partly in response, researchers and writers of various kinds were exploring the politics of work. Sociologists and psychologists addressed the subjective experience of labour as never before (see Mills 1951; Whyte 1956). In his 1964 book *Alienation and Freedom*, the sociologist Robert Blauner took up the concept of alienation suggested by Marx and Durkheim, and attempted to provide a more careful specification of it, so that it might act as the basis for research.[6] In our view, Blauner's discussion remains useful, because it is an unusually bold and transparent effort to develop normative concepts for the analysis of work. What's more, Blauner was helpfully clear that the concept of alienation had only an indirect relationship to questions of human happiness. In his view, work was rarely experienced as either entirely miserable or totally pleasurable. This is surely right. Our discussion will look primarily at elements of good work understood in terms of *the experiences of*

3 Marx's writings on alienation have been dismissed by some sociologists. They are accused of romanticism, essentialism, and all kinds of other sociological sins. It is true that Marx was not concerned with analysing varied experiences of jobs on the part of individual workers, or how different tasks might produce different degrees of alienation. This was not meticulous academic sociology or history, it was an attempt to understand the appalling conditions being newly faced by millions of people.

4 Or, as Braverman (1974) points out, about its organisation – another issue that is of major concern to us (see Chapter 4).

5 See Bell (1956) on this crisis, which is retrospectively apparent in myriad literary, theatrical and film representations of the time. Examples from different work and national contexts include Arthur Miller's play *Death of a Salesman* (1949, filmed in 1951), Sloan Wilson's novel *The Man in the Gray Flannel Suit* (1955, filmed in 1956) and Alan Sillitoe's novel *Saturday Night and Sunday Morning* (1959, filmed in 1960).

6 Blauner's study was of factory workers in four different manufacturing industries, and he was interested in the way that new forms of automated technology might actually serve to reduce alienation. Our concern here is not with this aspect of his book but with its conceptualisation of good and bad aspects of work.

individual workers. By good experiences, we do not mean happiness, joy or even pleasure – though these may be fleetingly part of the experience of work. Labour often involves an element of struggle, difficulty and compulsion, even for those who 'like' or 'enjoy' their work. To seek happiness in work might be to invite disappointment, as it inevitably involves frustration and struggle. We need other conceptions of good and bad work (or unalienated and alienated work, in Blauner's terms) beyond happiness and pleasure.

Blauner provided a thoughtful outline of four types of work alienation that he felt were of particular significance in modern societies: powerlessness, meaninglessness, isolation and self-estrangement. There are problems and contradictions in his categorisation, his choice of terms and his discussion. We point to these in what follows, and develop our own conceptualisation, building on Blauner's thinking, and that of other social scientists and philosophers who have studied work in the interim.

The first type of alienation identified by Blauner involved *powerlessness*, control and manipulation by others or by systems, and an inability to change or modify situations. The opposite of such domination was *freedom* and *control*. Blauner distinguished four main types of powerlessness that had concerned previous analysts: a lack of ownership of the means of production, inability to influence managerial policies, lack of control over employment conditions, and workers' lack of control over their own immediate work process. Distancing himself from Marxism and socialism, Blauner discounted the importance of the first two, and suggested that US workers had come to accept their powerlessness, and so did not experience alienation in these respects. He was concerned primarily with the latter two aspects, and especially with control over the work process.[7] Blauner helpfully pinpointed key dimensions of this: control over pace, freedom from pressure, freedom of physical movement, control over the quantity and quality of production, and control over choice of technique.

A second type of alienation was *meaninglessness*. For Blauner, meaning in work depended on the worker's relationship to the product, process and organisation of work. The character of the product itself was crucial:

> Working on a unique and individuated product is almost inherently meaningful. It is more difficult to develop and maintain a sense of

---

7 Our primary concern with the subjective experience of work means that we too, like Blauner, focus mainly on the latter two aspects of powerlessness and control. These are issues about which contemporary workers are most likely to express concern or satisfaction. All the same, control over the means of production and over managerial direction are not distant utopian concerns for creative workers. The assignment of rights associated with the authorship of cultural products is a crucial issue determining compensation and recognition. And a great many creative workers operate either as freelances and/or they work in small enterprises, where in some cases at least it may be possible to influence managerial direction. We return to these questions in Chapters 5 and 6.

purpose in contributing toward a standardized product, since this inevitably involves repetitive work cycles.

(Blauner 1964: 23)

Also important was the scope of the process. 'It is more meaningful', claimed Blauner, 'to work on the whole, or a large part, of even a standardized product than to perform one's task on only a small part of the final product' (1964: 23). Workers may lack a sense of meaning when their own role is so circumscribed that they lack awareness of the purpose or function of the product. These aspects of alienation were of particular concern in relation to what some felt was an increasing complexity of the division of labour, and the 'bureaucratisation' of societies. But meaninglessness was not just about relation to product, process and organisation, but about how it fit into life. 'A person experiences alienation of this type when his individual acts seem to have no relation to a broader life-program' (p. 30).

A third type of alienation, for Blauner, consisted of *isolation*, a state he defined as one in which 'the worker feels no sense of belonging in the work situation' and is either unable to identify with 'the organization and its goals' (1964: 24). Drawing on Durkheim's analysis of anomie and the decline of traditional forms of solidarity in modern societies, Blauner suggested that good work could provide a sense of 'industrial community', comprising 'a network of social relationships which are derived from a work organization and which are valued by members of the community' (p. 24).

Finally, Blauner used the term *self-estrangement* to refer to effects of work that encourage the worker's alienation from his own self, 'a kind of depersonalized detachment rather than an immediate involvement or engrossment in the job tasks' (1964: 26), one which 'does not express the unique abilities, potentialities, or personality of the worker' (p. 26). Conversely, unalienated or good work was to be found where work was experienced as fulfilling in itself, or when 'the work activity is highly integrated into the totality of an individual's social commitments' (p. 26). Self-estranging work produced boredom and threatened self-esteem. Some occupations were already of low status in society. But jobs within occupations vary in the degree to which they offer 'opportunities for control, creativity, and challenge' (p. 30). Jobs with these features can contribute to the worker's sense of self-respect and dignity, and enhance people's self-esteem, even in low-status occupations. Again, as with meaninglessness, self-estrangement was also about the relationship between work and the rest of life. 'When work is self-estranging, occupation does not contribute in an affirmative manner to personal identity and selfhood, but instead is damaging to self-esteem' (p. 31).

These various aspects of alienation had two features in common, Blauner felt. One was that each alienated state made it more probable that workers could be used as means, rather than ends in themselves (1964: 33). They therefore turned people into 'things' – his version of Marx's comments on how work alienated humans from their nature as humans. The distinction about ends and means is an important ethical one. But using the language of good and bad work, rather than alienation, allows us to avoid futile debates about whether such terms are essentialist in themselves. The second shared feature of these types of alienated work was a *fragmentation* in people's existence and consciousness. In this respect, Blauner, like Marx, overestimates the possibility and quite probably the desirability of an organic wholeness of the self. Identity is always fragmented. A better notion of successful personhood might be to think instead about well-being: whether the relationships between the different parts of our selves operate in a healthy way, whether they allow us to flourish over time. There is a social and collective dimension to this, as well as an individual one – some social arrangements (and work arrangements) might be said to allow such flourishing more than others. In Blauner's hands, the notion of alienation is linked to this 'organic' model of the self.

2.3 Towards a model of good and bad work beyond alienation

Partly because we do not share that model of the self and society, and also for reasons of simplicity, we refer to good and bad work, rather than alienated or unalienated labour. In what follows, we criticise and build on Blauner's thinking to develop a model of good and bad work.

We are not alone in considering explicitly what might constitute good and bad work. Writers have used various terms for 'good' and 'bad', and have developed various frameworks. Randy Hodson (2001), in his invaluable summary of numerous ethnographic studies, uses the concept of dignity as the basis of his assessment of contemporary work, and he outlines ways in which workers experience challenges to their dignity: mismanagement and abuse, overwork, incursions of autonomy, and problems of participation and involvement.[8] We draw on Hodson's useful deliberations, and comment on his categorisation below. His concept of dignity is a valuable one, but, as with alienation, we feel that simply to use the terms 'good work' and 'bad work' allows us more flexibility, and to cover the normative ground more easily.

Russell Keat (2009) makes a similar move to us, preferring the term 'good work' to the term 'meaningful work' as discussed by a number of political philosophers, such as Rawls (1971) and Schwartz (1982): 'work that is interesting, that calls for intelligence and initiative, and that is attached to a job that gives the worker considerable freedom to decide how the work is to be done' (Arneson 1987: 522). Keat suggests that the question of whether work is 'good' might be less important, normatively, than '(a) having any work at all, and

---

8 For other uses of the term 'dignity' in relation to work, see Simone Weil (1974/1951), discussed later; and Andrew Sayer (2007) who valuably extends the way the term is used in modern employment practice and sociology of work beyond harassment and autonomy to include questions of respect, recognition and vulnerability.

(b) having work that is *decent*: secure, reasonably well paid, and with acceptable working conditions' (Keat 2009: 123). However, it seems to us that all the features in Keat's category (b) could just as easily be categorised as features of good work. And what Arneson calls meaningful work covers only two aspects of our features of good work as discussed below: autonomy and interest.[9]

A helpful and comprehensive discussion of research on 'good jobs' is provided by the economist Francis Green, in his book *Demanding Work* (2006). Green identifies six aspects of job quality: skill levels (because skills are 'the means by which people have the potential for self-fulfilment', Green 2006: 16); work effort or intensity; personal discretion over job tasks and participation in workplace decisions; pay; low risks and security (in terms of health and safety, and job tenure); and job satisfaction and affective well-being at work. Green is dealing almost entirely with 'objective' aspects of work, in the sense that they would widely be agreed to be quantifiable and measurable.[10] It will become apparent that some of his categories overlap with ours, which focus on subjective experience. Leaving such issues aside, we repeat that our concern is primarily with the exploration of subjective states and people's reflections about them (and on forces that might shape such experiences); and this is best done through the kind of qualitative work that we have undertaken.

Let us now try to develop our model of good and bad work, via a discussion of Blauner's concepts. An alternative word for the freedom and control that Blauner sees as the positive opposite pole of powerlessness is *autonomy*. Hodson discusses the importance of autonomy, which he feels to be particularly central for professional and craft workers whose jobs 'depend on the daily exercise of autonomy in relation to tools, techniques, and work priorities' (Hodson 2001: 140). Workers in these *relatively* powerful and high-status forms of work often have a very uneasy relationship with managers, and greater power in relation to management than many other workers. Hodson also states that such workers often report greater levels of job satisfaction and meaning, and greater levels of creativity at work, than other types of occupation. Many creative workers, we will argue, can be thought of as craft and professional workers, and seek forms of autonomy – though with crucial

---

9 These debates about meaningful work are important because they are about the distribution of good work across societies. We return to this question in addressing the social division of labour in Chapter 10.

10 The obvious exception is Green's category of subjective well-being. The use of survey data to measure other aspects of well-being besides wages is a welcome development in economics, even though there are many very difficult conceptual issues surrounding the operation of terms such as 'job satisfaction' and well-being in surveys. The move is welcome because it goes beyond the one-dimensional model of the person in neo-classical economics (see Nussbaum and Sen 1993). Our concern is qualitative, but we would be very pleased if this made a contribution to the building of theory that might help to refine well-conducted survey work concerning labour.

differences deriving from the particular status of aesthetic autonomy. Autonomy is such a difficult and disputed concept that we devote considerable further attention to it in this and the next chapter. But, we argue, it is a crucial normative concept for work as a whole (not just the professional and craft workers that Hodson discusses) and perhaps especially for creative work.

Turning to the concepts of meaninglessness and meaningfulness, Blauner seems to use these in two different and rather narrow ways. One refers to the worker's sense of the whole process of production, or lack of it. But it is not clear here whether Blauner's main concern is the effects of this on a worker's individual autonomy (that they become unable to exercise discretion because their own role is strictly delimited) or on their level of absorption and interest (the job is *boring* because its relation to the whole is not understood, or felt to be of concern). The former aspects are best dealt with under autonomy. The latter are important aspects of work. It may be best actually to use terms such as *interest*, involvement and absorption, or detachment and boredom, rather than meaningfulness and meaninglessness, which might best be reserved for the second way in which Blauner uses them, to refer to awareness of the purpose or, better still, the social and cultural value of products, and linked to that, the goals of the organisation producing them. We think it is best to deal with issues concerning good work in relation to the social and cultural value of *products* separately from process, so we return to this question of value in the next section.

Blauner's discussion of isolation is marked by an appeal to the value of integration into a community that is not unusual for US sociology of the mid-twentieth century. One danger of Blauner's take on this is how easily integration into work organisations might, under profit-making systems, become a way of encouraging a false sense of unity among people in the interests of the firm. Yet, if we modify our conceptualisation of it, it may be possible to talk of isolation as a feature of bad work. The desirable opposite of isolation might be better conceived as *sociality* rather than membership, and the merits of sociality might be conceived of in terms of the values of friendship, solidarity, cooperation and *shared* enjoyment and interest. Hodson writes that co-workers 'provide the social fabric that is often crucial for meaning at work' and 'a significant line of both formal and informal defense against managerial fiat' (Hodson 2001: 18). We apply this conceptualisation of isolation and sociality in this book.[11]

Most problematic of all is Blauner's conception of self-estrangement. This merges three different aspects of good and bad work: discussion of the

---

11 As we shall see in Chapter 7, one prominent variety of modern Marxism, often referred to as autonomism, puts special emphasis on the possibilities that solidarity and cooperation in modern forms of work might encourage broader forms of social solidarity that could bring about revolutionary transformations in society. We explore this dimension of sociality in that chapter using our ethnographic fieldwork.

'alienating' experience of boredom or the 'non-alienating' experience of interest or absorption; questions regarding the relationship of people's work to self-esteem; and their sense of fulfilment and development over time. We have already mentioned above that the first of these, interest or lack of it, is a separate feature of our model. The second element in Blauner's discussion of self-estrangment, *self-esteem*, also needs to be separated out, as it is too important to be merged into a broader category. It matters that work can enhance or diminish our sense of self-esteem and, related to this, our sense of others' respect for us, and recognition for our work.[12]

The third element of Blauner's discussion of self-estrangement, people's sense of fulfilment and development over time, is in our view extremely important in relation to good work. Concepts such as career, vocation and calling indicate desires for people to sustain good work over time (we return to these concepts in Chapter 7). The term we want to borrow to refer to this aspect of good work is *self-realisation*. This has its origins in translations of Hegelian ideas about humanity's historical achievement of its own potential, and has come to refer to 'the fulfilment by one's own efforts of the possibilities of development of the self' (the *Oxford English Dictionary*'s definition). The idea has roots that go deeper than those of the English word. Articulated by philosophers such as Rousseau and John Stuart Mill, it is a core goal of post-Enlightenment thought. Later, Freudian psychoanalysis sought to increase the individual's understanding and awareness for the sake of the development of the self. By the mid twentieth century, however, the idea of self-realisation had become attached to popular therapy movements that some writers see as deeply bound up with problematic forms of individualism (Illouz 2007: 45). The humanist psychologist and early management guru, Abraham Maslow (1987/1954), placed 'self-actualisation' – realising one's own personal talent or potential – at the top of his famous hierarchy of needs: when other more basic needs (physiological needs, needs for security, love and esteem) were met, then self-actualisation, 'the desire to become more and more what one is', could serve as a motivating force for human action.[13]

One problem with the concept is that in contemporary culture, notions of self-realisation and its close relative 'self-actualisation' are often not far removed from narcissistic forms of competitive individualism. Life coaching guru Anthony (or Tony) Robbins for example offers books, recordings and classes that use the concept of self-actualisation to show us 'how to awaken

---

12 In recent years, matters of esteem have been pushed to the fore in political theory by contributions that have argued for and against the idea of *recognition* as the basis of justice and other normative claims. These are notably encapsulated in Fraser and Honneth (2003). See Rössler (2007) for discussion of the politics of recognition in relation specifically to work.

13 Creativity was tied closely to this. As Maslow himself put it, 'the concept of creativeness' and the concept of the self-actualizing, fully human person seem to be coming closer and closer together, and may perhaps turn out to be the same thing' (Maslow 1971, quoted in Illouz 2007: 45).

the giant within' (Robbins 1992).[14] It is possible then to see a focus on self-realisation as evidence of a 'culture of narcissism' (Lasch 1980). The German social theorist Axel Honneth has argued that increasingly, in the twentieth century, 'members of Western societies were compelled, urged or encouraged, for the sake of their own future, to place their very selves at the centre of their own life-planning and practice' (Honneth 2004: 469). As a result, individual self-realisation becomes linked to 'institutionalized expectations' and 'transmuted into a support of the system's legitimacy' (p. 467).

Do such developments make self-realisation irredeemable as a normative concept? Not necessarily (and Honneth does not think so either). The concept of self-realisation need not be an example of out-of-control narcissism or competitive individualism. Progressive collectivist political projects generally involve some kind of notion of self-realisation. Jon Elster claims, for example, that while Marx thought that communism would be better than capitalism for a number of reasons, he condemned the latter 'mainly because it frustrated human development and self-actualization'; this was the other side of Marx's much more sketchily portrayed concept of alienation. Communism was a society in which people could 'fully realize their potential as all-round creators' (Elster 1985: 83). Nor does the appropriation of the term by management gurus and therapists diminish its importance in understanding human life. The fundamentally ambivalent achievements of psychoanalysis (see Zaretsky 2005) include an emphasis on the pursuit of healthy self-realisation, and at its best this can involve working towards a reflexive understanding of the limits on this goal. Our aim here is not to advocate a Marxian or psychoanalytical concept of self-realisation, but to point out that the term need not be linked to competitive individualism or narcissistic fantasies about individual triumph. It can serve as the basis of ethical discussions concerning the place of work, and of creative labour, within conceptions of human well-being and social justice. It makes it possible for us to discuss how work, and other key elements, might contribute to a (pluralist) notion of successful development of the self over time. As with autonomy, we return to this concept below (Sections 2.5 to 2.7).

Some vital aspects of bad work appear to be missing from Blauner's breakdown of alienation. The improvements in working conditions in the United States in the 1950s and 1960s may have led him to assume that problems of job *security* and *overwork* were not sufficiently important to include in his framework. Or it may be that Blauner did not consider these to be aspects of alienation per se, but part of some broader problem of pay and conditions. Whatever the reasons, these surely need to be included in any

---

14 To add confusion, the concept of self-realisation is also widely used by religious and spiritualist movements, where the aim often appears to be a fantasy of self-mastery, or elsewhere something closer to self-abnegation in the face of materialism (for example, in the thought of Ivan Illich).

consideration of the quality of work as experienced by workers. It is true that under his categories of powerlessness and control, Blauner recognised that control over the pace of work was critical and constitutes 'the most insistent, the most basic aspect of a job' (1964: 21). But to subsume it under control seems not to do justice to this importance, and moreover, this is only one type of overwork.[15] Hodson categorises overwork as one of the major challenges to dignity in the workplace, and as well as the intensity of work, he also considers excessive hours. Employees work too hard and too long not only where they lack autonomy, but also in cases where there are 'contradictions of employee involvement'. Programs calling for heightened employee involvement, such as work teams, quality circles and so on, have the potential to increase responsibility and dignity at work, says Hodson, but 'they also can be used manipulatively to pressure workers to work harder and to increase output through intensified self-supervision and peer pressure' (Hodson 2001: 20).[16] All this relates to the question of balancing the emotional, physical and time demands of work with other aspects of life, including caring for the young and the elderly, contributing to communities, and simply enriching one's life through leisure.

Insecurity is an interesting term, because it has an objective, measurable sense, concerning conditions and length of job tenure, but it also has a widely used subjective meaning too. When we say we feel insecure, we suggest that we lack a sense of safety. This might involve threats to our physical health, through injury and contact with harmful substances, and physical effects of mental states such as anxiety and 'stress'. But we might also feel insecure about our futures. Workers on short-term contracts might especially feel this to be the case. But there are other dimensions too, related to ethnicity, class, gender and age. One of the most important contributions to sociology of work in recent years has been Richard Sennett's explorations of the 'corrosive' effects of flexible work (Sennett 1998). In his chapter on risk (Sennett 1998: 76–97), he writes about how the current conditions of corporate life are 'full of prejudices against middle age, disposed to deny the worth of a person's past experience' and treating the middle-aged as averse to *risk*; and he traces the disillusioning effects of this on Rose, a New York bar-owner who tried to break into advertising.

2.4 Good products as good work

We have now encountered a number of the main elements comprising our model of good and bad work, one which is substantially different from

---

15 Green (2006: 47–9) provides a valuable discussion of conceptualisation and measurement (through surveys) of work effort or work intensity.

16 As we suggested in Chapter 1, this kind of internalised commitment to work, resulting in overwork, is a key part of the critical case 'against' creative labour in recent years. We return to this issue in the next chapter.

Blauner's model of alienated and unalienated labour. To summarise so far, we have outlined a conception of good work as involving autonomy, interest and involvement, sociality, self-esteem, self-realisation, work–life balance and security. Conversely, this is a conception of bad work as involving control by or dependence on others; boredom; isolation; low self-esteem or shame; frustrated self-realisation, overwork and risk.[17]

These elements relate mainly to the experience of the *process* of paid work. However, as we indicated above in our discussion of Blauner's concept of meaninglessness, there are crucial further dimensions to our understanding of good work involving *the social and cultural value of products* (see Table 2.1).[18] There are two main dimensions of good and bad work in relation to products that we want to highlight. Bad work can be said to involve the production and dissemination of (a) *inferior* goods and services, and (b) *products that diminish the well-being of others* in society – or even harm them. When we say 'others in society' we mean primarily consumers of these products, but such harm can be indirect, for example when goods damage the environment. Conversely, then, good work involves producing goods and services that are *excellent* and that *promote aspects of the common good*. Of course, these two different aspects of good work, in terms of products, can float free of each other. A product may be created to the highest standards available and be dangerous or damaging to large numbers of people. This is true of explosive devices and it may also be true of television programmes.

Let us explain why we feel the need to include the issue of products in our notion of good work, even though our primary focus is on worker experience. This will also give us the opportunity to elucidate our understanding of the relationships between good work as good process and as good product. First, workers may experience many of the features of good work listed above, such as high levels of pay, long holidays and reasonable working hours, a strong sense of belonging and identity, high levels of autonomy, and yet still work in a situation where resulting products are not of a high standard. It seems dubious to apply the term 'good work' unequivocally to such a situation.

Second, and similarly, workers may have good experiences of work that is oriented towards limited, or even ethically dubious ends. This might be called the Oppenheimer problem. As Richard Sennett discusses, Robert Oppenheimer, director of the Los Alamos project that created the world's first atomic bomb, wrote in his diary: 'When you see something that is technically sweet, you go ahead and do it and you argue about what to do about it only after you have had your technical success' (quoted by Sennett 2008: 2). Or, to give an example from television, a producer may take great pride in putting together

---

17 Of course, risk can be good too, or at least exhilarating. We address this contradiction.
18 A notion of good work that involved only workers' experience of the labour process would risk severing the ethics of work from the ethics of production.

a programme that is slickly appealing and amusing about the pleasures of motor vehicles. But if this programme serves to trivialise and distort serious issues of consequence for societies, including climate change and consumerism, then should this really be understood as good work?[19]

We need to explore these issues further here, before returning to them when we consider how creative workers talk about their products and audiences (in Chapters 8 and 9). In their book *Habits of the Heart*, based on interviews conducted in the USA in the 1980s, Robert Bellah, Richard Madsen, William Sullivan, Ann Swidler and Steven Tipton (2008/1985) portray a society where people have little understanding of the social value of their work. Instead people seem to work for personal gratification and financial comfort. This suggests, as the political philosopher Russell Muirhead (2004: 111) points out, that contemporary versions of the work ethic are ethically fragile, shorn of their basis in the religious commitment to 'a calling' in the service of god, and resting 'on a combination of blind habit, a steely will to survive amid heartless competition, and the promise of status and physical comfort'. The solution for Bellah et al., and for others such as Gardner, Csikszentmihalyi and Damon (2001), is to rescue work by advocating a change in its meaning from 'private aggrandizement to public contribution' (Bellah et al 2008/1985: 289).

This move will be attractive to anyone committed to notions of the common good. However, it is worth defending the intrinsic value of work done well, separately from the question of social contribution. As Muirhead (2004: 151) points out, the social contribution of work may not be a sufficient basis for good work for everyone. It seems likely that there will be many people who may not wish to devote themselves to the common good. We need, says Muirhead, to consider the intrinsic value of work as well as its potential to contribute to the well-being of others. To grasp this, he turns to the Aristotelian concept of a *practice*, as developed by the philosopher Alisdair MacIntyre: a coherent and complex form of cooperative human activity 'through which goods[20] internal to that form of activity are realized in the course of trying to achieve those standards of excellence which are appropriate to, and partially definitive of, that form of activity, with the result

---

19 The main way in which such issues have been addressed in media studies is via ideology critique: the critical analysis of texts to uncover the ways in which they, often unconsciously, reinforce prevailing systems of power and inequality in society (see Thompson 1990; Downey 2008). Our focus on the experiences and products of cultural production as labour does not incorporate ideology critique but it is potentially complementary to it, because it reveals another, different way in which power and inequality manifest themselves.

20 'Goods' here is used in the sense of 'rewards' rather than 'things to be possessed'. And, in case it is not clear, the term 'practice' is being used here in a specific philosophical sense rather than in the broader sense, recently popular in social and political theory, to refer to the importance of understanding societies in terms of routinised forms of action and understanding (Schatzki 1996; Warde 2005).

that human powers to achieve excellence, and human conceptions of the ends and goods involved, are systematically extended' (MacIntyre 1984: 187).[21]

The notion of *standards of excellence* is extremely important. MacIntyre is defending the ethics of pursuing excellence.[22] *Goods internal to that form of activity* is a crucial phrase too. Internal goods or rewards 'are such that their character can only be identified by reference to the specific nature of the practice concerned and its particular standards' (Keat 2000: 23). External goods or rewards are by contrast not dependent on the nature of the practice through which it is achieved. These include money, power, prestige and status.

It is worth clarifying some potential misunderstandings regarding the contrast between external and internal goods. As Russell Keat (2000: 23) points out, this is not a simple contrast between 'altruistic and egoistic motivations', and practices do not have to involve self-sacrifice. For both internal and external rewards can benefit their recipients. Nor can the internal goods associated with practices be reduced to the pleasure or enjoyment of those undertaking them. Muirhead notes that pleasure might be available in all sorts of ways without doing anything demanding like learning to perform all the different aspects of a practice well. And both internal and external rewards can involve competition. The main difference is in the greater *exclusivity* of the latter. Success in achieving internal rewards is at least partly non-exclusive – the achievement of excellence can be a good thing for the whole community who participate in the practice because it enriches them. So, when Arctic Monkeys released their remarkable first album, they achieved money, prestige and status, but they also enriched the lives of those participating in the world of alternative or indie rock. Similarly, when Cristiano Ronaldo emerged as one of the greatest players football has seen, his speed, balance and power enraged supporters of opposing teams, but arguably enriched the lives of those who enjoy football.

Here then we see a potential link back to process from product in our model of good work, to ideas of meaning and purpose, self-realisation and autonomy. Internal goods are important partly because of a sense of shared participation in the attempt to achieve excellence, and as part of the evolving history of that practice. And this can lead to a further good, 'the good of a certain kind of life' (MacIntyre 1984: 190). Practices might only rarely give meaning to an entire life, and the effort to achieve excellence may detract from other aspects of our lives, but societies strongly oriented

---

21 Practices need to be sustained and of sufficient size to include numerous sub-activities. Planting turnips is not an example of a practice in this sense, says MacIntyre, but farming is. Kicking or throwing a football with skill is not a practice, but football is. But many activities are practices: 'arts, sciences, games, politics, the making and sustaining of family life' (MacIntyre, 1984: 188).

22 In Macintyre's conception, this means understanding that some know more about what constitutes excellence than others, although these standards may change. Some might argue that this represents elitism. But even socially just and equal societies will need experts.

Table 2.1 Conceptualising good and bad work

	Good work	Bad work
Process	Good wages, working hours, high levels of safety	Poor wages, working hours and levels of safety
	Autonomy	Powerlessness
	Interest, involvement	Boredom
	Sociality	Isolation
	Self-esteem	Low self-esteem and shame
	Self-realisation	Frustrated development
	Work–life balance	Overwork
	Security	Risk
Product	Excellent products	Low-quality products
	Products that contribute to the common good	Products that fail to contribute to the well-being of others

to practices, in MacIntyre's Aristotelian sense, will tend to be good ones.[23] Muirhead's suggestion is that the concept of a practice offers a way of grounding the promise of fulfilment (Muirhead 2004: 164; we prefer the term 'self-realisation') in the specific character of work, as opposed to alternative ethics based for example on being 'passionate' about one's job without any regard for what it consists of, or of sacrificing oneself to the common good.[24]

We are now in a position to summarise the main concepts that we intend to use in what follows (see Table 2.1).

However, as we mentioned earlier, two concepts still need further justification and clarification – autonomy and self-realisation. We address these now, and part of our concern is to defend these concepts from excessive critique associated with post-structuralism. We feel the need to do this, because post-structuralist analysis has been widespread and influential in the sociology of work and organisations, and in business and management studies; it has also influenced the cultural studies critiques of creative labour we discussed in Section 1.3.

2.5 Autonomy as a feature of good work?

In its most basic philosophical form, to be autonomous means 'to be one's own person, to be directed by considerations, desires, conditions, and characteristics that are not simply imposed externally upon one, but are part of what

---

23 There is a link to social justice here, which we shall return to in the final chapter of this book. Muirhead's hope is that, by considering the internal rewards of numerous jobs – remember that these serve human flourishing and the common good in MacIntyre's conception – we might gain a better understanding of what reforms may be necessary to spread meaningful work better across societies and individuals.

24 On the use of 'passion' to legitimate neo-liberal values with regard to work, see Nick Couldry and Jo Littler's compelling article on *The Apprentice* (2010).

can somehow be considered one's authentic self' (Chrisman 2009: no page). For some social and political theorists influenced by post-structuralism, the Enlightenment concept of autonomous subjectivity is highly compromised through its links to humanism.[25] Yet, as many theorists have pointed out, including some influenced by post-structuralism (e.g., Fraser 1989; Knights 2000) to dispense with the concept of autonomy altogether takes away a potentially valuable tool for probing freedom and independence in modern societies. This would include the domains of labour, and creative labour.

Although the significance of autonomy was initially derived from its centrality in Kantian and utilitarian philosophy's conceptions of the person, and of personal morality, it has long since multiplied in its uses beyond philosophy, and it cannot be dismissed on the grounds of its associations with those traditions. We use it to refer to 'self-determination', but we recognise that autonomy cannot simply be understood as freedom from others (MacIntyre 1984: 205, 221).[26] For all autonomy is limited, in that individuals and groups are, to some extent at least, socially constituted by others beyond themselves. This 'limitation' can be seen as a desirable aspect of human sociality. Total autonomy in any sphere of life – whether artistic, scientific or ethical – is an impossible ideal, because there is no life without constraints or determinants.

We intend the term in a sociological sense that retains its connections to these philosophical origins. It is often applied to groups, including groups of workers, as much as to individuals. A difficulty in the present context is that the concept of autonomy as self-determination is widely used in at least two quite different ways relevant to our study of work in the cultural industries. One is autonomy at work or *workplace autonomy* – the degree of self-determination that individual workers or groups of workers have within a certain work situation. The other is *creative autonomy*, the degree to which 'art', knowledge, symbol-making and so on can and/or should operate independently of the influence of other determinants. Here we focus on questions of workplace autonomy, beginning from a couple of useful sociological interventions

---

25 By humanism, post-structuralists tend to mean not the attempt to seek meaning in the human rather than divine or spiritual, but what Foucault (following Heidegger) in his book *The Order of Things* (1973) identifies as a modern discursive formation. This is the project by which modern Enlightenment thought sought to achieve the triumph of human beings as subjects by, in Nancy Fraser's gloss, 'achieving autonomy by mastering the other in history, in society, in oneself, of making substance into subject' (Fraser 1989: 40). This project, for many post-structuralists, is 'self-defeating, self-contradictory, and can lead in practice only to domination' (ibid.). Foucault provides a way of criticising objectionable practices without resort to humanism. The problem for Fraser is that he fails to set up an alternative grounding of values but instead insinuates that values can neither have nor warrant justification (Fraser 1989: 42).

26 As Gary Breen (2007: 400) helpfully puts it, discussing the philosopher Alisdair MacIntyre, this view of autonomy as 'freedom from others' is a mistaken one that can be found in Nietzsche, Sartre and much liberal thinking; rather, autonomy is based on interdependence, but with the possibility of independent active practical reasoning.

that serve to concretise the necessarily abstract discussion we have engaged in so far. We defer our discussion of creative autonomy to the next chapter (Section 3.6).

2.5.1 Two accounts of workplace autonomy

Mike Sosteric (1996) has addressed the issue of the degree to which relative autonomy in the workplace might be thought of as a feature of good work.[27] He bases his account on a distinction between two strategies of organisational control, made by a Marxian sociologist Andrew Friedman in 1977. Friedman distinguished between two types of strategy that senior managers use to exercise authority over labour power – direct control and responsible autonomy. The former tries to limit labour power by coercive threats, close supervision and minimising the responsibility of individual workers. By contrast, the other strategy of responsible autonomy

> attempts to harness the adaptability of labour power by giving workers leeway and encouraging them to adapt to changing situations in a manner beneficial to the firm. To do this top managers give workers status, authority and responsibility. Top managers try to win their loyalty, and co-opt their organisations to the firm's ideals … ideologically.
>
> (Friedman 1977: 78)

Both strategies have been present throughout history, says Friedman, but responsible autonomy 'has been applied most consistently to privileged workers and the Direct Control type of strategy to the rest' (1977: 79). With the rise of monopoly capitalism, involving a greater size and complexity of firms, along with increasing resistance by workers during the early twentieth century, management becomes better organised and more conscious, and this for Friedman led to a rise in the relative importance of responsible autonomy. Friedman was highly critical of the notion of responsible autonomy, which he saw in Marxian terms as an ideological trope: responsible autonomy does not remove alienation or exploitation, it 'simply softens their operation or draws workers' attention away from them' (ibid.). As we shall see below, this pessimism is echoed by later post-structuralist researchers.

In his ethnographic study of workers in a Canadian nightclub, Sosteric observed a shift in the nightclub from a version of responsible autonomy to an attempt to exert direct control. At the beginning of his time at the club, staff and servers were allowed to develop 'highly personalised service styles'

---

27 To be clear, we are not conceiving of nightclubs as cultural industries here; bars are better understood as part of the food and drink industry – which has important relations with the cultural industries. We focus on Sosteric's study because of its unusual normative clarity about questions of autonomy. A context for his study is the desire to extend debates about 'meaningful' or 'good' work into service and especially retail industries.

(Sosteric 1996: 301). This included an 'unceremonious' attitude to the removal of difficult customers who harassed waitresses or otherwise showed little respect to staff. However, the clientele seemed to appreciate this non-standardised service and the club was extremely popular. There were good relations between customers and staff, a low turnover of staff, a high degree of consumer loyalty and repeat business, and good job security. Training in the working practices of the club was provided informally in after-work staff gatherings. Serving staff formed an extremely tight-knit relationship with each other. Sosteric provides a summary of work in the club:

> Clearly, employees enjoyed considerable control, responsibility and autonomy. Direct forms of control were almost never exercised against tenured staff. It is of course possible to argue that this was because the employees had internalised the mechanisms of control. But the success of the system was based primarily on its ability to balance the needs of the staff with those of the organisation. The organisation itself enjoyed long-term success and a degree of market security unusual in this type of service business that normally is characterised by short life-spans.
>
> (Sosteric 1996: 305)

However, these more individualised forms of service led to some complaints from customers. These were directed further up the hierarchy to upper management, who were not involved directly in the nightclub, but who worked for the small hotel chain that housed the club. On the grounds of 'quality' and the need for 'attitude adjustment' on the part of staff, a new manager was introduced who brought in increasingly direct control of the work carried out in the nightclub. All intermediary supervisory positions such as head waitress, head bartender and head doorman were eliminated, concentrating power in the hands of the manager and assistant manager. Performance was closely monitored, including by covert observation, and, in order to gauge the appropriateness of responses, via deliberate provocation of staff by hired visitors. The response of staff to these new measures of direct control was to withdraw 'authentic emotional exchange and substitute it with the minimum level of superficial agreeability' (Sosteric 1996: 309), a form of industrial sabotage that resulted in the disintegration of the sociable character of work in the nightclub.

Sosteric recognises that the relations between labour and management in this nightclub were always 'asymmetric' and that working relations involved the construction of subjectivity on the part of workers, in the interests of making profit for the nightclub owners. He also takes the view that the very nature of the nightclub ('a sexual marketplace') may involve exploiting the individualism and even isolation widespread in modern societies. Once 'socialised' into the nightclub, workers were prepared to put up with a number of questionable aspects of the club. While conceding all these aspects, however, Sosteric argues that, perhaps especially in jobs involving extended social interaction by workers, the codification and standardisation of behaviour can have negative consequences for workers – and indeed for capitalists (after all, the club's business fell apart with the introduction of direct control).

This study provides some useful context for understanding creative labour in the cultural industries. Only some work in the cultural industries offers the high levels of control, responsibility and autonomy to be found in the Canadian nightclub. But Sosteric reminds us, through his close study, that these can be genuinely desirable aspects of work, with positive consequences for employees and for owners. The problem that remains though, both for creative labour and other forms of labour that offer relatively high levels of autonomy, such as the nightclub workers studied by Sosteric, might be put as follows. Is workplace autonomy really better understood as a mechanism to distract workers' attention from the 'real' exploitation and alienation lying beneath the surface of their working life? Friedman's Marxian analysis resulted in a 'yes' to this question. As we shall see in Section 2.7, other writers, especially those influenced by post-structuralism, take a related but different approach. The positive elements of work are seen in effect as compensatory mechanisms, or even as forms of 'seduction'.

2.6 Self-realisation as a feature of good work?

Before exploring these issues further, we now turn to the other element of our normative framework that, as we recognised above, might be controversial, perhaps especially for some post-structuralists: self-realisation. Although he does not explicitly use the term, the sociologist Douglas Ezzy has addressed this issue in an article that considers the problem of how to adequately conceptualise the difference between work that is ' "alienating" or "liberating" ' (Ezzy 1997: 429) – his language for what we are presenting as the broader problem of distinguishing between good and bad work. To do so, Ezzy turns to the philosophy of Simone Weil. For Weil, as for Marx, pay and conditions are only part of the problem of work. But whereas Marx addresses the problem of good or bad work through the concept of alienation, Weil conceives the problem in terms of the way that the organisation of contemporary work 'prevents the worker understanding or experiencing the task as a dignified use of his or her faculties' (Ezzy 1997: 438). Highly routinised work,[28] for example, is oppressive because the work is performed out of *fear*, 'rather than within the framework of an awareness of the purpose or value of the task' (p. 439). Good work, in Ezzy's reading of Weil, involves work being part of a life narrative in which current activities promise to lead into a desired

---

28 Often known as Taylorised work, after Frederick Taylor, associated with the development of 'scientific management', which sought to routinise labour tasks in order to maximise efficiency. The neo-Weberian 'MacDonaldization thesis' (Ritzer 1994) sees work as increasingly technologised, rationalised and deskilled.

and valued future. Importantly, this requires a cultural and social context in which shared cultural discourses construct the work as worthwhile; and in which work provides the worker with the opportunity to fulfil commitments to other people and society in general. It should be clear that this is a notion of good work that combines some of the features of our own model, including self-esteem and a version of sociality. But in invoking a sense of a person's development over time, it particularly emphasises what we are calling self-realisation.

As Ezzy recognises, this requires an adequate notion of the self. His emphasis on a context where activities are constructed as worthwhile (self-esteem) is linked by Ezzy to a theory of the subject derived from hermeneutics, especially the work of Paul Ricoeur, which considers what constitutes 'a good life', including an ethical life.[29] Reflexive narration (if only to oneself rather than to others) is key to this, for it can provide a sense of connectedness and temporal unity to a person's being. In articulating this vision of selfhood, Ricoeur, for Ezzy, captures a middle ground between conceptions of identity and work that place too much emphasis on agency, and those that overly emphasise the linguistic and contextual sources of the self. This, then, is a particular notion of work as potentially part of a human project of self-realisation, but one which is grounded in a sociological appreciation of problems of constraint and freedom, structure and agency. Ezzy is seeking to move beyond a dilemma in Marxian and post-Marxian labour process research, whereby 'the person tends to be either depicted as a passive reflection of social structure, or as an active autonomous subject resisting the influence of oppressive social forces' (Ezzy 1997: 428).

2.7 Post-structuralist critique of work and the problem of values

Ezzy, then, provides some pointers for how we might think about aspects of good work in relation to notions of self-realisation, including a conception of the self.[30] This is of course a philosophical minefield, and it would be foolhardy to stray too far into it. The main way we wish to proceed is briefly to defend the (broad) conceptions of self-realisation and autonomy outlined above against one particular critique. First, though, we need to defend the

---

29 The (Aristotelian) idea that ethical reflection on what constitutes a good life is valuable does not in itself imply that there should be one 'single conception of self-realization of the good life that is universally shared', as Nancy Fraser (in Fraser and Honneth 2003: 30) oddly claims, though of course it means making normative claims that some lives are lived better than others.

30 For a much more extended and philosophical (rather than sociological) approach to questions of work and self-realisation, see Murphy (1993). Writing from an explicitly Aristotelian perspective on 'moral economy', Murphy (1993: 225) argues that self-realisation is central to human flourishing, so we need to consider what it means, what kinds of work foster it, and what ought to be done to create more opportunity for self-realization in work.

very idea of constructing a model of good and bad work. For to construct such a model at all is to work against the grain of many critical studies of work and organisations, which have been characterised either by an outright rejection of normativity, or by hazy conceptualisation of normative principles. This rejection of normativity is particularly marked among post-structuralist researchers in the field of business, management and organisational studies.[31] Central here are debates about subjectivity.

In the emerging business schools, the post-war crisis in work (discussed in Chapter 1) helped to fuel an increasing interest in 'post-bureaucratic' forms of organisation, including 'craft' forms.[32] It was at this point, as we saw in Chapter 1, that the term 'creativity' emerged as a major part of the management lexicon, as part of a growing advocacy of the individual responsibility and autonomy of workers. Bureaucracy was portrayed by critics of capitalism as stifling of adaptability, enterprise, individuality and creativity. The celebration of these qualities by managers and academics was later to be a powerful way of countering the critique and crisis of capitalist work, as Luc Boltanski and Eve Chiapello (2005/1999) show in their study of the 'new spirit of capitalism'. For many Marxists, however, the post-war crisis in work was better understood simply as a product of the exploitation of labour, and organisational forms and management techniques were therefore of little interest. This was changed by Harry Braverman's Marxian analysis (1974), which, condemning management's separation of mental and manual labour and the historical degradation or deskilling of working-class jobs, reinvigorated the sociology of work, and launched a new sub-field that crossed the sociology of work and organisations and critical management studies: labour process theory. However, Braverman paid little attention to subjective understanding or experience of work.[33] One strand of the new generation of critical workplace studies began to fill this gap by analysing worker experiences and subjectivities via ethnography or observation, sometimes within a Gramscian framework (Burawoy 1979; Cockburn 1983).

Another strand of organisational research, drawn to the notion of labour process, but less inclined to Marxism and more towards post-structuralism, found such studies guilty of setting up simplistic dualisms of structure and agency, control and resistance (e.g., Willmott and Knights 1989). These post-structuralist studies suggested, following the work of Foucault and others,

---

31 We should explain that our own position towards post-structuralism is generally ambivalent rather than hostile. Post-structuralist researchers have, in many respects, enriched understandings of subjectivity, history and work – three key themes that we wish to address in this book.

32 In fact some of the earliest studies of cultural-industry organisations emerged out of such an interest, notably Hirsch (1972), referring to Stinchcombe's (1959) comparison of craft and bureaucratic administration of production.

33 He did so because he felt that 'what is needed first of all is a picture of the working class as it exists' (Braverman 1974: 27) rather than of its consciousness.

ways in which particular 'technologies of the self' underpinned modern capitalism and contemporary forms of work. Individual entrepreneurship and self-realisation were presented as superficially desirable but fundamentally problematic aspects of modern labour (Rose 1999). The post-structuralists were supported by other more ethnographically oriented analysts, who emphasised the way that employees might 'internalise' organisational goals and values. For example, Gideon Kunda's study of corporate culture in an engineering company found that productive work there was 'the result of a combination of self-direction, initiative, and emotional attachment', one which combined the firm's 'interest in productivity with the employees' personal interest in growth and maturity' (Kunda 1992: 10).

That attention to the politics of subjectivity in the post-structuralist litera-ture on work and organisations is potentially valuable and we attempt to engage with the best elements of such research in this book. The high degree of personal investment that many in the cultural and media industries put into what they do, an investment that may derive from the residues of artistic, craft and artisanal forms still found in creative labour, mean that these studies of 'internalisation' offer a useful resource for our understanding of good and bad work in the cultural industries.

There are, however, serious limitations to this contribution from post-structuralism, and the most prominent derive from the way in which post-structuralist analysis usually addresses questions of normativity. To explore these limitations, and to clarify our defence of the normative, we now wish to examine a critique of Sosteric's and Ezzy's approaches by two leading post-structuralist researchers Damien O'Doherty and Hugh Willmott (2001). Our immediate goal is to defend the taking of any normative position in rela-tion to labour. But in doing so, we also seek to clarify further our use of the concepts of self-realisation and autonomy (see also Hesmondhalgh 2010a).

2.7.1 *Good work: critique of a critique*

O'Doherty and Willmott (2001: 469) accuse Sosteric of paying insufficient attention to the contradictions involved in worker autonomy and offering only 'a familiar labour process meta-narrative' where the work of employees is deskilled and degraded. According to O'Doherty and Willmott, this is the narrative underlying Braverman's 1974 account of the general history of capitalist work in the twentieth century, and they see this as underpinning Sosteric's much more specific account. They accuse Sosteric of seeing power as something that is exercised only during the phase of direct control, and not the phase of work in the nightclub where considerable autonomy was given to staff. They also claim that post-structural analysis is much more fruitful than this supposedly unsophisticated approach, because it 'understands power relations to be co-implicated with existential concerns and identity, together with the economics of managing the employment relation' (O'Doherty and Willmott 2001: 470). Sosteric, in O'Doherty and Willmott's view, 'seems to ignore the extent to which employees were already disciplined by their own sense of self-identity during the period preceding the imposition of rigid criteria of service'; and he shows 'no appreciation of how employees may become entranced by an idea of themselves as independent subjects' (2001: 469).

O'Doherty and Willmott do not criticise Sosteric on the grounds of the inaccuracy or implausibility of his empirical work. Their critique is of his failure to see that what he presents as a 'reasonably successful and harmonious workplace' (ibid.) was in fact a kind of illusion: the employees were being disciplined by their own sense of self-identity, their naive notions that they were actually enjoying their work more; they were, in O'Doherty and Willmott's words, 'entranced'. No evidence specific to the nightclub is provided to support this interpretation, and so this claim is presumably based on one of two possible views that O'Doherty and Willmott hold about the employees observed by Sosteric. The first, indicated in the extracts quoted above, is that (seemingly) all employees in capitalist modernity are *entranced* in this way, *seduced* by an illusion of freedom. The second is that the workers' pleasure in their work during the phase of relative autonomy was based on a problematic self-identity that somehow made them more vulnerable to the changes that came later. This is indicated when O'Doherty and Willmott write that the nightclub workers were 'ill prepared' to resist the later changes that challenged their earlier sense of independence, because they were '[m]esmerised by a sense of autonomy that was formed prior to their employment at the club' (2001: 469). What is striking about this critique of Sosteric (and his nightclub workers) is the seeming impossibility of any hope of good work in capitalist modernity. The quality of any apparently good job, it seems, is in reality based on a seductive illusion of freedom. The possibility of a good life for anyone in this highly disciplined society seems even more distant. For all workers are, apparently, entranced by their own sense of personal self-identity and autonomy.

Ezzy is also strongly criticised by O'Doherty and Willmott. Claiming that he sees the context in which work is done as determining whether employment is experienced as good work or as alienating and degrading, O'Doherty and Wilmott (2001) accuse Ezzy of relying on an 'analytical disjuncture' between, on the one hand, work, and on the other, 'the shared social context that provides the resources and opportunities within which work can be made dignified' (2001: 472). '[T]he seemingly benign language of "good work"' (ibid.), they say, attempts to reconcile and seal a traditional sociological dualistic division – between work and a broader social context. That division is 'the product of a more profound theoretical intolerance towards thinking the processual, the complex and the paradoxical' (ibid.).

This is important for our present concerns because O'Doherty and Willmott are taking Ezzy to task for the way in which he attempts to develop an account of 'good work', and in particular the way in which work might fit, or fail to fit, into projects of self-realisation – in Ezzy's terms, a person's more or less coherent sense of their own subjectivity over a lifetime. Whether or not the particular account of subjectivity used by Ezzy, based on a notion of 'narrative identity' derived from Ricoeur, is fruitful, O'Doherty and Willmott's post-structuralist analysis seem to swat aside *any* discussion of the possibility of good work in relation to an individual's sense of its value and meaning. Their basis for doing so is thin. For they are not at all clear why the idea that the meaning of work for individuals might be affected by its context – the way others might interpret that work as more or less dignified or valuable – fails to address 'process, complexity and paradox' (2001: 471). They rely on the following description of what their preferred theories – Althusserian Marxism, post-structuralism and deconstruction – are able to provide instead:

> an analysis of 'the subtle inter-articulation and relational tensions that lie between the "macro" and the "micro", the "part" and the "whole", or "work" and the cultural and social context' that comes before the category definition and entity stabilisation in the volatility of agency-in-action. If we avoid the challenge of thinking in – and of – this fathomless space, a space moreover of struggle and strife – we risk accepting the restrictive ontology of dualistic categories that occludes and closes down the unformed swarm of social activity diffuse across the labour process.
>
> (O'Doherty and Willmott 2001: 471)

Such attacks on dualisms are a common feature of post-structuralist writing (though not always formulated quite as opaquely as this). However, distinctions of the kind listed by O'Doherty and Willmott – work and context, macro and micro – are not necessarily 'restrictive' in and of themselves, as is implied here. Indeed, such distinctions are often valuable, even crucial, for cogent social analysis (see Archer 1995; Layder 1997: 165). What is more, at no point does Ezzy deny that there are 'tensions' between work and its context. In fact, his argument seems precisely to concern such tensions.

Returning now to the issue of models of selfhood, O'Doherty and Willmott find Ezzy's borrowing from Ricoeur problematic. Ezzy, they say, is guilty of relying on a notion of a sovereign rational individual, one that is problematised by post-structuralist writers, especially Foucault. This is because, according to them, Ezzy has a conception in which '[t]hrough the exercise of reflexive self-consciousness the individual acts as the sole obligatory point of passage, or bridge, between the experience of degradation and meaningful, dignified, self-worth' (2001: 472). In this erroneous conception, good work 'is something that is possible through the subjective will-to-power of individuals and collectives who, it is implied, are capable of constructing, by means of negotiation and dialogue, a re-envisioned Habermasian style project of socio-political utopia' (p. 472). But we can find no evidence of utopianism (whether Habermasian or otherwise) in Ezzy's piece. In fact, Ezzy clearly acknowledges the limitations on subjects imposed by discourse and social location, and he does so in ways that suggest complexity and paradox, using Ricoeur to attempt to mediate between overly determinist and overly voluntaristic accounts of subjectivity. O'Doherty and Willmott seem to be over-reacting to a conception that invokes *any* sense of agency or a valuable reflexive self-consciousness – as well as to any sense of the possibility of work being good at all. They seem to confuse the discussion of individual experience itself with adherence to a particular conception of individuality or personhood.

So it becomes very hard to see what for O'Doherty and Willmott might constitute good and bad work in modern societies, or even work that is something less than dreadful. O'Doherty and Willmott's response to Ezzy's account of 'good work' is to claim that some rather vaguely stated abstract categories ('the processual, the complex and the paradoxical') are missing from his account, without explaining at all clearly where they might appear in an alternative critical account. It is also hard to see what conception of human agency and action they might have, given their rather unfair critique of Ezzy's supposed reliance on the notion of a sovereign rational individual and their view of Sosteric's workers as inevitably and always mesmerised by their own desire for autonomy. This seems to be a post-structuralist version of a certain Marxist viewpoint. Whereas a crude Marxism would resist the idea that there could be any 'good work' under capitalism's exploitative relations of production (Friedman's original piece seems to come close to this) O'Doherty and Willmott imply that the notion of the 'sovereign rational individual' held by employees similarly renders all work *equally* implicated with power.

This may be because, as admirers of Foucault, O'Doherty and Willmott are influenced by the way that Foucault's genealogical method suspends the modern liberal normative framework, which distinguishes between legitimate and illegitimate forms of power. Foucault does so in order to concentrate on how power operates. As Nancy Fraser (1997: 18–19) suggests, to some extent this bracketing of questions of normativity is fruitful, in that it allows Foucault to bring to light important new dimensions of modern societies. But at the same time it gives rise to difficulties, ones which are very much present in the work of some of Foucault's followers. It can sometimes appear that all normative notions are being suspended, and not just conventional liberal ones. This problem is apparent in O'Doherty and Willmott's critique, but the problem of normativity is a more general one for critical social science. When we undertake criticism, we presumably do so because of some kind of belief that life might be made better. Yet, as Andrew Sayer (2000: 172) remarks, critical social scientists have been 'coy about talking about values'. Sometimes values in social science are rejected on the basis of a dubious objectivism, where values are seen as beyond justification through argument because they are based on emotional, a-rational responses. As Sayer observes, values need to be 'subjected to scrutiny and justified as carefully as would any explanation' (2000: 172). He remarks that there are other ways in which normative questions have been refused or suppressed in critical social theory, more associated with the post-structuralism that O'Doherty and Willmott advocate, or the postmodernism that is often its close relative. One is the postmodernist view that defences of particular moral positions universalise and hence conceal the situated character of their origins.[34] Sayer (2000: 175) points out that this is indeed a major problem with regard to normative questions, but that the criticism needs to be made in relation to specific cases, rather than used as an a priori reason for abandoning normativity. Our claim has been that this criticism is not made successfully by O'Doherty and Willmott in their analysis of Sosteric and Ezzy and this appears to us to be indicative of a more general tendency towards effacing reasonable normativity in post-structuralist studies of work.[35]

2.8 Subjective experience

Finally, we now need to say something more, in addition to our comments in Chapter 1, about how we intend to use our normative framework, and in particular about the question of subjective experience. This focus on experience does not require us to agree with the beliefs of the workers we observed and interviewed, or approve of their behaviour, 'nor need it involve overestimating the extent to which they deliberate on their actions and views' (Sayer 2005: 21). Our intention is to take creative workers' accounts seriously. This is somewhat different from an attitude once widely held by critical researchers, especially those influenced by Marxism, who tended to be highly suspicious of 'psychologising'. An important early text in critical organisational studies claimed that people should be understood 'not as subjectivities, as unique individuals or social psyches, but as the bearers of an objective structure or relations of production and reproduction which are conditioned not by psychology but by history' (Clegg and Dunkerley 1980: 400, cited by Thompson and McHugh 2009: 15). We reject this position, but we do believe that the various forces that shape people's experience need to be considered (and, ultimately, ways in which people's experiences might in turn shape those forces). These include economic, political, regulatory, technological, cultural and organisational factors, and the relative emphasis on each will vary depending on the circumstances being explained. Given our focus

---

34 Another related, but more radical, ground for rejection of normativity often emerges from Nietzschean post-structuralism, which tends to see normative problems as the product of camouflaged interests asserting their will to power. It is not uncommon to hear researchers influenced by post-structuralism express this view. But, as Sayer points out, such an argument undermines itself, because if this is a basis for criticism of other arguments, it must be applied also to those making the argument. The result is a disabling and nihilistic anti-intellectualism (Sayer 2000: 177).

35 Whether or not this is true, it suggests that some reasons given by post-structuralists for questioning accounts of good and bad work may be dubious.

on creative labour in the cultural industries, we need to examine how these factors operate in the specific field of work that is the cultural industries. This, as we explained in Chapter 1, means considering some facets of work that are particular to the cultural industries, or at least take a heightened form there. Our next chapter addresses these matters.

3　The specificity of creative labour

3.1　Outline of the chapter

Building on the discussion of work in the previous chapter, we now examine what assistance research on cultural production can provide us in analysing experiences of work in the cultural industries. Our fundamental claim is that only through an understanding of the specificity of creative labour can we adequately carry out such analysis. As explained in Chapter 1, our aim is to examine subjective experience, but also to draw on existing research to offer explanation of the forces that might be seen to shape such experiences. Our treatment proceeds as follows. We begin by examining three contrasting paradigms of research on cultural production that will make regular appearances in this book: political economy of culture (PEC), organisational, business and management studies (OBM) and cultural studies, briefly examining their contributions and limitations (Section 3.2). As an aside, we then note a remarkable fact: that the study of cultural production *as work* has been mainly neglected in these different paradigms (3.3), and we briefly offer an explanation of this fact. In Section 3.4, we then lay out the differences between two major exceptions to this general neglect, from within PEC, one approach (that of Bernard Miège) emphasising the remnants of artisanal production in modern, industrialised, cultural production, the other (that of Vincent Mosco) arguing against the specificity of creative labour, and turning instead to the concept of knowledge labour. For an account of that specificity, we turn to Raymond Williams, who argues that creative workers are involved, more than any other occupations, in the communication of experience (3.5). Our view is that a neglect of the specificity of culture leads to a neglect of questions concerning the social class of creative workers as a whole, and different groups of creative workers (3.7); and of the vital issue of creative autonomy (3.6). For the latter, we draw on other writing by Raymond Williams, and on Pierre Bourdieu and Andrew Bowie. Clarifying the concept of creative autonomy further, we differentiate between two major components of it: artistic/aesthetic and professional autonomy. We then turn in Sections 3.8 and 3.9 to the recent critiques of creative labour that we mentioned in Chapter 1. These are mainly influenced by cultural studies and by post-structuralism, and ultimately they see creative autonomy and other features of the specificity of creative labour as controlling or disciplining mechanisms that serve to subordinate creative workers. We acknowledge the importance and partial validity of some of these perspectives, but also recognise evaluations of creative labour which, in our view, allow us the possibility of holding on to the remaining emancipatory possibilities in creative labour. We then summarise the implications of all this for our understanding of good and bad work in the cultural industries.

3.2 Three approaches to cultural production

Before proceeding further, we need to outline the main approaches that have been taken to cultural production that are relevant to this book. For these approaches provide many of the theories that we seek to test and build on in what follows. Inevitably, in painting this picture of vast tracts of research, we need to use broad brush-strokes.

The political economy of culture approach (PEC) focuses, in Graham Murdock and Peter Golding's (2005: 60) well-known definition, on 'the interplay between the symbolic and the economic dimensions of public communications', and aims to show how 'different ways of financing and organizing cultural production have traceable consequences for the range of discourse, representations and communicative resources' available to different publics 'and for the organization of audience access and use'. For our purposes, it represents a superior alternative to media and cultural economics (see Hesmondhalgh 2007: 29–49 for further discussion). The dual emphasis in PEC on the commercial and symbolic aspects of the media and popular culture, in relation to questions of power and social justice, ought to be a crucial element in any analysis of creative labour.

Political economists of culture have carried out some sociological studies of workplaces, but more often focus on conceptual analysis based on overviews of contemporary developments drawing on secondary data. A second set of approaches comes from the often intertwined fields of organisational, business and management studies (OBM).[1] Researchers from these fields offer a greater sensitivity to the specifically organisational dimensions of cultural production, including, in early sociological work, an emphasis on routines, rituals and values (Tuchman 1978; Gans 1980). Encouraged by the rhetoric of creative industries policies, OBM analysts began in the 1990s to see the cultural or creative industries as a potential route for understanding innovation and imagination in workplaces and this fuelled new studies (such as

---

1 An interest in cultural-industry organisations developed in US sociology departments in the 1970s (Hirsch 1972; DiMaggio 1977) and an important strand has been the 'production of culture approach' (Peterson and Anand 2004). But it has been in management and business schools that the approach has flourished.

Davis and Scase 2000; Lampel et al. 2006). Like a certain strand of PEC ('the cultural industries approach' associated especially with Miège 1989 and Garnham 1990) some OBM approaches (such as Hirsch 1972; DiMaggio 1977) usefully take into account the specificity of cultural production as opposed to other forms of production. Such approaches permit analysis of the specific ways in which creative labour is organised and managed, including how this varies across particular cultural industries. At the same time such approaches and others in OBM allow for the recognition that creative labour often takes place beyond the boundary of formal organisations, and certainly beyond traditional workplaces, in entities that might in some cases be better thought of as networks (Saundry et al. 2006). Both these insights will be important in what follows. However, many contributions from within the OBM fields have been much less directly concerned with normative questions of power and social justice than has PEC. And in its most intellectually significant versions (such as Garnham 1990; Murdock and Golding 2005) PEC aims to offer historicised explanatory accounts of the systemic and structural forces shaping cultural production in a way that no OBM account has done (apart from Ryan 1992, who explicitly draws on PEC).

A third tradition of production analysis has identified itself closely with the intellectual practice known as cultural studies, which sought to take popular culture seriously and to understand its imbrications with socio-historical forces. In so doing, it was reacting against approaches in the arts and humanities that had tended towards formalism, aestheticism or the treatment of history as mere 'context'. Against reductionist forms of Marxism and positivist and functionalist social science, some cultural studies, drawing on post-structuralist social theory, turned their attention to questions of meaning, subjectivity and power in relation to culture. In the early years of cultural studies, however, many key researchers seemed to view analyses of production as per se very closely linked to reductionist or 'economistic' forms of Marxism. A later generation of researchers sought to fill the resulting gap by invoking cultural studies theory to claim that 'processes of production are (themselves) cultural phenomena ... that construct certain ways for people to conceive of and conduct themselves' (du Gay 1997: 4) and they examined the 'cultures of production' of culture-making organisations. Others emphasised 'broader culture formations and practices that are within neither the control nor the understanding of the company' (Negus 1999: 19). The interest in 'cultures of production' has involved considerable convergence with organisational and management studies, or with sociological and anthropological studies of meaning and ritual in production contexts (see Caldwell 2008). This has been particularly evident in the rise of media production studies (Mayer et al. 2009; see Hesmondhalgh 2010b). The stress on meaning, power and subjectivity to be found in some cultural studies of media production is valuable, but it brings with it some problems, which we discuss below.

As is always the case with analytical traditions, a number of separate sub-fields and approaches are subsumed within broad categories such as these.

Many of the best studies of production combine interests from these different approaches, or transcend the divisions altogether (for example, Todd Gitlin's (1983) study of the production of US prime-time television; or Georgina Born's (2004) anthropological study of the BBC). And there has been some synthesis. Bill Ryan (1992) partially fills the gap between PEC and OBM through his combination of political economy and historical sociology. Bourdieu's 'field theory', now being taken up by other researchers, and which we also discuss below, can be thought of as a fourth tradition or approach. Nevertheless, this rough way of dividing the field can serve for now as a heuristic device to make sense of some recent research debates and conflicts which we seek to intervene in and draw upon.

3.3 General neglect of labour in studies of cultural production and possible reasons

These studies of cultural production are a major context for our study. But before we explain how we seek to test and build upon some of these theories and studies, we need to draw attention to a remarkable fact. Until recently, only a very small proportion of these studies of cultural production focused on the creative labour that is fundamental to that production. It is worth pausing to consider how this could have happened. For Marxists, one reason might be the commodity fetishism that encourages forgetting of labour in general in societies that take the work of others for granted. Some would argue that, in modern societies, there is a particular tendency to forget or ignore labour in the cultural industries. Richard Maxwell (2001: 2–3) suggests two reasons for this amnesia: that so much of the labour relevant to cultural production is submerged and dispersed in the international division of labour; and that there is a glamorous 'enchantment' about cultural products that encourages us 'to forget about the work in culture'. In communication and cultural research, the forgetting or devaluation of work can take a number of different forms. One, apparent in some arts and humanities studies, is a focus on individual producers rather than on the complex division of labour which, as the sociology of culture has shown (in valuable accounts such as Becker 1982; Wolff 1993), is the basis of most cultural production. Another is an emphasis within certain schools or traditions, notably cultural studies, on consumption, at the expense of production. Some cultural studies and communications researchers seem to assume that consumers have the vital final say in determining meaning and, given the importance of meaning in culture, that this makes it more important to study consumption than production. Such views may have played a part in the rise of an overwhelming focus on consumption, audiences, texts and theories of popular culture in cultural studies in the 1980s and 1990s, where questions of production were relatively muted, and where creative work was hardly even mentioned. As we shall see, this situation has changed radically in recent years.

More recently, though, the devaluation of work in communication and cultural research has taken a new form. Digitalisation has led to a proliferation of new forms of amateur and semi-professional production; blogs, Wikipedia and various forms of interactive games were the most cited examples during the 2000s (the noughties, as the British tend to say). In response, many researchers have celebrated a new age of cultural production, and many have argued that the very distinction between production and consumption is becoming outmoded. A German researcher Axel Bruns (2008: 13–14), for example, claims that production and consumption are old-fashioned 'industrial age' concepts, and that in the Internet age, where access to the means of producing and distributing information is 'widely available', consumers can become cultural producers and distributors, bypassing 'traditional' organisations via peer-to-peer and 'many-to-many' (rather than 'one-to-many') communication systems, leading to a new form or model known as 'produsage', a mixture of production and use. Wikipedia and open-source software are, without doubt, fascinating examples of cultural activity based on a resistance to commodification, and on the pleasures and rewards of cooperation. But caricatures of supposedly surpassed eras of production are no substitute for analysis. Moreover, as Andrew Ross (2009: 23) notes with reference to open-source software, it is not clear how such new technologies might act 'as a model for sustainable employment'. Even intelligent celebrations of these new technologies of cultural production and distribution (for example, Benkler 2006) ignore questions of employment and occupation entirely. These apparently egalitarian analyses of 'ordinary' creativity are usually silent about how cultural producers are going to earn money in the new digital environment. This is a silence that can have profoundly inegalitarian consequences.

3.4 Political economy and the specificity of creative labour

More surprising, given its Marxian heritage, has been the general neglect of labour in PEC. A major exception is to be found in the work of Bernard Miège.[2] His most important study, originally published as a 1983 UNESCO paper (and revised as Miège 1989: 65–97) portrays 'artists and artistic creation' – his preferred terms for those involved in creative input – as 'the forgotten factor in thinking about the cultural industries' (p. 66). Miège wanted to counter approaches that, 'out of a kind of arcane respect for a social activity that is prized in almost all societies', implicitly portray art or creativity as 'contaminated' by industry or commerce, and reduce artistic

---

2 Other notable exceptions include various contributions by Janet Wasko (e.g., 1994); Sussman and Lent's 1998 collection; reflections by Toby Miller on the 'New International Division of Cultural Labour' (e.g., Miller et al. 2005); and, as discussed here, Vincent Mosco (see also Mosco 1989). Mosco and Wasko (1983) was a significant early collection.

workers to victims (p. 66). Instead, argued Miège, we need to understand how capitalism organises the functioning of creativity.

In providing a starting point for such an understanding, Miège decisively distinguished his own approach from that of Adorno and Horkheimer's famous 'Culture Industry' essay (1979/1947). They had rightly drawn attention to decisive transformations in the production of art, but had failed to explain why the artisanal or 'handicraft' structure of artistic creation had continued in the era of the industrialisation of culture. Equally though Miège was dissatisfied with contemporary analyses of cultural industries (notably those of Augustin Girard) who, because key elements in cultural production such as creative talent and a sense of contact with the public were unique and non-reproducible, saw cultural production as impervious to industrialisation and commodification (Miège 1989: 71–2). By contrast, Miège detected in artisanal remnants of creative autonomy *pseudo-independence*. For 'artistic professionals' (or creative workers as we are preferring to call them here) themselves bear the costs of producing commodities that are high risk, likely to fail, and involve considerable conception costs. These costs are spread by cultural businesses across a catalogue or repertoire, so that the very few hits cancel out the many misses. But, for Miège, creative workers themselves 'bear the costs of conception inasmuch as they earn little (except for the small minority who are overpaid' (p. 83). This was achieved by the existence of reservoirs of creative labour, including professional workers on the margins of the cultural industries such as academics, but especially 'non-professional artists, those who work occasionally and those who have to take other jobs but continue their artistic activities' (p. 84). Royalties and reproduction fees pay only a small proportion of these costs. And it is not just creative workers who serve to subsidise high conception costs. They in turn are supported through public expenditure and other, related commercial sectors, such as live commercial entertainment, which serves as a testing ground for new ideas and talent.

Miège, then, provides an account of the political and economic forces that shape work in the cultural industries. In doing so, he raises the fundamental issue that we signalled at the beginning of the chapter, concerning the specificity of creative labour. He links this to a historical account of artisanal and artistic autonomy. But he recognises that autonomy is contradictory, and is linked, in the case of the contemporary cultural industries, to a set of difficult conditions for creative workers.

However, his work has not gone without criticism – and one criticism in particular concerns the issue of specificity that we need to address. In his overview of *The Political Economy of Communication*, Vincent Mosco (1996: 158) criticised Miège for his emphasis on the contradictions arising from 'artistic input', and suggested that he had underestimated the effects of concentration and rationalisation in the cultural industries. The specificity of creative labour was being reduced, Mosco claimed, and the artisanal or 'handicraft' elements that Miège thought were central to understanding cultural industries were diminishing as vast entertainment corporations grew. However, it is hard to see that this has happened in the intervening years since Mosco's assessment. Rather, studies of artistic labour markets suggest that Miège's notion of reservoirs that serve to offset conception costs on to other workers and agencies – including the state – has been amply confirmed (see, for example, Menger 2006).

Mosco has returned to the question of labour more recently in research with Catherine McKercher (McKercher and Mosco 2007a; Mosco and McKercher 2008) and it is significant that here, rather than labour in the cultural and media industries, the focus is on the broader category of knowledge work. Superficially, this may seem an attractive move, but we shall explain why we think it is a mistake, as it will help to clarify our focus on specificity.

McKercher and Mosco operate the widest possible definition of knowledge work, to encompass all those who handle and distribute information (McKercher and Mosco 2007b). They argue against a definition restricted to creative labour, in the sense of work involving the direct manipulation of symbols (which is roughly what is meant by Miège's translated term 'artistic input').[3] Instead they want to broaden the term out to include workers such as postal transportation workers and librarians. They give two main reasons for wanting to do so. First, 'an increasing amount of the work involves making use of information to efficiently and effectively deliver an information product. The line between what is and what is not creative labour in the knowledge field is fuzzy' (McKercher and Mosco 2007b: x) and workers who appear to be more marginal to production nevertheless add tangible value. Second, 'the meaning of knowledge labour is not measured simply by external criteria but by how it is subjectively experienced by workers themselves' (ibid.). We agree with these statements, if the word 'also' is inserted after the word 'but' in the last sentence. But McKercher and Mosco do not in fact address how workers categorise their own work. What is more, most boundaries between concepts are fuzzy; that does not mean that the concepts are not useful or valuable.

A third reason for operating a very broad notion of knowledge labour is given in a later book by Mosco and McKercher (2008):

> Since much of the research on knowledge work tends to see inclusion in that category as a positive development for the workers who make the move, the type of definition one accepts is also an implicit decision about

---

3 Mosco and McKercher (2008: 24) associate this definition of knowledge work as creative labour with Richard Florida (e.g., Florida 2002) and see this as part of a tradition beginning with Peter Drucker (1959) and Robert Reich (1991). We do not share Florida's conception, which has the same problems of breadth as McKercher and Mosco's definition, but none of its socialist inclusiveness of non-professional workers. Rather, our focus on creative workers owes more to writers such as Raymond Williams, Bernard Miège, Nicholas Garnham, John Thompson and Georgina Born, none of whom is discussed by McKercher and Mosco.

who and how many are privileged. ... A more heterogeneous vision of the knowledge-work category points to another type of politics, one predicated on a question about whether knowledge workers can unite across occupations or national boundaries.

(Mosco and McKercher 2008: 25–6)

Is this not a more inclusive and democratic conception of work than our specific focus on work in the cultural industries? Underlying McKercher and Mosco's move is an admirable desire to understand and support new forms of unified resistance among different constituencies of workers. We strongly support the idea of forming trade union alliances across occupational groups and we return to this issue in our final chapter. Let us be absolutely clear here too that we consider the working lives of librarians and transportation workers to be of no less, or more, intrinsic interest or worth than those of workers involved more directly with symbol-making. But when it comes to the analysis of creative labour in the cultural industries, our view is that the move out to a very broad conception of knowledge work will, in the name of inclusiveness and the recognition of fuzzy boundaries, lead to the exclusion of certain key issues, and the erosion of crucial distinctions. In particular, such a broad conception risks eliminating the specific importance of *culture*, of *mediated communication*, and of the *content* of communication products.[4] Cultural producers can be seen as having, compared with other groups in society, the capacity to make texts (primarily symbolic, aesthetic and informational artefacts, intended to inform, edify and/or please audiences), which are then circulated, to greater or lesser effect, to wider groups, primarily through the institutions and technologies we call the media. The sociological analysis of cultural production and of the media, not entirely but to a pretty large degree, has been based on an interest in the specific nature of cultural products, with their ability to shape and influence societies, be they films, songs, news bulletins, documentaries, reality TV shows, pornography or sports magazines. It may be valid to study knowledge workers as a corpus, as do Mosco and McKercher (though there are reasons to doubt the cohesion of concepts such as 'knowledge economies' and of the 'information society'),[5]

---

4 We mean culture here in the sense of 'the *signifying system* through which necessarily ... a social order is communicated, reproduced, experienced and explored' (Williams 1981: 13, original emphasis) rather than the very broad anthropological sense of 'a whole way of life'. See Paul Jones (2004) for a dissection of Raymond Williams's definitions, and a rigorous defence of the conceptions of culture and society Williams developed in his later work.

5 There can be no doubt of the proliferation of information and knowledge in modern societies, a long-term 'informationalisation of life' and of economies. It is also the case that in many capitalist economies, there has been a considerable growth in the middle classes, including professional occupations. Once we move beyond such established facts, though, things become less clear. Many critics doubt whether there is a coherent body of enterprises and institutions that we might call 'knowledge industries'. See Webster (2005) for a fine exploration of these and related issues.

but there are also good reasons to study creative labour specifically. It would surely be strange to conduct a study of workers in the cultural industries that did not recognise that those industries are *especially* involved (i.e., other industries are too, but not as much) in the production of symbols and of social meaning. It would imply, for example, that television workers are no different from call centre workers. In the general social division of labour, workers in the cultural industries are involved in the creation and dissemination of very particular kinds of products, ones that are mainly symbolic, aesthetic, expressive and/or informational. Of course other products involve these elements. The point is that television programmes, recordings of music and magazine articles *primarily* have these characteristics, rather than functional ones (see Hesmondhalgh 2007: 12–13 for further discussion).

3.5 Raymond Williams on the specificity of creative labour: the communication of experience

For an account that will help us to understand the specificity of creative labour in greater depth than Miège and other political economists of culture were able to provide, we now turn to Raymond Williams, a key figure in the development of cultural studies, but also a major contributor to the political economy of culture. The title of Williams's book *The Long Revolution* refers to 'the rising determination, almost everywhere, that people should govern themselves' (Williams 1965/1961: 10). Williams chose to begin his book on this long democratic revolution with an essay on 'The Creative Mind' which sought to establish that art and creativity are *ordinary*. Williams's argument is rooted in a sweeping historical survey of thinking about art and creativity, which also draws on contemporary cognitive science. His views are of great importance in the context of this book because they defend the notion of creativity against those who would too quickly dismiss it and those who would too zealously celebrate it.

Williams pointed to the tendency for evaluations of creativity to polarise, whether derived from classical theories of imitation/mimesis as the function of art, or the post-Renaissance humanist notions of creation that eventually displaced them. When art is understood as imitation, it can be revered as a form of learning or record or scorned as second-hand reproduction. When art is understood as creation, it can be valued as revelation or dismissed as fantasy or delusion. 'Plato or a Puritan or a modern Practical Man can dismiss art as inferior. Aristotle or a Renaissance theorist or a modern Romantic or aesthete can praise art as superior' (Williams 1965/1961: 35).

For Williams, these overly polarised evaluations derive from the error of setting art against reality. Such a contrast of art and reality is false, Williams claimed, for human experience is both objective and subjective, always involving interpretation and meaning (subjective factors) but always involving non-human reality (objective ones).[6] Consciousness and reality interpenetrate. This means that we all, as part of our lives, attempt to formulate, describe and communicate experience. Symbolic creativity – or 'the arts' in Williams's 1950s parlance – should be understood then as particularly intense forms of this ordinary human activity. Creative workers are ordinary too, for they share with everyone else the general capacity to find and organise new descriptions of experience. Ideas that art always involves newness or special levels of inspiration are therefore mistaken. Symbolic creativity is better thought of as incremental, involving small steps, building on what others have done (c.f. Toynbee 2001: 8).

But Williams also examines ways in which creative workers are different from other workers. The creative worker makes the communication of experience her central work in life – 'the artist's work is the actual work of transmission', says Williams (1965/1961: 42) – and uses learned skills to transmit that experience.[7] Some are more able, through genetic endowment, motivation and practice, to transmit that experience in a way that audiences can understand and feel. Creative workers then are far more ordinary than traditional views of 'art' would have us believe. There is nevertheless something extraordinary about them. Their work is the communication of experience through symbolic production.

3.6 A critical conception of creative autonomy and its two variants

Only through an institutional analysis of the way that organisational forms mediate the specificity of creative labour can we really understand work in the cultural industries. This will serve as a meso level of analysis between our ethnographic focus on worker experience and the account of the systemic and structural features of cultural production provided by the best versions of political economy of culture (as in 3.4 above). Our normative model in the previous chapter presented some key organisational dynamics as they bear on good and bad work in general. A key issue identified by many sociologists is work autonomy. Understanding the specificity of creative labour helps us to understand that work autonomy takes on particular significance – and particular organisational forms – when placed in the context of the cultural industries. That significance arises in relation to a particular set of

---

6 This does not mean that Williams thought that objective knowledge was impossible. For this is a different meaning of objectivity than that involved in the object/subject distinction – see Sayer (2000: 58–62). Williams's position is close to contemporary critical realism. In its emphasis on the communication of experience, it is also potentially compatible with some aspects of philosophical pragmatism (see Dewey 1980/1934). Negus and Pickering (2004: 23–4, 37–8) reflect on this latter issue in a rare and thoughtful discussion of Williams's essay.

7 For Williams, this does not entail relativism – some art communicates experience more effectively than others.

historical developments regarding creative autonomy.[8] An appreciation of the complexities and contradictions of creative autonomy is therefore necessary for understanding organisational aspects of autonomy in the cultural industries. But to gain such an appreciation means overcoming mistaken and simplistic critiques of the concept.

Our conception of creative autonomy, based on our interviews and ethnography, involves two main components to it, which we call aesthetic or artistic autonomy, and professional autonomy. We deal with aesthetic autonomy in the following section, and professional autonomy after that.

3.6.1 Variant 1: aesthetic autonomy

Aesthetic autonomy is usefully defined by Andrew Bowie (2003: 2) as 'the idea that works of art entail freely produced rules which do not apply to any other natural object or human product'. In a widely cited critique, Janet Wolff (1987: 1) attacked the 'ideology of autonomous art', which she equated with the 'notion that Art – at least Great Art – transcends the social, the political and the everyday'. Wolff (1987: 6) saw this ideology as a romantic conception 'still dominant in the twentieth century', with precedents in the Renaissance, and particularly linked to the idea of 'the artist as creative personality and free intellectual worker' in discourses – and especially in academic analysis – of art. For Wolff (1987: 3), 'the individualism of the liberal-humanist thought associated with mercantile capitalism and with the bourgeoisie confirmed and reinforced the aesthetic ideology of the artist as sole and privileged originator of the cultural work'. This in turn helps to legitimate the high/low culture split, which drew upon and reinforced class and gender inequalities.

As with the concepts of personal autonomy and work autonomy discussed in Chapter 2, post-structuralists are particularly sceptical of any Enlightenment-tinged understandings of creative autonomy as liberation or progress. Martha Woodmansee (1994) for example, portrays the emergence of aesthetic autonomy in the late eighteenth century as a defensive measure adopted by the bourgeoisie against the increasing vitality of popular culture. Jonathan Hess (1999), meanwhile, sees aesthetic autonomy as a response to a crisis in Enlightenment public culture, a displaced attempt to establish some ground, any ground, where agency could take place. In Hess's view, this displacement of politics and agency onto the aesthetic realm undermines modern public sphere theory and its claims to be reliant on rational foundations.

Such analyses contextualise the emergence of creative autonomy and suggest some of the limits on its application as a critical concept. Wolff and others are absolutely right to point to the way that the 'freedom' of bourgeois

---

8 It is this historical dimension that is all too often missing from OBM, and from cultural studies approaches to cultural production (and as indicated above, it is only intermittently present in PEC).

creative workers, newly released from patronal bonds, was linked to 'many other kinds of unfreedom and new constraints' (Wolff 1987: 3), including those deriving from the social division of labour. But some critics of creative autonomy, echoing post-structuralist critiques of autonomy in general, risk missing the historical ambivalence of the concept.[9] The question raised by such accounts is whether we retain any kind of notion of autonomy at all, given these contradictions. Our view is that we need a critical account of creative autonomy that takes account of social justice and equality within and across different societies.

We can gain a sense of that ambivalence by seeing the quest for autonomy in cultural production as the product of a varied and complex set of historical pressures. The focus of early modern European aesthetic thought on human creative powers represents a hubristic celebration of human potential in the face of the decline of religion. But it also represents a quest for other sources of meaning. It is a product of mercantile and bourgeois individualism, but also reflects the need to counter emergent capitalism's manipulation and control of nature, and the subjugation of beauty to instrumental value. What is more, we should not miss the political battles that took place over the defence of these conceptions, with industrialists and financiers dismissing the realm of the aesthetic as mere fantasy (see Williams 1965/1961) and indulgence.[10]

The importance and value of knowledge, art and culture has been recognised in all major civilisations. But for historical reasons, partly connected with the need for mediation in increasingly complex and specialised societies, meanings and symbols have come to be imbued with special significance in modern life.[11] In *Culture and Society* (1958), Raymond Williams argued that the concept of culture emerged in the eighteenth and nineteenth centuries in relation to the changing meanings of other key words: democracy, class, industry and art. This emergence involved a complex fusion of two responses

---

9 According to Andrew Bowie (2003), post-structuralist accounts often also miss the way that those who forged the idea of aesthetic autonomy in the eighteenth century criticised the limitations of their own focus on the aesthetic.
10 Bourdieu (1996: 48) for example quotes a leading French capitalist of the nineteenth century:

> I repeat each day to my children that the title of *bachelier* [high school graduate] will never put a piece of bread into their mouths; that I sent them to school to allow them to taste the pleasures of intelligence, and to put them on their guard against all false doctrines, whether in literature, philosophy or history. But I add that it would be very dangerous for them to give themselves over to the pleasures of the mind.

> Surely his descendents are the many bourgeois parents who direct their children towards vocational and professional degrees, seeking to protect them from the lure of intellectual and artistic pursuits?

11 We defer for now the question of whether this significance is exaggerated out of a kind of narcissism on the part of intellectuals, as Frow (1995: 163–9) suggests, seemingly advocating extreme reflexivity as the only viable politics of knowledge.

to economic and social change. The first response was a 'recognition of the practical separation of certain moral and intellectual activities from the driven impetus of a new kind of society' (Williams 1965/1958: 17). It was felt, in other words, that moral and intellectual activities were not subject to the same laws as industry and the making of money. The second response, though, was to emphasise these moral and intellectual activities 'as a court of human appeal', one that would be 'set over the processes of practical social judgement' – in other words, to be placed above such processes like a supreme court would be placed over an ordinary criminal court – and yet also 'to offer itself as a mitigating and rallying alternative' to such processes (Williams 1965/1958: 17).

These changes were linked to transformations in cultural production taking place in the nineteenth century, as Williams was to emphasise in his later work (Williams 1981). These transformations can very roughly be summarised as the transition from patronage to markets, but both include a highly variable set of arrangements. Market relations include artisanal and 'post-artisanal' forms, the latter involving the use by independent producers of distributive intermediaries such as booksellers. These 'early' market forms, like patronal relations, persist today, but with the introduction of contracts, copyright and royalties in the nineteenth century came the rise of market professional relations. This allows a specific kind of social relationship, 'professional independence within integrated and dominant market relations' (Williams 1981: 47–8). This new phase, including this key idea of professional independence, means that production for the market, 'as a purpose taking priority over any other', is widely evident; yet in Williams's view, 'any full identity between cultural production and general production has been to an important extent resisted' (Williams 1981: 50).

Williams is – rightly in our view – at pains to capture the ambivalence of this resistance. It includes, for example, distinctions between what is creative and what is useful, and distinctions between artisans and artists. These distinctions can undoubtedly serve the interests of certain class fractions and occupational groups over others. Williams also stresses that most relations of cultural production have indeed been assimilated to the terms of the developing market. But he also says that it would be seriously reductive to claim that the general market order has transformed all cultural production into market commodities.[12] For efforts to defend culture from assimilation to the market continue, including the invocation of 'creative activities'. This has never been satisfactory in terms of definitions and clear distinctions, says Williams. Cultural producers are often willing, and are sometimes eager, to engage in market relations. Complacent conventional distinctions between

---

12 It is possible to read Adorno as making this claim for example. Such a view certainly seems to be a feature of the *Monthly Review* strand of the American New Left, for example Baran and Sweezy's (1966) analysis of 'monopoly capital' – which has had considerable and under-acknowledged influence on some radical media studies in the USA.

'commercial' and 'creative' or 'authentic' cultural forms are never adequate. However, says Williams (and this is crucial), 'it would be quite wrong to disregard the actual or attempted social relations, of an alternative kind, which [such] attempts at differentiation, and the initiatives and marginal institutions corresponding to them, undoubtedly represent' (1981: 51). To put this another way, these distinctions may sometimes be applied clumsily, but they, and the institutional forms to which they may give rise, represent an ongoing attempt to forge social relations outside the market.

Another version of this story is told by Pierre Bourdieu (1996) in the first part of his book on the development of 'the literary field', *The Rules of Art*. Bourdieu provides a detailed account of the emergence in the mid nineteenth century of what he sees as a persisting tension between two 'principles of hierarchization' which, between them, structure various fields of cultural production in France, right up to the time he was writing in the 1990s. One is the heteronomous principle 'which favours those who dominate the field economically and politically (for example bourgeois art)' (Bourdieu 1993: 40). The other is the 'autonomous principle', favouring in the context of bourgeois society, the dominated fraction of the dominant class. This autonomous principle is seen at its extreme in notions of art for art's sake, but it should not be equated with pure aestheticism. This is only one of the positions taken by cultural producers, as they oscillated between different ways of seeking to exercise autonomy from political, economic and religious power. Bourdieu is often read as a critic of aesthetic autonomy. This is partly on the basis of his critique of Kantian aesthetics in his remarkable book on cultural taste (Bourdieu 1984). It is also because Bourdieu is wonderfully scathing about the way those involved in 'restricted production' seek, through a disinterested stance, symbolic profits that can be turned into economic profits in the longer term. Bourdieu, then, surprised many readers when, in the late 1980s, he began advocating (most notably in the 'postscript' to Bourdieu 1996, first published as an article in 1989) an 'Internationale of intellectuals committed to defending the autonomy of the universes of cultural production', in the face of what he saw as historically unprecedented threats to this autonomy resulting from 'the increasingly greater interpenetration between the world of art and the world of money' (Bourdieu 1996: 344).

Bourdieu and Williams, then, provide the theoretical and normative underpinnings for our explorations of how notions of creative autonomy are mobilised and countered in contemporary cultural industries (though without our embracing the full Bourdieuvian vocabularies of habitus, capital, *illusio* and so on). To summarise, this sees autonomy as contradictory and ambivalent, and that means that in spite of the many problems associated with it, we should not lose sight of the aspiration to human freedom that it embodies.[13]

---

13 The critic Brian Holmes has made important contributions to understanding this – see Holmes (2004).

That aspiration is linked to the social value of culture and communication. If we lose sight entirely of that potential value in the name of anti-romanticism or some kind of populist anti-elitism, we risk a crude reductionism.

3.6.2 Variant 2: professional autonomy

Debates about autonomy in the cultural industries have tended to focus heavily on artistic or aesthetic autonomy. This neglects the importance of a rather different kind of autonomy from that which Williams, Bourdieu and numerous others saw emerging in the nineteenth century. Many creative workers are not involved so much in aesthetic or artistic production. Instead they occupy jobs centred on the construction and dissemination of what might be called interpretive information or knowledge. This is true of profes-sional book authors, such as encyclopedia editors, but the largest group involved in such work is journalists. Journalists have rarely been considered in comparison with artistic-creative workers, even though they coexist in the cultural industries. The autonomy sought by journalists is closer to that sought by professional groups than to the aesthetic autonomy traditionally sought by 'artistic' creative workers (although, as we shall see in Chapter 4, this professional creative autonomy itself has variants). Other similar groups, such as the documentary producers that we interviewed for this book, also seek a kind of professional autonomy similar to that pursued by journalists.[14] This is perhaps especially true in public service broadcasting systems. Our claim then is that for analysis of creative labour, we need an understanding of two different kinds of autonomy: aesthetic and professional. Journalistic autonomy needs to be placed in the context of professional autonomy.

There is a vast literature on the professions, but Hallin and Mancini (2004) have provided a valuable entry point to issues relevant to analysis of creative labour in their comparison of different national media systems (see also Aldridge and Evetts 2003). Autonomy, they say, has always been central to definitions of professionalism. But journalists have failed to achieve the levels of autonomy present in other, 'classic' professions such as law and medicine, partly because journalistic knowledge is not esoteric. Journalists are often salaried employees and where they are freelance they tend to be vulnerable, rather than owners of their own means of production. Nevertheless, groups of journalists have been able to achieve some level of autonomy within media organisations, though this varies widely across different media systems and organisations.

There are some significant ways in which journalists have developed distinct professional norms of the kind often identified as forming professional cultures. Journalists might agree broadly on criteria of newsworthiness for example; they might tend to judge other's standing according to criteria

---

14 See also Kennedy (2010) for an intriguing study of discourses of professionalism and professionalisation among web designers.

generated by themselves rather than others. This 'enclosed' feel helped to generate widespread suspicion of the professions in the 1960s and 1970s on the part of the countercultural left and many sociologists (see Larson 1977 and in media studies, Elliott's brilliant 1977 study). And so just as artistic or aesthetic autonomy came under critique, so did the kinds of professional autonomy to be found in journalistic organisations. Again, though, as with aesthetic autonomy, we wish to hold on to the ambivalence of the concept, including the way that professional values may help to provide some resistance to the encroachment of commercial goals, such as the influence of advertising, or the requirement to serve the goals of those tied to political parties and governments.

Hallin and Mancini's primary focus is comparative and objectivist whereas ours is conjunctural and experiential. We sought to gather experiential data from our interviewees concerning the degrees of autonomy they believe are present in their everyday work, along with the pressures that they feel are being exerted on their professional autonomy. However, as explained in Chapter 1, we interpret and triangulate their perspectives by examining the political, economic and organisational forces shaping their experiences. We continue our analysis of these forces now by addressing the question of social class, which continues to be fundamental for anyone who seeks to understand the relationships of work to social power.

3.7 Creative work and social class

While cultural producers as a whole are engaged in the collective production of ideas, and therefore undertake a specific role as intellectual workers within the *social* division of labour – a fact with implications that we explore further below – there is also an *organisational* division of labour within cultural production. Some of those involved in cultural production are managers; some are, in the broadest sense of the term, professionals (such as journalists or highly trained musicians); some might best be defined as craftspeople (such as carpenters specialising in set construction, or film editors); and of course in the broadest sense of people who work for cultural-industry organisations, even though they are not involved directly in the cultural production aspects of the business, there are also unskilled workers carrying out relatively mundane and routine tasks (sorting and delivering mail, cleaning and so on). This makes the task of considering the class position of cultural producers, and therefore the task of better understanding their relative power, privilege, status and interests, quite complex.

This problem can be explored via consideration of what Erik Olin Wright has called 'the problem of the "middle class" – people who do not own their own means of production, who sell their labour power on a labour market, and yet do not see themselves as part of the "working class" ' (Wright 1997: 19). Wright's aim is to move beyond crude Marxist class distinctions based purely on ownership of the means of production, according to which there are only three class locations: the capitalist class, the working class and the petty bourgeoisie (who own means of production but do not hire workers). In order to gain a clear sense of class dynamics such as class consciousness, class formation and class conflict, says Wright, we need some way of understanding divisions among the population of employees. Wright believes that two dimensions of such divisions are particularly important: the relationship of employees to authority within production; and their possession of skills or expertise.

In terms of *authority*, managers and supervisors occupy what Wright calls 'contradictory locations within class relations' (1997: 23): they exercise domination on behalf of capitalist class members but they are controlled by capitalists and their labour is exploited. At the same time, such managers and supervisors have a privileged position within exploitation relations. Their high earnings are a kind of excess payment or rent to gain their loyalty. In terms of *skills* or *expertise*, these are usually scarce in labour markets, in terms of credentials but also often in terms of talent, and so owners of scarce skills gain wages 'above the costs of producing and reproducing their labour power': in other words, owners pay a kind of skill rent. This control over knowledge and skills makes it difficult to monitor and control skilled employees. Again, as with managers, this can result in loyalty enhancing mechanisms – good conditions, higher wages, etc. The result is a map of middle-class locations (not classes), as reproduced in Figure 3.1. As in any industry, the cultural industries contain workers occupying most of these positions. But there is a strong tendency for creative workers to occupy the lower-authority, higher-skilled locations here: i.e., experts and skilled workers with little or no supervisory or managerial powers.

Relation to means of production

		Owner	Employees			
Number of employees	Many	Capitalists	Expert managers	Skilled managers	Nonskilled managers	Managers
	Few	Small employers	Expert supervisors	Skilled supervisors	Nonskilled supervisors	Supervisors
	None	Petty bourgeoisie	Experts	Skilled workers	Nonskilled workers	Non-management
			Experts	Skilled	Nonskilled	Relation to authority

Relation to scarce skills

Figure 3.1 Wright's map of (middle) class locations

This means that the creative workers we are dealing with here may seem privileged compared with those in other occupations, but this is not the same thing as having a powerful position within the general structure of modern societies. Meanwhile, significant changes in creative labour markets are altering the way we might potentially understand the class positions of creative workers. As Graham Murdock (2000: 19) points out, within the overall category of intellectual and cultural workers, a new cleavage may be opening up 'between groups with relatively secure conditions of employment or their own successful businesses and those operating in conditions of permanent insecurity and independence'. In such a context, the issue of class becomes yet more complex, as some workers constantly drop in and out of having any kind of employment. The term 'proleterianisation' has been widely used to refer to this growing aspect of creative work. This term might usefully draw attention to the ways that cultural-industry businesses might be imposing harsher conditions on workers. But it is only helpful if it is not understood too literally, for even these workers tend to be middle class, educated employees.

This links up to another significant issue arising from these discussions, one which is both sociological and political. To what extent is our interest in creative labour directing us towards the analysis of a particular privileged group within society? And given that we are of course ourselves intellectual workers, even if employed by educational rather than cultural-industry institutions, are we not guilty of a kind of bourgeois narcissism? Why analyse creative workers when there are many jobs in which people seem likely to suffer more? A brief answer to such questions is due here. We would stress the potential ability for skilful and ethical professional and craft work to serve the common good and to enrich human life. Of course, in modern societies, much professional and craft labour falls far short of the standards necessary to contribute to the common good, and takes place in contexts where many people are often deprived of access to their skills and services for reasons of income and/or education. Short of an eradication of the division of labour,[15] the quality of life for nearly everyone in modern societies is likely to be compromised unless professionals and craftspeople undertake their work in an effective and ethical way. In the case of the cultural industries, a key factor is the importance of the communication of experience that we discussed above. Bad creative work may mean the making and dissemination of products that fail to enhance people's knowledge, their sense of belonging to, or feeling distinct from, wider communities, and their emotional and affective lives. This surely matters. And this also means that the conditions and experiences of creative workers matters. If workers undergo difficult and pressing circumstances, and find it difficult to sustain a reasonable quality of

---

15 We return to the questions concerning the feasibility and desirability, or otherwise, of moves to reduce the social division of labour in order to achieve social justice in Chapter 10.

life themselves, and if in the longer term their work is unlikely to contribute in any way to their well-being, then the quality of their work is likely to suffer.

3.8 Cultural studies on creative labour: subjectivity and self-exploitation

Having established an understanding of some of the historical forces shaping work in the cultural industries, and of the 'objective' position of creative workers within the general structure of social class in modern societies, we turn now to the question of subjectivity that is fundamental to our approach in this book, and to some of the debates that we seek to intervene in.

This is where we part company with even the best aspects of political economy of culture. For that approach shares a problem with much of the Marxian labour process theory we discussed in Chapter 2: a lack of attention to questions of subjectivity and experience.[16] These issues though have been of central interest to more critical management studies and some sociologies of work, although these groups of analysts take somewhat different approaches. More recently, this interest in subjectivity has been taken up by cultural studies-influenced researchers and has been applied to creative labour, and to a neighbouring set of labour practices, in new media. As a result, a series of studies have added to a growing sense of 'a turn to cultural work' in the social sciences and humanities.[17] On the face of it, like political economy's general neglect of creative labour, the fact that this research has come from analysts influenced by cultural studies is perhaps surprising, given the hostility that cultural studies showed towards scrutiny of production, and its almost complete neglect of questions of creative labour in earlier times.[18] A large part of the motivation here has been to counter some of the complacency surrounding creative and new media work on the part of policy-makers (including creative industries policy) and some of their academic cheerleaders who extol

---

16 This point is also made by Wittel (2004). But his critique of PEC relies on a mixture of postmodernist and autonomist Marxist assertions about fundamental changes in economic life, away from the industrial towards the 'immaterial'; and his programme for bringing subjectivity into studies of creative labour relies on vague Deleuzean statements about the need to understand the workings of desire and affect in cultural production.

17 These cultural studies writers have not been alone in paving the way for the 'turn to cultural work'. Film studies made notable contributions (e.g., Wasko 1994; Gray and Seeber 1996; and the British Film Institute's studies of television workers conducted in the 1990s, see for example Paterson 2001). There have also been significant recent studies from disciplines such as geography (Pratt 2000; Scott 2005; Christopherson and van Jaarsveld 2005; Christopherson 2008) and sociology (Neff et al. 2005; Huws 2006–7). We draw on many of these in this book.

18 Ross (2008: 31–2) claims that this is true even of the work of Raymond Williams, but this is not really the case. As well as comments in *The Long Revolution*, there is also the remarkable 1983 essay 'Marx on Culture' (Williams 1989: 195–225). See Paul Jones (2004: 46–51) for excellent commentary.

the benefits of creativity and entrepreneurship. These cultural studies-influenced writers have drawn, to varying degrees, on sociology and social theory concerning work and organisations for their examinations of new media and creative labour. In some analyses, the influence of post-structuralist studies of work and organisations has been particularly apparent. We now turn to a number of significant critiques of creative labour that have appeared in recent years. As with Mike Sosteric's account, discussed in Chapter 2.3, questions of autonomy are central. And as with Ezzy's, and O'Doherty and Willmott's critique, discussed in Sections 2.4 and 2.5, so are the relations between self-realisation and the systemic requirements of work organisations and of capitalism. We want to examine the normative assumptions underlying some recent cultural studies accounts, and we also want to address the implications of such accounts for constructing a *politics* of creative work, including the kind of emancipatory social action necessary to make access to good work, including good creative work, more equal and just.

Gillian Ursell's (2000) early contribution was significant because it paid attention to the particularly high levels of personal investment in creative labour – something that had increasingly been noted by sociologists of work concentrating on other fields (such as Kunda 1992). Building on ground-breaking studies of the formation of 'consent' in workplaces by Marxian sociologists such as Michael Burawoy (1979), Ursell acknowledged that processes such as union de-recognition and considerable reductions in labour costs and earnings provided plenty of evidence to support a Marxist reading, focused on exploitation and property. But she also noted 'an intensification of the self-commodification processes by which each individual seeks to improve his/her chances of attracting gainful employment' (Ursell 2000: 807) and analysed how television workers had, in the era of casualisation and increasing freelance work, come to take on the work of organising their own labour markets. This element of 'apparent voluntarism' needed to be acknowledged, Ursell claimed, and she turned to Foucauldian theory not to dispense with labour process theory concerns but 'to approach them more substantially' (Ursell 2000: 809). In particular, she drew on Nikolas Rose's (1999: 145) idea that, in advanced liberalism, freedom is redefined as 'a capacity for self-realisation which can be obtained only through individual activity'. Rose (1999: 244) also believed that work played an increasingly key role in modern identity formation, and that 'subjective desires for self-actualisation are to be harnessed to the firm's aspirations for productivity, efficiency and the like'. The reference to individual as opposed to collective activity is significant; here Rose's Foucauldian approach shows some similarities with parallel developments in other branches of sociology that were also emphasising individualisation.[19] But whereas writers such as Ulrich Beck (1992) emphasise

---

19 Rose stressed the importance of commercial consumption and lifestyle choices – and risked downplaying the continuing importance of education, media and religion.

the ambivalent results of such individualisation, in that it potentially frees subjects from the bonds and demands of tradition, Rose and Ursell emphasise the negative results, where individuals are left to fend for themselves.

Discussing how notions of creativity, talent and work are being redefined in those burgeoning micro-businesses of the cultural sector associated with young people, including fashion and design, but also entertainment industries such as clubbing, recording and magazine journalism, Angela McRobbie (2002a: 523) echoed Ursell in pointing to the 'utopian thread' involved in the 'attempt to make-over the world of work into something closer to a life of enthusiasm and enjoyment', and in focusing on how this leads to a situation where, when things go wrong, young people entering these creative worlds of work can feel they only have themselves to blame. In this respect, McRobbie usefully broadened the study of creative work to include a wider set of conditions and experiences, including the way in which aspirations to and expectations of autonomy could lead to disappointment, disillusion and 'self-blaming'. She also pointed to the gendered aspects of these conditions, with women now expected to find full-time work, uninterrupted by family commitments, satisfying and enriching (McRobbie 2002a: 521). The context for McRobbie's critique (see also McRobbie 2002b) was the then UK Labour government's creative industries policy, and their general valorisation of labour, where 'work comes to mean much more than just earning a living; it incorporates and takes over everyday life' (McRobbie 2002b: 99). McRobbie was usefully questioning the 'ideal of self-expressive work' (2002a: 101) and its place in Labour's advocacy of 'a new youth-driven meritocracy', involving a labour of love and self-exploitation.

Similar issues have also been explored by other researchers in relation to work in the IT sector, forms of work sometimes unhelpfully blurred with creative labour in governments' conceptions of creative industries. Andrew Ross (2003: 9) observed how, in the eyes of a new generation of business analysts in the 1980s, Silicon Valley 'appeared to promote a humane workplace not as a grudging concession to demoralized employees but as a valued asset to production'. 'New economy' firms, he argued, aimed to provide work cultures that 'embraced openness, cooperation and self-management' (ibid.). But this, showed Ross, was closely linked to long working hours and a serious blurring of the line between work and leisure. Whilst the dot.com working environments of the 1990s offered 'oodles of autonomy along with warm collegiality' they also enlisted 'employees' free-est thoughts and impulses in the service of salaried time' (Ross 2003: 17, 19).

Also writing about new media work, Andreas Wittel (2001) saw there a paradigmatic case of an emergent form of community that he calls 'network sociality', one which appears to be individualistic and instrumental, involving an assimilation of work and play, while Tiziana Terranova (2000), from an autonomist Marxist perspective, provided an early analysis of the

'free labour'[20] underlying the emergent digital economy, countering the optimistic visions of Marxian utopians who hoped that gift economies might
undermine capitalism from within. Ros Gill (2002), in a study of European
freelance new media workers, found evidence that features of the work that
seemed superficially attractive, such as its informality and high levels of
autonomy, were in fact particularly problematic for women because of the
lack of clear criteria for evaluating work and especially because of the difficulties such informality caused when seeking new contracts.

More recently, a significant intervention has been made by Matt Stahl,
who, more than most of these cultural studies writers, brings systemic political economic questions to bear on creative labour and, in so doing, advances
debates about the relationships between capitalism, autonomy, self-realisation
and creative labour in intriguing and often valuable ways. Stahl's starting
point is how 'the personal and political-economic dimensions of the alienation and domination characteristic of capitalist society appear in attenuated
forms in popular music' (Stahl 2006a: 1).[21] This combination of attention to
both political economy and subjectivity is helpful, and of course is in line
with our own concerns in this book. Drawing on the cultural industries
tradition of political economy, Stahl recognises that various historical forces
protect the creative worker from the full force of alienation and expropriation
associated with capitalism, according to many of its Marxist critics, most
notably the contradictions arising from the creativity–commerce relations
discussed above. This, along with the attachment of ideals of self-realisation
to 'artistic' careers, makes music and other creative labour *desirable*.

Stahl's aim is to puncture this apparent desirability. In a fascinating range
of cultural sites Stahl sees evidence of intense struggles over the value and
meaning of musical production. Hierarchies of production, between performers and audiences, haunt the attempts of indie musicians to create spaces
where cultural equality can thrive. Rock ideology provides discourses of
authenticity that superficially allow for musicians to struggle against cultural
capitalism, even boy bands such as the Monkees, but this discourse is used
by television producers to capture the identification and desires of audiences.
Idol shows provide narratives of meritocracy, offering drastic warnings to
those who would seek to aspire beyond their abilities, whereas contemporary
rockumentary, exemplified in the film *DIG!* (2002), offers moral tales about
the dangers of taking bohemian excess too far. In all these cases, Stahl claims,
we can see signs of the way in which authenticity and authorship are central
to accumulation through cultural production. This is particularly apparent in
battles between record companies and artists over contracts and legislation

---

20 By which Terranova meant unpaid work, rather than work not undertaken under conditions
of slavery or serfdom, which is how the term 'free labour' has been more generally used.
21 But also animation (Stahl 2006b); and he makes frequent reference to struggles over meaning
and status in film and television (e.g., Stahl 2006a: 7–9).

concerning creative labour and the rights deriving from it. Just as the primitive accumulation of modern Europe enclosed common land in order to render it private property, copyright provides 'a new, inexhaustible common stock out of which new productive property can be generated and a new class of capitalists established' (Stahl 2006a: 224).

Stahl explains these roles for subjectivity, autonomy and authenticity historically. The original primitive accumulation of medieval Europe (extended to other realms by European imperialism; see Harvey 2003) forced production out of the family into waged employment outside the home. For Stahl, borrowing from Zaretsky (1976), this created a separation between work and life, with the latter 'more free' than the former, and this helped to create more personal forms of subjectivity by compelling men and women to look to themselves for meaning and purpose.[22] Eventually, as mental labour becomes increasingly incorporated into production in the twentieth century, such 'personal' subjectivity became more important – even central – to capitalism. At the same time, however, the historical compacts between businesses, states and labour, where the latter traded in autonomy and ownership for decent pay and working conditions, were relinquished. Stahl suggests that the incorporation of subjectivity into capitalism acts as a kind of pacifying device in the era of neo-liberalism and that popular music's democratic promise that 'you can do this too' is a particularly salient way in which 'liberal society' (a term that seeks to cover both capitalism and democracy) promises an end to alienation and appropriation by offering independence and autonomy (Stahl 2006a: 23). This has an important economic as well as a cultural aspect. Musicians seem to bypass corporate control by commodifying their identity as property which can then earn monopoly rents through the copyright system. But this apparent autonomy masks alienation and domination. Only a very few musicians really gain the autonomy and ownership associated with authorship; most musicians operate 'below the line' in ways that render them little better than wage slaves. Stahl suggests that the desirability of creative labour is a version of the way, for the Frankfurt School theorist Herbert Marcuse, culture serves to affirm capitalist societies.

There are two important theoretical strands underlying Stahl's analysis. One is a concern, derived from post-structuralism and autonomist Marxism (Read 2003) with 'the production of subjectivity' (and with what might be better called 'the productivity of subjectivity'): the way that certain modes of subjectivity are necessary and central to a given mode of production. This is apparent in the way that discourses of authenticity seem to offer a challenge to capitalism, permitting a certain amount of conflict in workplaces (possibly a distinctively popular music version of creativity–commerce relations). Ultimately, though, these discourses are presented by Stahl as sustaining new

---

22 This is an account which, it could be argued, pays too little attention to the declining but continuing role of religion in modern life.

variants of capitalism, or at least masking alienation and domination. This understanding derives from the other main theoretical strand in his research, which is a very strong critique of the profoundly undemocratic nature of the relations between employers and employees.[23]

3.9 The debate about creative work

In a variety of different forms, then, these cultural studies-influenced critics of creative work have found autonomy and self-realisation to be tied to conditions such as self-exploitation and self-blaming. In the strongest version of such critiques, involving political-economic as well as subjective processes, self-realisation becomes a systemic requirement.

In an important contribution, Mark Banks (2007) has partly endorsed the pessimism of many neo-Foucauldian accounts of creative work (and also, to some extent, critical theory and political economy accounts) but has also qualified that pessimism, drawing on his own empirical work and on a range of social theorists. Drawing on the writing of Ulrich Beck and Elizabeth Beck-Gernsheim (2002) on individualisation, Banks finds hope that transformations in modern life have enhanced the possibilities of social action and reflection. For Scott Lash and John Urry (1994) the cultural industries themselves have provided flows of signs that have enabled genuine reflexivity and independent creativity in modern societies. This is a world away from Adorno and Horkheimer's 'culture industry' thesis (1979/1947) of standardisation and pseudo-democratisation. Banks sees evidence of such individualisation and reflexivity in a number of aspects of contemporary cultural production.

First, says Banks, there are widespread signs that 'social creativity and independent artistic production are actually on the increase' (Banks 2007: 102) and a willingness to explore counter-rational and radical creative impulses remains alive. The aesthetic 'continues to provide resources and inspiration to a whole range of social actors, not just artists and creative cultural workers' (Banks 2007: 103). Regardless of whether or not this realm is a creation of bourgeois society, a practical belief in this realm has proven persistently inspiring. This is linked to a broader democratisation of aestheticisation. This provides new opportunities for commodification, but it also broadens the constituency of people who can live a life governed less by accumulation than the pursuit of aesthetic goals. Related to this, Banks (2007: 108ff.) turns to the concept of practices (see Section 2.4) to argue that the pursuit of internal rewards continues to provide a very important part of the

---

23 Stahl refers approvingly to Ellerman (1992), for example, who sees work in capitalist modernity as based on an illicit hiring and renting of people, which, in the private sphere, fundamentally contradicts democratic norms and values established in the public realm. Capitalist modernity is therefore seen as at odds with itself. The problem is that this relies heavily on a notion of self-ownership which, Cohen (1995) convincingly argues, undermines collectivist claims for justice.

motivation of cultural producers. Drawing in particular on Russell Keat's (2000) modification of Alisdair MacIntyre's ideas, Banks asks his readers to explore the possibility that there is enough variation within the institutions of contemporary capitalism that practices might endure in modern cultural production. Internal and external rewards may not be quite so mutually contradictory as is implied by stances that see the market as necessarily eroding quality.[24] What is more, practices can flourish at the expense of market-led imperatives. Firms can act as profit-satisfiers rather than profit-maximisers, summed up in the idea of doing it for the love and not the money. This can lead to self-exploitation, but it has another side too, encouraging resistance to the pursuit of external rewards. Furthermore, Banks (2007: 120) claims that moral systems of trust, honesty, obligation and fairness remain present in contemporary capitalism, and he provides examples of the resilience of social and cultural values amongst the creative workers he interviewed in previous research. Later in his book, Banks (2007: 184) extends this by suggesting that we need to think of creativity–commerce or art–commerce relations in terms of a triad, composed of orientations towards creativity, commerce and the social. The thought is that such a conception would allow us to consider the degree to which creative workers seek not only to live an aestheticised life, but also actively seek to intervene in social relations. Political and aesthetic goals may often be in tension, in that many may feel that pursuing morality through artistic production undermines aesthetic and 'practice'-like aspects of production; others may be looking for some kind of synthesis of the two.

In terms of the division identified earlier between notions of aesthetic autonomy and of professional autonomy, Banks tends to focus on the former almost exclusively. But his contribution is a valuable one, because it suggests the possibility of a more balanced appraisal of the relationships between subjectivity and creative labour than that provided by the cultural studies critics. So too does the work of Georgina Born. In an essay on the way in which aesthetic value has been treated in television studies, Born (2000) trenchantly critiques debates about quality in television for their relativist unwillingness to adjudicate between producer and audience discourses of quality, and she argues for the importance of analysing the discourses of media professionals. In particular, Born suggests that researchers should attend to

> a category of specifically media intellectuals whose task is to mediate the generic dynamics that bridge the past, present and future of media output. Their skill is in the art of judging how to progress a set of generic

---

24 A perspective that was to be found in post-war cultural policy for example; see Garnham (1990: 158) for criticism of this tendency.

possibilities in given conditions, and how to balance the enhancement of the entertainment, pleasure and education of the audience.

(Born 2000: 406)

Crucially, this puts emphasis on the *positive possibilities* of cultural production, by asking when its powers might be used 'responsibly, creatively, inventively in given conditions, and when not' (ibid.). It also suggests the importance of theorising agency, reflexivity and value. In later work, based on her own ethnographic research, Born analysed the 'situated ethics and aesthetics' of BBC television producers in documentary, drama and current affairs (Born 2004: 84–7; see also Born 2002). Born does not claim that reflexivity always results in better television; rather, she argues that a key analytical task is to consider how the reflexivity, intentionality and agency of cultural producers conditions the creativity and innovation possible within a given medium. This task in turn she locates within the context of genre theory, stressing the difference between various attitudes to generic change: 'nostalgic repetition, the rich mining of the familiar, which may itself be achieved in more and less inventive ways'; 'a self-conscious exceeding of the previous horizons of expectation'; and the production of generic stasis, involving the entrenching of given codes (Born 2000: 421).

The tensions between the pessimistic accounts discussed above and Banks's and Born's critical insistence on a more balanced appraisal brings us right back to the problem which, as we explained in Chapter 1, will be central to this book: the possibilities of doing good work in the cultural industries. For if the high levels of autonomy and the enhanced possibilities for self-realisation that some sociologists have identified as features of good work lead in the end only to self-exploitation, then these supposedly desirable forms of labour look bleak indeed. Is creative labour, then, really barely disguised 'bad work'? Might it even be a particularly modern form of bad work, where the subject's desires for autonomy and self-realisation become folded into systems of discipline and accumulation? It seems to us that these debates rely fundamentally on assumptions about and interpretations of the subjective experiences of workers, and it seems only right to listen and observe creative workers reflecting on their work, while taking into account the probability that their relationship to their own experience will often be opaque. For that reason, we draw on the theorised, historicised account of the forces shaping cultural production that we have outlined in this chapter. And as we have explained, an important 'intermediate' level, between the subjective experiences of workers and the historical and systemic forces structuring those experiences – and in turn being at times structured by them – is that of the organisation: of how work in the cultural industries is managed, coordinated and divided. That is the subject of the next chapter.

Part Two
Empirical study

4 The management of autonomy, creativity and commerce

4.1 Creativity, commerce and organisations

In the previous chapter, we outlined how the principle of creative autonomy has come to structure cultural production – and therefore creative labour. Struggles over aesthetic and professional autonomy generate tensions and contradictions in cultural production. How these tensions and contradictions are labelled varies between authors. They are usually expressed as between some kind of contrastive pairing: for example, between art and capital (Ryan 1992), art and commerce (Banks 2007), culture and commerce (Slater and Tonkiss 2001), creativity and commerce (Negus and Pickering 2004), culture and commodity (Frow 1996), and culture and economy (Ray and Sayer 1999). The result of these tensions, according to various sociological traditions, including Marxist, Foucauldian and liberal ones, is, in Mark Banks's words, that 'artistic desires for creative autonomy and independence exist in uneasy tension with capitalist imperatives of profit-generation and *controlled accumulation*' (2007: 6, original emphasis); the same can be said of journalistic and other professional desires for autonomy and independence.

If we compare the main approaches to cultural production discussed in Chapter 3, it is clear that one element of organisational, business and management studies (OBM), with its roots in sociology of culture, has paid considerably more attention to the implications of creativity–commerce tensions than has political economy of culture (PEC). For PEC has paid rather little attention to 'institutional imperatives, organisational routines and working exigencies' in spite of an early call from leading PEC exponents to do so (Murdock and Golding 1977: 34).[1]

---

1 It is true that a separate though related strand of research, radical media sociology, has complemented PEC by paying attention to organisational power dynamics, including creativity–commerce relations, sometimes using ethnographic methods to do so (Elliott 1972; Gitlin 1983). But, as pointed out in Chapter 3, neither there nor in PEC itself has much attention been paid to the specificity of creative labour and to the role of creativity–commerce tensions in constituting that specificity.

In an early account from OBM, Paul DiMaggio (1977: 442–3) remarked that nearly all culture-producing organisations include 'brokers' who mediate 'between the aspirations of artists for creative expression and the desire of management to be able to predict and control' and provided a categorisation of brokerage systems. This categorisation included 'pure' brokerage, where the broker serves both management and creative workers, 'acting as mediator, double-agent and advocate for both, with ultimate loyalty to the former' (DiMaggio 1977: 443). There were two variants on this pure system, entrepreneurial brokerage at one extreme and centralised brokerage at the other. The former, DiMaggio wrote, is associated with the most turbulent and competitive sectors of popular cultural production, and where managers abdicate control over acquisition and production decisions to the broker. The latter was associated with industries marked by high unit costs and strong government regulation and where management exerts strong pressures on creators. This usefully moved understanding of cultural-industry organisation beyond Hirsch's (1972) earlier and seminal analysis of cultural organisations, which was presented in terms of whether cultural industries followed 'craft' or 'bureaucratic' forms of management, and which therefore downplayed the distinctiveness of the cultural industries. However, DiMaggio, like many other innovative analysts of cultural industries, tended to underestimate the hybridity of cultural organisations, assuming that larger conglomerates produced standardised cultural goods lacking in innovation, while smaller firms were more oriented to creative diversity and innovation. This somewhat crude opposition (many innovative cultural goods are made by artists working for huge bureaucratic companies; the Beatles on EMI; *The Simpsons* at Fox) perhaps partially explains why the issue of 'aspirations of artists for creative expression' referred to by DiMaggio remained unpacked. But our emphasis here is on the need for a greater historical understanding of the notion of creative autonomy.

By the turn of the century, OBM analysts were more explicitly taking the perspective of managers. Davis and Scase (2000: 52) envisaged creative organisations as typically a place of 'negotiation, mutual adjustment and compromise' between commerce and creativity. Lampel et al. (2000) saw the management of creativity as an attempt to seek a balance between creative freedom and commercial imperatives. A key problem, in Lampel et al.'s (2000: 265) words, is that 'creativity comes from individuals whose talents and inputs can be organized and controlled only up to a point'. They provided an interesting categorisation of the tensions arising from this problem (and from the uncertain nature of demand for the expressive, non-utilitarian goods produced). Managers need to reconcile artistic values with economics; novelty with familiarity; existing demand with transformation of the market; vertical integration with outsourcing; and systems with individual inspiration.

For Davis and Scase, and for Lampel et al., then, management in the cultural industries is an act of navigation, a tentative 'balancing act', an attempt, from the perspective of managers (rather than of citizens, or audiences, or some other entity) to find that 'point' up to which creative individuals are willing to be controlled. Similarly, Davis and Scase write of the *paradox* of control and creativity. 'It is a paradox', they say, 'because the problem of reconciling openness, intuition, personal networks and individual autonomy (which serve "creative" ends) with instrumental criteria and rational business methods can never be completely resolved' (Davis and Scase 2000: 52).[2] However, from our perspective, all this leaves open the question of how we might understand the historical and structural factors behind such paradoxes, and how we might evaluate issues of the conflicts and unequal power relations lurking behind metaphors of negotiation and navigation. To quote Banks (2007: 6) again, creative labour in the cultural industries is 'routinely presented as an arena of political struggle' – but you would not know that from reading some of the research that emerges from business and management studies (see also Lampel et al. 2006; Caves 2000). By portraying such tensions primarily as challenges for managers to navigate, such perspectives potentially marginalise the political and historical nature of these contradictions.[3] A more satisfying synthesis has been provided by Bill Ryan (1992), though this has gone uncited by many accounts that purport to analyse cultural and creative industries, whether in PEC, OBM or cultural studies (Murdock 2003 is among the exceptions). Ryan, building on the work of Raymond Williams and Nicholas Garnham, but also drawing upon organisational sociologists such as Hirsch and DiMaggio, constructs a Marxian–Weberian explanation of what he calls art–capital relations. We shall now discuss Ryan's account, because it provides important insights into the structuring of creative autonomy and commercial imperatives in the cultural industries.

4.2 The creative management function

To summarise briefly, Ryan's view is that, in spite of their overwhelming motivation to produce profit (to accumulate capital), capitalist businesses cannot make artistic input completely subservient to the drive for accumulation. This is because art is generally understood, in most societies that can be characterised as modern and capitalist, as centred on the expressive individual artist. This attachment of artistic value to the expressive artist leads to a tendency for artistic objects to appear as the product of recognisable persons, and this means that in cultural production, unlike most other forms of work, the concrete and named labour of the artist – a particular and relatively privileged form of creative worker – is paramount and must be preserved.

---

2 See also DeFillippi et al. (2007: 511) on 'the paradoxes of managing and organizing creativity in the cultural economy'.

3 A striking recent exception from OBM is the fine research of Doris Eikhof and Axel Haunschild (e.g., 2007).

It resists the abstractness and alienation that Marx attributes to pretty much all other work under capitalism. This causes a constant problem for capitalist businesses.

This may seem to accept a romantic picture of creative labour as exceptional and somehow resistant to capitalism. But Ryan recognises that many capitalists make a very nice profit out of cultural goods. For him, they do so by *rationalising* cultural production, both at the creative stage and the circulation stage. Indeed, most of Ryan's book is framed as an examination of the extent to which capital has succeeded in achieving such rationalisation. This is achieved in different ways, at different stages. At the creative stage it is achieved through what Ryan calls *formatting*, especially the use of genre-based and star-based series of production, which go beyond the usual conventions associated with cultural production, to act as an identifiable marker of the kinds of experiences that cultural products aim to offer. At the circulation or distribution stage, it is achieved through the institutionalisation of marketing within corporate production, in order to produce a more controllable sequence of stars and genres. So cultural products are organised and marketed as 'a horror film' or 'a talent show' or 'a Tinchy Stryder recording' and so on.

It is the task of *creative management* to direct this work (Ryan 1992: 114–23, 178–82; and see Hesmondhalgh 2007: 24, 66–7 for further discussion). According to Ryan's account, as cultural-industry enterprises grew and professionalised, especially in the twentieth century, a stratum of creative management consolidated, fulfilling the functions of design and interpretation, and conversely relegating performers and other creative personnel to the status of directed executants. But creative management is unlike the top-down, inflexible supervision found in many other industries. It is less directive and has 'a muted and accommodating style' (Ryan 1992: 121) which partly flows from the view that symbolic creativity cannot be reduced to set rules or procedures. So this 'soft' but nevertheless rationalising creative management is always struggling against the relative autonomy given to creative workers, especially for 'star' creators, which further fuels the a-rationality of the creative process. For capitalists, creative workers represent an investment in variable capital that consistently threatens to undermine profitability.

An interesting political problem here is whether Ryan's account and any like it that would emphasise the concrete, named nature of creative labour, based on the status of the expressive individual artist, potentially renders the romantic myth of authorship the basis of creativity's resistance to commodification.[4] Rationalisation is then imposed on that creativity from outside. In reality, as we have already observed, artistic-cultural production is based on a

---

4 For Matt Stahl (2006a), discussed in Chapter 3, authorship is central to the politics of creative labour, because it creates hierarchies and inequalities among cultural producers. Like many authors, Ryan understates the importance of rights and contracts. We too pay insufficient attention to these issues, and hope to return to them in future work.

complex division of labour. Ryan's point might be more feasible if it were rephrased as resting on how the value of artistic-cultural production is very widely *perceived*, so that this 'myth' ends up having unexpected progressive consequences. Leaving aside the problems of his particular explanation of creativity–commerce relations, Ryan's account points to the importance of understanding how the *specificity* of creative labour, based on the production of culture, 'art' and knowledge, leads to certain organisational dynamics in cultural production, and to the value of understanding these dynamics in the context of power relations. There is quite simply no rival account that does so – or even attempts to do so – to anything like the same degree of detail, based on theoretical and empirical work.

One way of cutting through the conceptual thickets surrounding creativity–commerce relations is suggested by Keith Negus and Michael Pickering (2004). They usefully distinguish three positions to the creativity/commerce split lying behind everyday value judgements and academic approaches:

- A romantic, pseudo-political position that acting creatively is perpetually and inevitably at odds with being controlled industrially
- A populist, market liberal position that commerce is the condition which inspires creativity
- A sociological position that commerce and creativity have become so inextricably bound together as to be indistinguishable.

In a manner that we believe to be consistent with Ryan's account, Negus and Pickering prefer to see creativity and commerce as distinct dynamics that are nevertheless intertwined, producing a series of tensions – including organisational ones. In what follows, we seek to explore such tensions, organisationally and in terms of the experiences of creative workers. We discuss relations between the concept of autonomy and creativity–commerce tensions. Importantly, we aim to contextualise these organisational dynamics and worker experiences by reference to some of the conjunctural forces structuring worker experiences. These include: the general push on the part of businesses and their allies in government towards neo-liberalism and marketisation (the process whereby market exchange comes to permeate societies); changing business strategies, including a shift towards 'the service sector' and the rise of ideas such as the knowledge economy and the information society, which radically boosted the growth of the telecommunications and cultural industries; socio-cultural changes, including populist attacks on the authority of intellectuals and experts, even as certain experts, such as economists and financial analysts, gained unprecedented power; technological changes, notably the rise of multi-channel television and the Internet, closely associated with an increasing distrust of professional cultural production.

In the next two sections (4.3 and 4.4), we outline management strategies and discourses across two of the three industries we studied: magazines and music. In each case, we emphasise how the creative management function is carried out, in terms of the division of labour in the particular industry.[5] We discuss how managers and creative workers understand what constitutes quality, how to produce quality products, and the degree to which autonomy is explicitly central to their goals. In keeping with the perspective outlined in the previous chapter, we show that aspirations to creative autonomy, deriving from the historical and structural conditions discussed there, remain central to power dynamics in the cultural industries.

In the latter part of the chapter, shifting towards the subjective experiences that are the main focus of our empirical fieldwork, we show that considerable conflict and anxiety surrounds these aspirations in contemporary creative labour. We track a number of forces threatening artistic and professional autonomy in the contemporary cultural industries, using empirical evidence. The main forces we focus on are: marketing and efficiency; attacks on public service broadcasting and centralisation of control; and 'the obligation to network'.

4.3 Managing creative autonomy: magazines

In the magazine industry, the key creative management role is carried out by editors – though of course this role can be delegated to deputies, administrators and so on. A number of analyses of the cultural industries have emphasised their distinctive characteristics (Hirsch 1972; DiMaggio 1977; Garnham 1990; Caves 2000; Hesmondhalgh 2007). As we have already seen, some emphasise the special nature of creative labour (Ryan 1992; Stahl 2006a; Banks 2007). Creative managers and workers tend to vary in how they talk about this distinctiveness. Some of them, as we shall see later, tend to deny it, downplaying the differences from other industries, in a seeming attempt to avoid being labelled as 'whining artists'. However, many creative managers discuss their work in terms of managing the distinctive nature of creative labour. Here Wayne, the editor of a small but successful dance music magazine, described how he managed his staff:

> I think that monthly magazines in particular and weeklies, although less so, they are a creative business and you have to manage people as creative individuals not as office staff. What that means is that people don't get told off if they turn up half an hour late, they won't get told off if they turn up two hours late, but ultimately the important thing is that they excel in what they do, that they are imaginative, passionate, informed, funny and entertaining.
>
> (Interview 5)

---

5 We focus on the creative management function because this seems the most concise way to approach the organisational aspects of creativity–commerce tensions we are discussing here.

Here then is a strong statement of how 'creative', cultural-industry businesses such as magazines differ from other businesses. It is directly linked to a valuing of autonomy, of the ability of journalists to operate with relative freedom as long as they produce results imbued with creativity. In order to produce this creativity, according to Wayne, managers of magazine journalists need to exercise the gentlest possible controls in terms of routine, behaviour, comportment and so on. Like many other creative managers in the three industries we examined, Wayne was himself still active as a 'creative', regularly producing articles himself, for other magazines, under the supervision of other creative managers. This emphasises the potentially quite close links between creative managers and creative personnel – though ultimately the creative manager will have to obey the dictates of commerce in hiring and 'releasing' staff, and this hiring will take place according to the conventions of employment contracts.

> I think what I try to do is get the best out of native talent and passion for the subject matter. I think the kind of magazines that we publish here and the magazines I work on, they're not exactly fanzines but they're not far off. There is no substitute for somebody who has been really, really obsessed with the subject for a long time and who knows a lot about it and can communicate that in an entertaining and passionate manner.
>
> (Interview 5)

This emphasis on the distinctive strategies needed for managing creative labour are contrasted with businesses which, while dealing with creative products, nevertheless fail to respect the distinctiveness of symbol-making.

> I mean I've worked in different kinds of organisations and [another magazine company] was a very, very managerial environment where they were into being Investors in People and HNDs[6] and all this kind of stuff, as if you can apply a professional qualification to this kind of thing, and I actually don't really think you can.
>
> (Interview 5)

Similar principles were applied by the same editor to freelance staff. Here long-term informal relationships built on trust were seen as key to managing 'people who do not like rules' – another feature of artists, constructed as in opposition to routine, bureaucracy and regulation:

---

6 Investors in People is a government-backed accreditation scheme whereby employers can demonstrate that they are investing in the training and development of their staff. Higher National Diplomas are the main form of vocational Higher Education qualification in the UK.

Well, I mean it's management in the sense that you are trying to get people to do what you want them to do and you're trying to get the best out of them, but it's enormously informal, and every time I've seen any attempt at formalised relationships, particularly with freelancers, with contracts, with notification of rights and duties and obligations and so forth, it doesn't really work very well. I think it is the kind of business that attracts people who do not like rules and want very informal relationships, and I think the success of the magazines that we publish and the ideas that go into them, it's down to those informal relationships.

(Interview 5)

Here we have an explanation, from the viewpoint of a creative manager, of the reasons for respecting autonomy. It is a matter of attracting creative people, and these tend to be people 'who do not like rules' and who value informality. This allows relationships to thrive which feed into ideas.

In other magazines, though, there was much less of a conscious sense amongst managers and creative personnel of the magazine industry as a cultural industry or creative business. This was true of the very different genre of the building and construction trade press. The readership of these magazines consists almost entirely of people who work in the building and construction businesses. There was a strong ethos of serving the professional needs of the trade, as demonstrated here by one editor, Reggie:

One of the three things that we are as a magazine is that everything we write has to be useful for our professional readers, it has to be authoritative, and it has to be adventurous and fun. So, what's really, really important in terms of that knowledge is the authoritative. If we lose that ... this week we wrote about the train crash, and we have to make sure that what we write is correct, or else people write in. The week before we published a massive thing in the UK with nuclear power stations and we got them in the wrong place by a hundred miles. We got calls from people saying you've got it in the wrong place. Our readership are very, very accurate in the way they think, so we have to be accurate.

(Interview 50)

There is still an emphasis here on the creative and the aesthetic – 'adventurous and fun' – but there is even greater emphasis on accuracy and authority. These latter qualities supposedly ensure an appropriate distance from the requirements of the civil engineering trade, and this equates to a kind of professional autonomy, as is indicated by the emphasis that Reggie places on 'independence' from the professional institute to which the magazine is contracted:

We remain fiercely independent, but we keep them onboard as partners. They can't influence what we write, which is a very unique position to be in that we have a contract, and we call ourselves the magazine of the [Institute], but they have no access to our editorial and we are independent. From their point of view they are probably a bit pissed off about the fact that they can't say anything. We reach 57,000 people every week that are members of the Institute, and they can't influence anything that we say. They can influence, but they can't directly put anything into the magazine.

(Interview 50)

How then are tensions over autonomy manifest in this genre of the magazine industry? Some indication of this is provided by Aggie, a features editor who has some supervisory responsibility but who works beneath editor Reggie, a more senior creative manager. Here she discusses supplements: special sections of her trade magazine covering a particular topic, and aimed at attracting advertising from a particular sector of the building and construction industry, such as concrete.

I have a team of four, including me, and some of them have other duties. They don't just exclusively write features. Some of them exclusively write for me, and [there is] also a sort of roster of freelancers. It's my job to come up with good ideas for general features constantly, also to encourage the team to generate ideas themselves, and sometimes that's more successful than others. We also have a massive programme – because it's a big commercial operation – of supplements which go into specialist sectors, which is where I would say the creativity goes downhill a little bit because these are areas which we put on our publishing calendar because it's easy for the sales team then to talk to advertisers and say 'hey, we've got a special coming up on concrete, why don't you advertise?' For that reason those supplements tend to be big and we are always under pressure to feature certain companies. I would say there is a big tension between editorial and sales because they are always trying to push us to write more about their clients, and we are trying to do more general issue based stuff, and also they don't want us to upset their clients. I mean our front page story almost every week will be upsetting someone and they will be threatening to pull advertising. So, it's always a very tricky one, but because we are a big paper – this is what I love about [this magazine] – we can do it. Other papers I've worked for you just get bullied and you sort of go down.

(Interview 18)

For Aggie, autonomy involves independence from the interests of the industry on which she reports. Even at its most developed, this is a qualified form of autonomy, in that journalists will only be able to be critical of developments in the industry to the extent that its business readership will feel comfortable enough to continue subscribing. However, magazine supplements,

aimed primarily at gaining revenue through advertising, undoubtedly represent a less autonomous area – 'here', as this journalist put it, 'the creativity
goes downhill a little bit'. Aggie also hints at an important organisational issue: the creativity–commerce tension is structured into 'a big tension
between editorial and sales' – editorial representing the 'creative' pole, sales
the commercial.

Another concrete example of tensions over autonomy in the magazine
industry is copy checking. This is where representatives of companies will see
a draft of features before publication. Magazines sometimes grant permission
to companies to check copy in return for access to elusive interviewees and
other information. This may particularly be the case with less prestigious
publications. But there is no mechanism to show readers that copy has been
checked; there is no code of practice that says that copy checking should be
acknowledged. Therefore those magazines which choose not to undertake
copy checking in order to maintain enhanced autonomy from the business
sector that they report on say that they have to work much harder in order to
gain interviews for features.

We explained in Section 1.2 that we designed our study of three industries
to take account of the importance of genre in understanding the sociology
of cultural production. How might we understand the effects of genre on
the organisation of cultural production using the above examples? The
emphasis among music journalists is on a kind of operational autonomy.
Workers are given the freedom to dress and behave 'as they wish', though
of course they still follow sets of social codes and conventions in doing
so. This allows an informality, and a focus on working relationships which
in turn permits good ideas and good writing to flow. Among trade press
workers, autonomy is conceived as independence from the industry that they
report on.

It seems then that, at least in the case of these contrasting cases of magazine journalists, the effects of genre are mediated through *content*, and
through the specific histories of the material that creative workers deal with.
Music represents a distinctive form of social communication in modern
societies, with marked elements of performance, ritual and self-expression.
These elements are carried over into the related but separate industry of
music journalism, as music journalists identify strongly with the traditionally
very high levels of creative autonomy sought and occasionally obtained by
successful musicians. Music journalists adhere to certain conventionalised
forms of conduct – a semi-politicised bohemian hedonism – and are certainly
restrained by the commercial ties of the magazine organisations they work for
to record companies and musicians. After all, these magazines and record
companies are tied together by mutual interest, with magazines reliant on
record companies and musicians for material and stories, and record companies partly reliant on magazines for publicity. Nevertheless, music journalists
tend to identify with the high levels of autonomy sought and, at least in myth,
attained by the most prestigious musicians. Building and construction are, by

contrast, social activities founded on accuracy and professional competence. Here too, journalists echo the values of the world they report on, in terms of how they conceive of their products. Accuracy, precision and professionalism are highly valued.

While genre of product affects organisation of cultural production, we need to remember that there can be considerable variation *within* particular genre cultures about how genre codes are put into operation. This is perhaps especially the case when it comes to levels or degrees of autonomy. So within the music press too, as within the building and construction press, there is considerable variation in autonomy. Some trade press magazines carry more supplements and allow more copy checking, potentially reducing the costs involved in securing stories, but this potentially damages the prestige of the magazine and its writers. Meanwhile in music magazines, the genre of music reported on plays an important role, creating a system of music magazine sub-genres. Rock and dance music journalists are likely to be quite different from classical music journalists for example. Workers in some sub-genres of music magazines seem to emphasise autonomy more or less than others. So-called 'urban' music magazines – those reporting on the 'urban' genres of hip hop, R&B and genres such as soul and funk that feed into them – seem to have less space for such autonomy, perhaps as a result of the economic fragility of the sub-genre, but perhaps also because of a relatively lesser emphasis on notions of creative autonomy. Lakshman, a music journalist, explained:

> I've found in the last few years a lot of magazines from like *Rewind* to *Echoes* and *Blues & Soul*, and even *Hip Hop Connection* actually, they are kind of at the mercy of advertisers to a degree. ... I do know of a lot of instances where I've had to review or interview somebody simply because their label or company has taken out a large amount of ads with such and such magazine. So it's kind of 'we'll take out this many ads, so do you think you can squeeze our artists in or review their product?' or whatever. I do know of instances where people are paid for covers and they are paid for features, they are paid for a certain amount of page space over a certain amount of time. If somebody is doing that you're not really going to let anyone say anything remotely negative about them in your magazine. It's unfortunate, but I kind of understand why it happens. It is kind of hand in hand with editorial.
>
> (Interview 41)

Lakshman would like to experience greater autonomy in this context but recognises that in the smaller music magazines the separation of 'editorial and advertising ... [is] not always that clear cut'. As with the trade press, it will often – though not always – be workers for less prestigious and less well-resourced magazines that have to sacrifice independence for access to information, interviews and so on.

4.4 Managing creative autonomy: the case of music recording

Whereas the management function in magazine journalism mainly inheres in the figure of the editor, in the recording industry there are two main types of creative manager. Each acts as an intermediary between creativity and commerce, but with somewhat different allegiances. The first type, 'A&R' (artist and repertoire) staff, operates within a recording company. In a major record company or a large independent, they will usually carry that title but in a smaller independent, where jobs are more mixed, the role may become blurred, as a label boss may effectively carry out the role. Their main jobs are to seek out creative talent, and arrange for these acts to release their music through the label; and to work with established acts to ensure that they build on previous work in a successful way. The second main type of creative manager in the music industry is the artist manager, whose job is to represent the artist, not only in negotiations and interactions with recording and music publishing companies, but also in arranging promotional and publicity work, live concerts and other activities.[7] Artist managers, in most recorded music genres, act to further both the commercial and creative interests of their clients (and of course their own interests too), but in cases of conflict, the job of the artist manager is to protect clients from demands on the part of other, commercial entities – most notably record and publishing companies. The record company may, for example, wish to bring in a certain record producer to modify the sound and feel of an act's recordings in a certain direction; the act and their manager may prefer a very different producer, with a different style and musical sensibility. In general, then, in terms of the contradictions between artistic creativity and commerce that we are claiming is fundamental to the cultural industries, artist managers are more oriented towards the pole of creativity and A&R staff more towards the pole of commerce. But within the specific organisational setting of the record company, A&R staff are more oriented towards creative personnel than their colleagues in marketing, whose interests are more directly framed in terms of profit maximisation (see below). This is partly because A&R staff have to maintain a close working relationship with musicians and artist managers.

An indication of some of the tensions involved in these organisational relationships of creativity and commerce can be gleaned from the following discussion by Ryan, an experienced artist manager who has managed many successful UK rock musicians. For Ryan, 'a good A&R person helps you work out the situation, helps you work out what to do, gives you good advice as to what songs work and what don't work'. The problem though is that such A&R personnel 'don't have the influence with the marketing people and

---

7 This 'type' is better thought of as a 'function', for any aspect of this role can be delegated or even outsourced.

their bosses'. This leads to an apparently friendly relationship which can mask deeper, structural antagonisms.

> He is as it were your professional mate, but in the end he is paid by the other side. He has got to answer to the people who pay his wages and although he appears to be your mate, you know, 'we're all in this together', at the end of the day he knows who butters his bread ... To some extent he is the guy who is posing as your mate whilst actually trying to get you to do what the marketing men and the corporation want you to do. He's like a stalking horse, but I think sometimes they will stand up and really become your mate, they become involved and they really do help, and then they usually get fired.
>
> (Interview 8)

Another scenario that brings conflict between A&R personnel and artist managers is excessive intervention on the part of the former in the work of the musicians that managers (ideally) seek to protect. For example, Ryan commented on an A&R man who helped to bring about the initial success of the principal act he managed:

> I mean he did a fantastic promotion job and all the press he gave us ... But he was an absolute nightmare as an A&R man, and we couldn't stand him in the end. It was like he was always phoning up at all times of day and night and we all breathed such a huge sigh of relief when our relationship stopped with him because he was all over us. But in a way when we were coming up, that [...] sort of maniacal enthusiasm was fantastic. If only he could have backed off and still kept that sort of discipline, and in that sense you wanted a more impersonal thing. So [we went to another record company] where they just distribute our records for us and they suggest what we should do and I say yes or no and I even work out the marketing budgets with them.
>
> (Interview 8)

A&R personnel, the key creative managers in the recording industry, then, can achieve success through a very 'hands-on' attitude, but taken too far, this can alienate musicians and their artist managers. Once established, the artist manager can, acting on behalf of the artist, serve as an equally powerful figure. This has become even more the case in recent years as the recording industry has undergone a crisis associated with digitalisation. Ryan explained the issue in the following terms:

> Well, going back a few years when A&R departments were still sort of fairly significant and doing something, which they're not really now, the classic [situation] was that A&R would make the record and then they'd just walk into marketing and go, 'here you go', and run away. There would

be no dialogue or conversation about the band or where they had come from or where they were going. ... So I think it was always the manager's place to then jump in at that point and be the person to take the vision and describe it to marketing and help them form a plan. But more and more now management, or management companies, are forming a greater part of the A&R process. I mean certainly with [this manager's best-known act] we deliver finished records, and it's happening more and more across the board.

(Interview 8)

These developments have been part of a process whereby, as record company budgets and business confidence have shrunk, A&R personnel 'have seen their status and numbers diminish' (Simpson 2009). In this situation, A&R personnel are increasingly taking on the less prestigious role of talent scouting, including the coordination of such scouting by teams of younger people hired to check out a series of live gigs. Note however that this does not mean any less importance for the function of creative management as we are analysing it here, or for the tensions between creativity and commerce that this function is supposed to contain. The point is that key aspects of that function are now taken on outside record companies, by artist managers.

What of the role of genre in the recording industry? It is perhaps even more important here than in magazine journalism in determining the precise shape of creativity–commerce tensions. Here 'genre' refers essentially to a particular type of musical 'style', such as rock, rap, pop, reggae and so on. The major record companies nowadays tend to divide themselves up by imprint – 'labels' or groups of labels within the company (sometimes based in separate offices) that serve particular market niches. For example, Universal Records, the world's biggest record company, included in 2008 Island-Def Jam for black musical styles including rap and R&B, Interscope-Geffen-A&M for pop and rock; and Machete for salsa. Each company division then has multiple smaller labels under its wing. Not all of these fit neatly into the genre divisions indicated, and this demonstrates the messiness of musical categorisation as well as organisational life. These 'styles' are also to some extent marketing categories. In fact, though, these terms are bigger than styles or marketing categories, because they involve an entire set of institutions, discourses and meanings. As Simon Frith (1996: 88) puts it, new genres are 'constructed and then articulated through a complex interplay of musicians, listeners and mediating ideologues' and are built on a sense of exclusion as well as inclusion.

Following such development of new genres, the recording industry then seeks to draw and maintain genre boundaries, but musicians, listeners and mediators such as writers, DJs and so on continue to construct the meaning of the music, usually in a way influenced by the origins of the genre. Keith Negus (1999) showed this in his analysis of the US recording industry. He analysed how rap, country and salsa carry with them a particular set of meanings in relation to place and ethnic identity, but also how these genres tended to have their own particular institutional arrangements: country, for example, is much more reliant on radio than is rap, where there is greater emphasis on informal networks of 'performances, posters, magazine articles, community events, parties, the actions of DJs and word-of-mouth chains' (Negus 1999: 175). However, the importance of genre is ultimately constrained by the greater significance of attitudes towards autonomy and authenticity. In Bourdieu's (1996) terms, there will be producers who are oriented towards restricted audiences, or limited niche groups in modern marketing parlance, emphasising autonomy; and there will be other producers who are oriented towards larger-scale production. In the recording industry, these differences are mediated through emphasis on 'organic' and 'synthetic' development of artists respectively (Negus 1992: 54–5). The organic 'ideology' sees the role of the record company as enhancing the already existing qualities of the act, which has been largely formed in some separate musical sphere – for example, in live performance in a certain region. The synthetic 'ideology' sees the role of the record company as 'a catalytic bringing together of various elements' (ibid.). In creating a pop act such as a 'boy band', for example, there will be collaboration with artist managers but the record company may well have considerable input into what record producers, songwriters, video directors, stylists and so on may be used. Lloyd, a head of A&R, explained:

> I actually believe with some artists you have very little input. You might go down to the studio and say 'great', but some artists know exactly what they want. They know how they want their songs written, they obviously write their songs, they know how their songs will sound in the studio. The A&R will obviously say they are genius. However, conversely, sometimes you will work with a pop act and you kind of produce it, you become part of the band, part of the artists. You get much more involved in the writing, the arrangements, everything about that act. So again, A&R do very broadly different roles, depending on the genre of the artists ... Genre is essential. An R&B act, the album could consist of maybe eight to ten collaborations with different producers or writers. So the A&R could be very active putting together and coming up with ideas, and supporting the idea together. Whereas a guitar band album, you make one phone call to the producer and they go off and make the record.
>
> (Interview 60)

Genre, to put it in the analytical terms employed here, determines the grounds on which creativity and commerce are negotiated.

4.5 Pressures on autonomy (1): marketisation in broadcasting

Having outlined the main organisational features of two of the three industries, and examined the degree to which genre might modify and nuance these features, we now examine the ways in which these organisationally embodied tensions between creativity and commerce might currently be going through changes. We understand these changes as continuing renegotiations of the power lines between creativity and commerce in an era of pronounced marketisation. We begin by addressing the case of television, at first outlining briefly the main organisational dynamics, as we did for recording and magazines above, but here focusing on *changing* dynamics of autonomy, creativity and commerce.

In television, as in the recording industry, the creative management role is split. One key role is that of the producer, who serves as head of a project team working on a programme, whether a one-off or a series. The producer must mediate between, on the one hand, the writers, directors, actors, camera operators, and on the other hand, more senior management, including the other key creative manager in British television, the commissioner or controller. The commissioner acts as head of a department, and departments are defined by genre, such as documentary, drama, religious affairs, arts, etc. The relationships between commissioners and creative personnel can be highly effective, or it can be another source of potential conflict, as Samuel, a freelance producer, outlined:

> But generally I think if you are working on a film where you are actually the director of the programme, I suppose there are a number of places where that vision is not matched. It might not match with your executive or the company you are working for, and it might not match with the commissioning editor of the channel. Ideally they will, and I think it depends a lot on the commissioning editor and the relationship you've got with the commissioning editor. I think it's often said, but I don't think there are that many great films made or great series made without great commissioning editors. In a way, what I think that means is that they tend to be more hands-off than hands-on, and that varies.
>
> (Interview 21)

In the case of the television talent show discussed in detail in Chapter 7, Marcus, the show's executive producer, described the commissioning editor as 'probably quite hands on ... She was very much an ally really, almost like another senior member of the production team who would give her opinion' (Interview 55). This 'collaborative' but more interventionist approach was contrasted by Martha, a commissioning editor, with that which prevailed in the early days of independent production in the UK, in the 1980s:

> It's a very different market to the market it was in say '82 when Channel Four started and there were far more smaller independents and it was slightly more fly by the seat of your pants stuff really. You know, you commissioned something it would arrive, it may not bear any relation to the thing you thought you commissioned, but it would go on air anyway

and some people would like it and some people wouldn't. It is now much more of a business. It's very focused about what it is you want and how it's going to be delivered.

(Interview 6)

This more business-oriented approach involved providing considerable autonomy until the final stages of production. However, that autonomy is increasingly based on what creative managers call 'trust' – a knowledge of what kind of product they are likely to get:

> Different people work in different ways. I tend to establish a relationship with different production companies over a number of different projects and I'm sure everyone will say the same thing but I only work with companies and people who I have a trust and belief in and who have something of a pedigree. We have quite a lot of discussion at the beginning of a project about the talent which is very important for me, and the content, and then to an extent I'll let them get on with it and then pick it up again at the rough cut stage where it's the opportunity to see what they've done.
>
> (Interview 6)

Importantly, however, there has been a shift in the relative importance of these two key types of creative manager, and a considerable centralisation of power in the hands of commissioners. Producers tended to work very closely with creative personnel such as writers, and were expected to monitor only a limited number of projects.[8] This tended to lead to quite close relationships, and a certain amount of shared sympathy. The downside of this was that, in the small world of British television up until the 1980s, producers and their associates may well have shared similar social backgrounds, leading to the exclusion of others (given the often-noted tendency for managers to 'recruit in their own image'). Television has traditionally been the preserve of white, upper middle-class employees – including of course some extremely talented people, with the vision to portray worlds beyond their own in a powerful and affecting way. As television expanded in terms of its budgets, hours of availability and channels in the 1990s and early 2000s, it grew as an industry, and now employs more people, from a wider range of social backgrounds (Paterson 2001). Under a different system, this may have led to an unleashing of creativity. However, this change coincided with a much greater degree of senior managerial control, particularly at the BBC, as the public service ethos

---

8 A notable example would be the BBC producer Innes Lloyd's (1926–91) collaboration over many years with the great Yorkshire playwright and screenwriter Alan Bennett. On the role of producers, see Tunstall (1993) for a study from when some of the changes outlined above were already underway.

of British broadcasting came under increasing scrutiny, in an era of neo-liberalism, where marketised and entrepreneurial forms of organisation were considered to be superior to supposedly state-bureaucratic institutions such as the old BBC (Born 2004). Commissioners are now responsible for a large body of programmes, very much greater in number than those of the producers who were previously the 'centre' of creative management in the industry. With the rise of independent production, these commissioners are also expected to sift a huge amount of programme ideas. This can sometimes involve conflict, but in other cases highly effective collaboration between commissioners and creative managers.

Within European television, a major threat to autonomy has come from the erosion of public service broadcasting (PSB). PSB provided no guarantee of creative independence, and the quality of programming across public service systems was highly uneven. However, some PSB organisations provided a bulwark against the casualisation that became rampant in many television systems from the early 1990s onwards. Stable working conditions are fundamental to a secure sense of independence necessary for creative autonomy, and such public television funding can arguably provide such independence, as long as funding is operated at 'arm's length' distance from government and from political and other imperatives, as was the case with the BBC. But the size and nature of its defence against commercial pressures diminished as the BBC came under increasing assault. It shrunk in size, and increasingly resorted to certain techniques of contemporary managerialism, as Georgina Born (2004) shows in her ethnographic study of the corporation in the late 1990s and early 2000s.

4.5.1 Television documentary and factual television

We focus here on the genre of television documentary to explore these issues. Although certain programmes and sub-genres, such as internationally distributed wildlife documentaries, can be highly profitable, many European broadcasters show documentaries primarily out of (an increasingly residual) commitment to public service; it is generally considered to be a genre unlikely to make money. Creative autonomy for documentary makers therefore has tended to rely on the idea that it provides public understanding of social processes and private experiences. As Lilith, a documentary producer and production manager, stated: 'I don't want to do factual television; I want to make documentaries … that teach people about things, that throw light on something maybe people haven't heard before' (Interview 43). This is an idea not far removed from the notion of professional journalism as public service, but also influenced by ideas of artistic autonomy, because of the emphasis on aesthetic factors in documentary production. But the value of documentary as public service has come to be eroded. This can be seen in the reduction in dedicated slots for documentaries in the schedules. As Lilith said: 'looking at the schedule on the BBC there are very, very few slots for documentaries, any kind of documentaries at all … they are really squeezing them out' (Interview 43).

As the idea of the social value of broadcasting has diminished in the increasingly neo-liberal media climate of the 1990s and 2000s, broadcasters have come to see documentary as a high-risk medium. Consequently, our interviewees from the world of documentary reported that commissioning organisations spread their risk by providing only a small percentage of a budget, leaving it in the hands of documentary-makers to seek funding from elsewhere, such as international co-production and financing deals – for example, from an overseas broadcaster or TV channel that might be interested in showing the programme and, crucially, in retaining rights. Take this example from the world of arts documentary:

> I mean we made 17 pre-sales and we still had a shortfall of £100,000. With European money, it was a £300,000 budget, we basically got, more or less … a third from Channel 5, a third from Europe and these 17 pre-sales, and a third [the] shortfall. So all the sales we're making now, the advance we had from the distributor in Australia, we're still [making] a loss.
>
> (Interview 1)

The result is that documentary-makers need now to spend a great deal of time chasing these new financing sources and they also need to gain expertise in how to do so. Gaining funding can take time that is not available, especially in current affairs documentary-making. Esther, a head of documentary production, explained:

> it can hold things up, particularly if you are trying to film a current affairs film. We are currently filming in [two hot spots] and they are all potentially difficult subject matters, but we have to go *now* because it is happening now. So a lot of time we go off before we've received any funding at all, before contracts are signed, before we've got co-funding in place, it's a risk that we take and the broadcasters constantly remind us that it's our risk, even though the commissioning department wants us to do it. So it's a kick bollocks scramble to try and get funding in place, to get all the contracts, to get everything agreed.
>
> (Interview 40)

This general erosion of the authority of PSB means that managers are much less likely to take risks when it comes to supporting creative autonomy – including journalistic autonomy. Malcolm, an executive director of documentary film, commented on this, claiming that an increasing concern about risk has restrained cultural organisations, which have in turn imposed restrictions on what broadcasters can do.

> Fifteen years ago working for [a leading BBC current affairs programme]
> if I went out and interviewed somebody without a camera – a research
> interview – and came back and said 'I know that in the British army they
> are beating their recruits', they would say 'how do you know?' I would
> say 'well, all my instincts as a journalist and I went and checked the story
> out and I know this to be true and this was said to me and I can't report
> who the person is'. They would trust me as a professional, say 'yes, okay',
> and they'd go with the story. Now they want affidavits, and in other
> words the professionalism and the judgement is all being squeezed
> out, and the level of compliance that's been required is increasingly pre-
> venting hard, tough journalism being conducted. But across the board for
> all programming, the compliance officers are trampling on the creative
> process and on, if you will, the democratic responsibilities of broad-
> casters to reveal the world as it truly is, even if that world is difficult to
> prove completely ... Judgement, risk taking is all being squeezed out
> dramatically.
>
> (Interview 37)

This is a general social and cultural change, as this interview subject
acknowledged. Nevertheless, it could be argued that cultural organisations
have a responsibility to take a courageous stance in order to avoid stifling
creativity and the dissemination of knowledge.

A number of our interviewees discussed the emergence of a new entertainment genre, factual television, or factual entertainment. This is how Kieran,
an executive producer, described the difference:

> So the documentary, what you would have done, you would have been
> more interested in a longer narrative journey, which might last the whole
> film, with one particular character. You would have picked a good char-
> acter and they would have been there at different points in the film and
> their story, there would be some element of the story and the narrative
> carrying you through the whole film. Factual entertainment is not so
> interested in that, much more interested in the thematic subject and
> picking out the kind of best bits and the most outrageous bits and not
> interested in that substantial immersion of character and narrative
> throughout the whole programme.
>
> (Interview 20)

It would be too simplistic to portray this as merely a 'dumbing down' however.
The same executive producer described what he felt had been a useful intervention on the part of a commissioning editor in a documentary on women
and body hair:

> [The commissioning editor] is a lovely, lovely person, a highly intelligent
> woman, very, very direct, and we had never made a film for what you

might call factual entertainment. We had done documentaries and we had set out to make a film about the gender issues involved for women who are covered with hair. [The commissioner] took one look at this at viewing and said 'it's boring; it's boring, boring, boring! I mean where are your young British hairy cunts?' And you know what? She was dead right. We had to completely rethink the film and to make the film for what the factual entertainment take on it would be. ... So [the commissioner] for example wanted us to interview a load of young blokes and get them to talk about their attitudes towards women with hair. It was a really good move and it just lightened up the whole thing immediately and made it much more funny. So that was [the commissioner] putting in her necessary brief of being head of factual entertainment, on that programme, and we learnt a lot from that and it was a good process.

(Interview 20)

At other times, however, from the point of view of creative personnel, the intervention of commissioning editors might take some of the creative edge out of the finished product, depending on their vision of where the programme should fit on the continuum that runs from documentary through 'popular factual' to factual entertainment. Kieran provided an example of an experience his company had had with a different commissioner to the one discussed above. Here, the commissioner was surprised to see the programme already quite close to a 'finished version'.

It was the right length, it was in four parts, the parts are the right length, etcetera. He was quite surprised by that. He was used to seeing things in a much more fluid form and with Channel 4 having much greater influence a lot earlier on with the editing process.

(Interview 20)

The film had an experimental feel to it: 'The way we cut the film was very, very jagged and it was deliberately jagged. There was no narration voice to ease you into it, and it was kind of enigmatic and startling and quite alarming in places.' The commissioning editor's response was that 'it was too much for Channel 4 at nine o' clock. It was his view that the film needed warming up and making it more accessible to a wider audience', which involved 'bumping up the warmer material in the film'. 'So what was your response to Channel 4?' we asked: 'We do what they want. They are paying the money. I have always taken the view that they are paying for the product and who are we to say "that's not really what you want"?'

The way in which a number of creative workers choose to deal with this situation is to learn about which commissioning editors they can really work with. Kieran's preferred aesthetic is to work 'close to an edge of accessibility' and to avoid the cruelty of some documentary and factual television by 'being kind with people':

> I know commissioning editors who I know would always be trying to kind of push you over that line into areas which I think would be cruel about people, so we don't work for them. So you don't get into that area of discomfort.
>
> (Interview 20)

This is how creative workers accommodate the new more competitive, business-like arena of television. We return to the issue of how this affects questions of quality in Chapter 8.[9]

4.5.2 Television drama

Another change was taking place in UK television in parallel to the erosion of PSB which also has serious consequences for creative autonomy: the centralisation of control in the hands of newly powerful commissioners. One BBC producer told Georgina Born how in the mid-1980s 'singles', the department of the BBC responsible for creating one-off dramas, employed 'ten or twelve producers with some degree of autonomy, each with two or three slots a year they could make' (Born 2004: 309). The number of key gatekeepers had, by the mid-1990s, decreased to two 'controllers' (commissioners). Control had become centralised but at the same time, existing alongside the BBC's own in-house production, there was an increasing number of independent television production companies specialising in drama and in other genres. As a result, commissioners were required to sift through an enormous number of ideas. In addition, commissioners themselves were less and less creatively autonomous, because of a set of measures introduced by senior management to monitor and modify the BBC's institutional behaviour. This was also true in genres other than drama.

The effects of the kinds of changes studied by Born in the late 1990s were still being felt strongly in the television industry in the mid-2000s when we conducted our research. One independent drama producer, Ally, put it this way:

> The centralisation of power within broadcasters has changed things completely. When I was a script editor in-house at the BBC, it used to be that producers would pretty much get a certain number of hours that they could make. So the person who was head of the series department would be keeping an eye on what they were doing and helping them, but they

---

9 For a valuable ethnographic study of documentary production in the UK and Germany, see Zoellner (2009).

wouldn't be saying yes or no, and then it all started to change. I think it was John Birt where it all started, and then there was so much bureaucracy and accounting and everything. In many ways it was absolutely right because there were a lot of freeloaders at the BBC and people who weren't working that hard. But it's the same with ITV. Once that happened in 1992 or something, where the regions no longer got guaranteed amount of hours, they had to sell their stuff to ITV Network Centre ... Then it was all centralised. Granada made *Cracker* just before that happened, and it would never have got let through ITV Network Centre. It just becomes harder to get more interesting things.

(Interview 59)

Again, we need to focus here on how the discourses surrounding creative autonomy reflect and yet also come to constitute the prevailing conditions affecting creativity–commerce tensions. Even Ally, who mourns the effects on the quality and innovation of programming, speaks of the need for discipline on the part of creative producers. Also noteworthy in this extract from our interview is the way that workers discuss prestigious texts to invoke an era where creative autonomy was less constrained – a feature of many of our interviews. The acclaimed television drama *Cracker* (Granada Television, 1993–95) featured a number of storylines intensely critical of British institutions, featuring a flawed, cynical but perceptive police psychologist, based in Manchester. Such invocations can be overly nostalgic, in that they can marginalise the fact that innovative programmes continue to be made. But they also chime with evidence, such as that provided by Born's account, that certain storylines and characters may be harder to get on screen than before.

4.6 Pressures on autonomy (2): the rising power of marketing

One way in which marketisation renegotiates autonomy, and workers' understandings of creativity–commerce relations, is through the growing importance and influence of marketing in cultural-industry organisations. A long tradition of political–economic analysis (sometimes called 'the cultural industries tradition') makes clear that while symbol-makers may achieve operational autonomy in *production*, in conceiving and creating cultural products, businesses exert much tighter control over distribution and marketing, or *circulation*.[10] As indicated above by Ryan, the artist manager discussing A&R in the recording industry, marketers represent the imperatives of commerce over creativity. These imperatives may be temporarily sidelined during the creative

---

10 As Garnham puts it, '*It is cultural distribution, not cultural production, that is the key locus of power and profit*' (Garnham 1990: 161, original emphasis). See Hesmondhalgh (2007: 24, 68) on circulation: a better term than distribution, because it covers marketing, publicity and dissemination.

stage of production, but during the circulation stage, they may reappear with a vengeance. This of course can bring benefits to creative workers, in the form of increased sales and greater dissemination of their work. But it may bring a cost too in the form of a loss of control over the 'framing' of their products.

Our interviewees reported a strong influence over creative outcomes on the part of marketing departments. Although our aims were not to provide a historical comparison with earlier periods, it does seem that this influence has increased over time. Here is how one music PR company director, Jerry, answered our question about whether marketing and PR people now have greater influence than before.

> In terms of presentation of creation, how something is viewed, yes, definitely. We've been doing [artist] for [major record company], we came up with a whole heap of suggestions for that, and we said X, Y, Z should be done. So, in terms of artistic creation, yes, sometimes we do have input. More often we're in the background but it is starting to become more and more frequent. People are willing to listen to us a lot more.
>
> (Interview 54)

Jerry may be exaggerating his company's own power, but it should be remembered that there are reasons too for marketers to *downplay* their own influence. For the historical distancing of creativity from commerce means that workers in the cultural industries have traditionally viewed marketing with some suspicion. While marketers are not ashamed of their work, they have reason to be cautious about too strongly expressing their influence.

One reason to think that the importance of marketing has increased is that marketing budgets have increased – for example, for launches or relaunches of magazines, for individual albums (increasingly advertised on television as well as in print media) and even for television programmes. Organisational changes and decisions also play an important part here. For example, music magazine editor Wayne told of how one magazine publisher had shifted (in 2005) from a system of having a marketing person or two assigned to individual publications, to one where an overall marketing department covered all music publications within the company. The result was a much more forthright approach on the part of marketers, and one which quickly alienated 'editorial' (creative) staff. In fact, in this case, the company eventually reverted to something more like the original structure – but this was made possible by a high level of confidence amongst editorial staff about defending their autonomy. The editor's perspective suggests some of the difficulties involved:

> So instead of having a marketing person as well as an advertising person for each magazine, attached to that magazine you had a self-directing marketing department which has its own priorities, which shows [*sic*] its own decisions. It was a situation where the marketing department turned

up with [magazine X] and plonked it down on the editor's table. 'There's your new logo, we've designed your new logo.' The editor said 'What are you talking about?' 'No, it's the new logo for the whole of the [magazine X] brand. It's going to run across the magazine and the TV and radio and all the rest of it.' The editor was so furious that he left the room and subsequently moved to another job within [the company].

(Interview 5)

In television, marketing was seen as being less 'present' than in the other industries but evidence of its influence still leaked into interviewees' responses. For example, Lilith, a documentary producer, spoke of how the factual entertainment genre had increasingly displaced documentary from the UK television schedules: 'It's more cut-throat [than documentary], it's more commercially minded, it's more about getting ratings and marketing people leading things' (Interview 43).

4.7 Anxieties about autonomy

We now turn to the connected theme of the increasing anxieties surrounding high levels of creative autonomy in the cultural industries, using the recording industry as an example. Traditional music industry management techniques are often depicted as being 'hands-off' – an approach which is believed to foster creative output – and separate from marketing. As Ray, the manager of a small independent label, explained:

We trust ourselves and the people we sign just to come up with the best record they can. Our kind of attitude about that is that you, for the most part, allow them to do exactly what they want, and that's the way to get the best records out of people. Whereas ... when you've got marketing considerations, that can tend to queer the pitch as it were of the music production process, and you end up with records which aren't very good.

(Interview 39)

This describes the function of autonomy from the point of view of some creative managers in the cultural industries: autonomy is intended to produce quality. From such a perspective, then, marketing can threaten both autonomy and quality. Niall, an industry analyst with close links to the recording industry, described the kind of hands-off creative management associated with the record companies – or at least with certain sections of record companies. Relatively junior staff tend to be given the role of negotiating with musicians:

They [executives] don't want to be seen to be interfering and they don't want to be seen to be putting on too much pressure, but they also want to be putting on pressure because they've got to deliver albums within a certain financial period.

(Interview 17)

Stars, on whom profits depend, particularly in industries conforming to the 'editorial logic' of production (see Miège 1989 and Section 1.2 of this book), are given especially high levels of creative autonomy, leading in some cases to exciting innovation, and in others to self-indulgence.

There has always been some ambivalence within the cultural industries about such autonomy. Long-term trends towards marketisation in the cultural industries are giving greater power to the side of this ambivalent relationship that questions autonomy. This is apparent, for example, in an anecdote told to us by Niall about a senior executive at EMI, who was called upon to visit the musician Kate Bush, who had taken many years to record and release an album (*Aerial*, released in 2005, twelve years after her previous album).

> Nobody in the company had heard anything and she just put in a call and said 'tell Tony to come down to my house, I'll play him the album, it's finished'. So he went down and sat down and listened to it. Have you heard the album? She's got this track and the chorus is 'washing machine, washing machine, washing machine', and she's got another song called 'Pi', where she just recites pi to 20 decimal points. He [the executive] said 'I'm sitting [there] and I'm going to go back to the office to tell people, they're not going to fucking believe me.' He said 'with other artists, they very much want you to come and hear the demo stage and kind of get the feedback and then you've got other artists that have got a very clear vision'. He said 'you know with somebody like Kate Bush you just don't get involved'.
>
> (Interview 17)

Whether or not this anecdote is accurate, there is an almost gleeful revelling in the excesses of the music business in this story, the fact that it centres on the unpredictable, the bizarre, the eccentric. But lurking there too is anxiety about the consequences of the hands-off attitude necessary to allow such attitudes to prosper. This anxiety is revealed in the focus on the most unusual aspects of the album, rather than its more conventional moments. This anecdote echoed wider concerns within the recording industry and the business press during the period of our fieldwork about 'traditional' music industry management techniques. It is not accidental that this story in particular concerned EMI, one of the UK's most venerable cultural organisations, the record company that has been home to, besides Kate Bush, other leading British artists such as the Beatles, Radiohead and Pink Floyd. Armed with the cheap finance capital available in the mid-2000s, as global interest rates fell to historically very low levels, private equity groups swooped on many institutions, including cultural-industry ones. EMI was taken over by a private equity group, Terra Firma, run by financier Guy Hands, in 2007. The music industry had for many years been prone to criticisms for its failure to meet the challenge of digitalisation in an effective way. This allowed Hands and the financial press to portray EMI as antiquated and inefficient and, in some cases, Hands's reforms as providing a necessary injection of good business sense. Lucy Kellaway for example, writing in the *Financial Times* (Kellaway 2008) wrote of how her opera singer brother-in-law reported to her that he was 'now singing better than ever before'. The reason?

> Fear, he replied. He explained that when his existing contract ... ends he could find himself out of work. This fear was doing more to make him improve than rave reviews had ever done. I was reminded of our conversation last week as I read about the heroic struggle between Guy Hands, the fat, tousled-haired financier, and Robbie Williams, the toned, close-cropped crooner.
>
> (Kellaway 2008)

Kellaway goes on to explain that hands-off creative management is ruinous for business: 'loving neglect makes artists into spoilt toddlers who have no incentive to produce anything that their audience will like'. The tone is tongue-in-cheek but the attitudes are real enough. The *Financial Times* may not embody the attitudes of senior management and financiers directly, but its views are to some extent indexed to theirs.

These concerns link up with the factors discussed above concerning the role of marketing. In early 2008, Hands announced that he was taking control of the record company out of the hands of creative managers and putting it into the hands of the marketers: 'What we are doing', said Hands, 'is taking the power away from the A&R guys and putting it with the suits – the guys who have to work out how to sell music' (quoted in Wray and Gibson 2008). To some extent there already existed a blurring between the 'creatives' (in this case, A&R) and the suits (marketing) in regards to their input in artist development before Hands's involvement at EMI. In regards to another major company, the running of Artist Development meetings was led by the marketing team with the process described by Nathan, the marketing director, as follows:

> Week in week out we are discussing three or four acts per week probably, if not more, and the management comes in, obviously they are part of the strategy for it, and the kind of vision, the A&R man who has signed the acts has got some vision on it, and the agent is another key person as well ... we'll all have different opinions, but we tend to always find a way forward that suits the project ... those meetings will either be run by the marketing person, the marketing manager or by the head of the label who comes from actually – in our instance – comes from a marketing background.
>
> (Interview 48)

Indeed, this shift was also noted by Alana, a marketing executive at a small independent label who was formally a VP of marketing at a major:

> sometimes you find an A&R person is actually more of a marketing person ... There is a guy called [X] at [company Y] ... Now he used to be a marketing man and now he's head of a company, but A&R as well. So he has the whole vision in him.
>
> (Interview 22)

At EMI Hands's reforms have met with stiff resistance from artists and the artist managers who represent them. Ernie, an artist manager in the hip hop genre, remarked to us that 'particularly at places like EMI, they are picking up MBA graduates all the time and putting them in strategic marketing positions, and it's beginning to work for them' (Interview 63). The significance of such discourses for us is their relation to the responses by cultural industries to the challenges posed by digitalisation (on top of the usual problems of risk and uncertainty). One response, it seems, has been to portray creative managers, capitalism's way of mediating between commerce and creative autonomy, as seduced by aesthetic autonomy. Private equity is in turn represented as a new, dynamic sector of capital, which will sweep such old-fashioned concerns away. However, in this case hard-headed business seems to have been considerably less successful than such discourses would suggest. Key acts have left EMI, which has fallen even further behind its UK and global rivals in terms of market share. Earnings have expanded, mainly because of its music publishing wing, but in February 2010, it was reported that Terra Firma had to write down 90 per cent of its equity in EMI, and is struggling to repay its creditors at Citibank (*Financial Times* ft.com, 4 February 2010).

4.8 Pressures on autonomy (3): the obligation to network

The *obligation to network*, a feature of contemporary workplaces noted by other commentators (for example, Neff et al. 2005) may also be a force that threatens creative autonomy.

In television, a number of programme-makers noted the increasing amount of networking time necessary to engage with the now-powerful commissioners discussed above. This means actively working to form networks of friendship with commissioners. As drama producer Ally put it,

> Some of them are my friends and therefore I meet them socially. Sometimes that's difficult because you don't want to know what they are not going to make of yours – that is, which programme ideas would be rejected. But even when I don't know them that socially, [...] it's a very girly network. It's a completely female thing. So it's as much as 'oh hello,

you look gorgeous', or 'how are you looking after your childcare?' and then talking about commissioning.

(Interview 59)

Another producer, Leon, talked to us about his successful attempts to gain commissioning money for a documentary about a boy who had played around the huge sculptures of Buddha at Bamiyan, in Afghanistan, until they were destroyed by the Taliban in early 2001. He knew that the head of programming, above the level of the commissioner but also involved in commissioning decisions, was interested in Buddhist sculpture, and drew on this in pitching his idea. Of course, such personal connections can be a pleasurable part of any work, and links between creative managers and creative personnel are not necessarily insidious. Many of the producers we interviewed spoke highly of commissioners. This was no doubt genuine, but we cannot discount the fact that the livelihoods of producers depend on these creative managers, external to their organisations. Even if producers felt personal dislike or distrust of the commissioners, it would be necessary to suppress these feelings. On their part, the commissioners employ a modern, cooperative form of managerial style rather than charisma or arbitrary acts of cruelty and so at least on the surface warm relations can be maintained.

Given the relatively equal and often friendly relations between commissioners and producers, can we really understand these relationships as a constraint on autonomy? We believe they can, where relationships are constructed in the context of the centralisation of power in the hands of commissioners. Beneath the civility is a fierce struggle for the money that makes it possible to survive as an independent. Yet everyone must act as if relations were warm and friendly. Of course, commissioners themselves are not unaware of this. One television commissioning editor, Martha, told us the following story:

> I was saying to someone quite recently something about someone having laughed at one of my jokes and he said, 'well, you know, what did you expect?' I said, 'no, he's a friend', you know, but he's also an independent producer. I am a buyer and they are sellers and the balance of power is shifting a bit, but for most independent producers they want our money and I am the gatekeeper, the route in.

(Interview 6)

This tension can also be found more generally in relationships between managers and creatives in other cultural industries besides television. As Erik, a freelance writer for men's magazines, remarked: 'I tend to socialise with my editors in London once every two or three weeks, and I pretend that it's me being pally with them, but it's not really, it's me just maintaining relationships' (Interview 28). Ekinsmyth (2002: 235) found, in her analysis of the risk and insecurity to be found in magazine industry social networks, that '[u]nder the mantle of friendship and co-operation, a ruthless business model is operated'. This means that the cultivation of creative managers demands considerable personal and organisational resources and emotional labour, a form of work that requires the worker 'to induce or suppress feeling in order to sustain the outward countenance that produces the proper state of mind in others' (Hochschild 1983: 7). In their networking activities these workers are deploying emotional strategies, not always authentically felt, in an attempt to maintain or develop fruitful relationships with managers. We explore this concept more fully in Chapter 7 in our discussion of the production of an entertainment television series, with regard to the emotional labour of junior workers.

The networked relations we are discussing here are based on collegiality, but they are underpinned by tensions derived from the structural inequalities between commissioners and independents. Some independent producers took a much more cynical view of such relations:

> They [commissioning editors] are interested in having power and making decisions and seeing the global picture. It's not really about creativity, and you know how much that is important to them when you challenge them. If you challenge a commissioning editor face-to-face, that is it ... you will be on the blacklist forever and ever.
>
> (Interview 37)

Whether or not this is accurate, it reflects the insecurity that some independent producers feel with regard to their relationships with commissioners.

Mark Banks (2007: 78–80) has reported an interesting twist on the close cultural links between managers and creatives we have been discussing. Banks reports that cultural-industry managers increasingly claim that their own management practices are as 'creative' as anything that so-called creatives do; or, to put it another way, that one does not have to be a musician, film-maker, etc. to be creative. This is especially apparent in small companies, where many new media managers interviewed by Banks tended to downplay notions of creativity such as drawing, composing and designing in favour of a notion of creativity as problem-solving, negotiating solutions, selling the client the product and so on. We too heard expressions of this kind during our research. Here, for example, is Kieran, the owner-manager of an independent television production company, when asked if he thought of himself as a 'manager': 'No, because I think that would imply you weren't involved directly in the process you were managing, because most people who manage in the health service aren't doctors. I mean I get my hands dirty with what we do' (Interview 20).

These claims to creativity in management should be understood in the context of economic conditions 'where the need for "softer", more intuitive and innovative forms of leadership are routinely cited as crucial to success' (Banks 2007: 80). Such a claim may seem on the surface to represent a democratising move, in that it sees creativity as confined not only to symbol-makers, but instead as more widely dispersed. But as Banks suggests, this may in fact have the result of divesting creative work of its privileges. Given that these can be seen, as explained above, as 'compensations' for the considerable precariousness and insecurity faced by such workers, this is not necessarily a positive move. Nor, in spite of Kieran's (no doubt honest) claims to get his hands dirty alongside his creative personnel, should such views be seen as expressions of solidarity with symbol-makers. Rather, they can be seen as an attempt, however unconscious on the part of individual managers, to undermine the distinctiveness claimed by creative personnel as the basis of their relatively autonomous working conditions. This logic was rarely expressed in naked form in our interviews. However, at a seminar on 'creativity' one of us attended at the offices of Channel 4 during our research, there was a striking example of such discourse. In the course of a discussion of the distinctive nature of creative work, one web TV entrepreneur aggressively articulated his dislike of views such as those expressed by some of the creative managers quoted above. Instead, he claimed that his own creativity as a manager was just as formidable as that of any of the creatives he managed. Creatives, he said, were 'up their own arses' and needed to have their egos kept in check. This is a more direct expression of creativity–commerce tensions than we generally heard in our interviews. But there may be various explanations for this. First, it may well be that the kind of manager who is likely to consent to give an interview to an academic researcher may be less likely to conceive of his/her managerial role in this aggressive way. Most managers would at least be more ambivalent about their managerial role and those we interviewed generally adopted a 'soft' management style. For example Ingrid, a managing director of a factual television company, described her management style as 'inclusive, I hope. ... I am democratic, I suppose' (Interview 11). Second, creative autonomy is still resilient enough to make more aggressive attitudes unspeakable in certain cases – which does not mean that certain elements of managerial practice may not ultimately be hostile to autonomy; for example, when new marketing initiatives are launched, with the aim precisely of taking away such autonomy.

4.9 Conclusions

We have sought to show some ways in which creative autonomy represents a ground of conflict and negotiation in contemporary cultural-industry workplaces. This has been the case for many decades, but it seems that the expanded social and economic role of the cultural industries may have added to the impetus of those forces that emphasise commercial imperatives over artistic and professional ones. Indeed, it would be somewhat surprising if they had not, given the overwhelming push towards marketisation in the neoliberal policy regimes of the last thirty years. We have discussed some of the ways in which that was apparent in our interview material, but also some aspects of the resilience of autonomy – as struggles over changes in broadcasting and the recording industry illustrate. All this provides the fundamental organisational context in which creative work takes place. In the next chapter we turn to a more direct consideration of the ways in which that work is experienced.

5 Pay, hours, security, involvement, esteem and freedom

5.1 Quality of working life in the cultural industries

In the previous chapter we sought to establish how historical tensions between goals of creative autonomy and commercial success structure the dynamics of work and organisations in the cultural industries. We now examine how, within this context, workers understand the quality of their work. Here we begin to address explicitly the degree to which creative labour might offer good and bad work in the senses defined in Chapter 2. Each of the sections corresponds to a category of good and bad work as laid out in that chapter. Our emphasis, as we made clear in Part One, is on workers' experiences, values and attitudes, but we continue to pay attention to structuring factors. We begin with what is often considered to be the key way in which workers think of their work: how much work they do, and how much they get paid for it (Section 5.2). As a vital corollary to this, we examine how workers see the roles of trade unions in protecting creative workers. We then move on to explore questions of insecurity and risk in relation to creative work (5.3). Insecurity is a feature of a great deal of working life, but is arguably worse in the cultural industries than many other sectors, because of the uncertain and short-term nature of many cultural-industry job contracts, and the high level of subjective investment that many creative workers have in what they do. The esteem and recognition that creative work might bring to workers is the subject of Section 5.4, and we show that creative work is often marked by personal experiences of vulnerability and self-doubt. For workers as a whole, this is offset – if only partly – by a sense that the work they did was seen as interesting or desirable by outsiders. Section 5.5 examines the pleasures, rewards and difficulties associated with the interesting and involving work offered by cultural-industry jobs. In Section 5.6, we return rather briefly to questions of autonomy. Our treatment is curtailed because we have already discussed autonomy at length in the previous chapter, including some material on the perceptions of workers, but here we focus more on *experiences* of autonomy. None of the pleasures, rewards, difficulties and frustrations discussed here is unique to the cultural industries; as we present the workers' reflections on their experiences and conditions, we examine the degree to which it is possible to interpret the dynamics on display as a result of the specificity of creative labour.

5.2 Pay, working hours and unions

5.2.1 Pay

The large reservoir of labour from which the cultural industries can select its employees (see the discussion of Miège 1989 in Chapter 3) enables a form of exploitation of junior workers in the form of low pay, especially when we take into consideration the number of junior workers who are willing to gift their labour to companies in order to accrue the experience needed to eventually attain (better) paid positions. Take for example rates for freelancers working in factual television production. The Broadcasting, Entertainment, Cinematograph and Theatre Union (BECTU 2009) provides a rate-card detailing the 'basic rate' and the 'rolled up' rate for each grade or job title. The rolled up rate includes holiday pay and BECTU note this is the rate that is often quoted to freelancers by production companies but that, in fact, this practice is 'unlawful'. The rates they list are based on a 48-hour week because, as the BECTU rate-card states, 'the law does not allow an employer to require you to work more than an average of 48 hours per week, unless you sign a waiver in which you agree to work more'. The lowest paid worker in the production department is the Runner with a basic rate of £354 per week, with the grade up, Junior Researcher, getting £415 per week. In the middle of the pay scale sits the Assistant Producer with a going rate as of April 2009 of £800. The highest grade, Producer/Director, is quoted at £1,200. Using the BECTU rates, we can calculate that a freelance junior researcher, working almost every week of the year would earn under £21,000. This is a tiny amount when compared to senior management salaries in the BBC, for example, where the base salary for 2007/08 of Tom Archer, the Controller for Factual Production, was reported to be between £190,000 and £220,000 (Guardian 2009). Or indeed, when compared to the yearly salaries of the CEOs of independent production companies, specifically the smaller 'super-indies', which pay on average £200,000–£250,000 (Faulkner et al. 2008: 309).

These statistics suggest marked inequalities in pay. Our emphasis here though is on worker experiences, and on workers' own perceptions of the consequences of these labour market conditions on their lives.[1] Striking here was the use of language which expressed anxiety about the sheer numbers of young people competing for work. Factual producer Samuel spoke of 'an army' of graduates from media and journalism courses (Interview 21)

---

1 As explained in Section 1.5, we sought to balance a number of factors in our selection of interview subjects, including age, gender, ethnicity and the degree to which interviewees were established or successful in their industry.

who, as researcher Margie at the BBC explained, 'can't expect to graduate and magically fall into a TV job because everyone knows how competitive the industry is' (Interview 35). Production manager Lilith told us that 'hordes and hordes of kids ... will do anything' to get a position (Interview 43). And in our ethnographic research at a London-based independent television production company during the first half of 2007 workers expressed concern about their 'replace-ability' – recognising, from their own experiences of job searching 'between' contracts, the sheer volume of young freelancers competing for the same pool of positions (field notes, 14 March 2007).

This massive 'reservoir' (Miège 1989: 83) of labour means that wages are depressed, and in many cases workers – especially young people – are willing to work for free. In her study of the UK television industry Ursell (2000: 814) writes of the number of university students on work experience who 'gift' several weeks of free labour to production companies in the hope that 'their gift will bring career returns in the future'. When many of these students graduate from their course, says Ursell (2000: 814–15), they 'persist in working for nothing or expenses only, or cash-in-hand, or very low pay' and this then results in 'extremely low pay at the entry point to the industry'. Willis and Dex (2003: 124) concur, saying that the labour supply is swelling with 'graduates willing to work for free or for very low wages to get a foothold in the industry'.

Our fieldwork provided considerable evidence to support this. For example, William, a junior writer for a men's magazine, told us that 'on the fashion desk loads of them are working for free, up to a year and stuff, and people do work experience as writers for six months or so and they write for nothing' (Interview 12). In television the willingness to carry out unpaid or low-paid labour results, as production manager Lilith claimed, in 'abuses' of junior workers in companies producing reality and factual television: 'They don't get paid properly, but it's supply and demand ... they kind of churn people out and spit them out' leaving the young workers 'battered and bruised' (Interview 43). Two metaphors get mixed here, both disturbing in their implications. 'Churning out' workers invokes a sense of mechanistic dehumanisation, 'spitting them out' suggests an animalistic gobbling up of workers, before they are rejected as inadequate for consumption. This chimes with Ursell's (2000: 816) description of the television industry as a 'vampire, ingesting youngsters at low prices from a large pool ... working newcomers and established hands remorselessly, and discarding the older and less accommodating at will'.

Some managers were keen to emphasise that their companies made a point of doing things differently.

> I know some companies keep them on because they think experience is a good thing and don't necessarily pay them. But we find if they are actually doing a job and they are contributing so much to a production and that we couldn't do without them, then I think we should pay them, and we do. ... And we always pay expenses for work experience.
>
> (Interview 40)

Note, here, however, that these more reasonable conditions seem somewhat qualified. Only if the young people on placement are contributing so much that 'we couldn't do without them' will they actually get paid more than just expenses.

That so many workers, including graduates, are willing to sacrifice pay for a foot in the door has repercussions for the class composition of these industries. It is bound to limit mobility, because in most cases working for free is only possible with the resources of a relatively wealthy family to provide financial back-up.[2] It also has implications for those already working in cultural industries. As Ursula Huws (2006–7: 10) explains, when workers are 'putting in extra time, accepting lower pay or poorer conditions' they are 'either directly or indirectly ... constructing new bars for their own cages, or those of others'. Giles, a music writer we spoke to, said that this results in publishing houses having a sense that 'everybody wants to work for them' and, in the case of one particular company, becoming 'incredibly rude' and 'arrogant' towards their writers, treating them 'like plankton' (dehumanisation again) (Interview 4). This engenders an uncomfortable feeling in workers that they are dispensable: 'there is pretty much always somebody to replace you and do your job', as Lakshman, a freelance music writer, put it (Interview 41). This in turn leads to greater pressure, and great self-consciousness about how workers might be perceived:

> I try not to refuse work whenever I can, because then people think you might be being a bit too – not full of yourself – but something like that ... because if they need somebody to do that, then there's no reason for them to go elsewhere.
>
> (Interview 41)

5.2.2 Working hours

Problems relating to pay are frequently combined in the cultural industries with the issue of working hours. This relates to three key aspects: workers needing to be flexible with their time; workers not getting paid commensurate to the hours actually worked; and workers having to take on second jobs to make ends meet. Television, again, provides some interesting statistics here. *Broadcast* magazine's 2006 'Lifestyle Survey' of television sector workers showed that, of the 1,000 respondents, 38 per cent reported working ten hours a day or more. Of these 42.5 per cent worked in independent production. Those most likely to be working ten-hour plus days were middle management

---

2 This potentially has further ramifications for what kinds of texts might get produced by the cultural industries. It may be that encouraging efforts are finally being made to consider the potentially unjust effects of the internship system – the Social Market Foundation organised an event in London on Social Mobility and the Creative Industries in February 2010.

(24 per cent), and it was at this level, and also managing directors and chief executives, that respondents most often reported working seven-day weeks. The survey also found that 45 per cent of respondents reported not taking all their allocated holiday time. Not taking holidays was more common for freelancers (61.6 per cent) than for those in full-time employment (30 per cent) and while 52 per cent of respondents reported having 'flexible working hours', qualitative data went on to suggest that 'the flexibility is on the part of the employee, rather than the employer' (Bashford 2006: 18–19). Our own interviews with creative workers in television, and also in recording and magazine publishing, provide qualitative confirmation of the experience of working hours – its intersection with the issue of pay, but also its dangers.

According to Mark Banks, being a flexible worker in the cultural industries

> essentially means that one must do whatever is required to support commercial interests. It increasingly requires working longer or unsocial hours, taking on-board additional responsibilities, relocating according to company demands and certainly committing oneself to the commercial imperatives of the firm over and above non-work commitments.
>
> (Banks 2007: 36)

Much of this was confirmed in our research. Nigel, a documentary camera operator, explained how in television the contracted working hours have extended, though without an increase in pay:

> On commercials you used to have an eight-hour day, that was your basic working day, and then after eight hours you'd be on overtime. Most commercials you did ten hours minimum anyway so you'd work two hours overtime and then production companies and budgets got tighter and they started saying your basic day is going to be ten hours. The same thing as happened in documentaries. We never had an eight-hour day; it was always a ten-hour day ... But now people are trying to be sneaky and saying your basic day is twelve hours, but instead of saying you are going to be paid for an extra two hours, you get the same pay for working twelve hours that you did for working ten hours, which effectively means that you take a pay cut.
>
> (Interview 33)

However, as the cultural studies critiques of creative labour suggest (c.f. Section 3.8) one of the problems for creative workers is that they are often, at least on the face of it, 'free' to decide whether to take on such long hours. 'Pleasure in work' (Donzelot 1991; Nixon and Crewe 2004) is closely linked to self-exploitation. Elizabeth, a reviews editor of a music magazine, told us:

> I'm one of those people who really love being busy but then I risk taking on far too much ... and people presume you're going to do it and

then you realise you've got no time to do it. I went to my boss and said, ... 'I'm going to have a breakdown one of these days because I'm working ridiculous hours and working on weekends and doing all this crazy stuff'. I enjoy it, admittedly, but when it starts affecting you, that's really bad.

(Interview 30)

Interviewees also told us of the physical dangers of working long hours. One factual producer, Adele, spoke of a friend who after working extended hours on a regional shoot then had to drive back to London, exhausted, and ended up having a car accident (Interview 27). Simon, a freelance camera operator, told us: 'Crews do crash on the road sometimes because they get overworked and flogged and they drive off the road or they crash and even get killed occasionally, and that's because there's a lot of pressure' (Interview 29). Whether this is really the case or not, Simon can be understood as externalising his own fears about the pressure put upon him. Even as an established camera operator who tries to pace himself, say no and 'be sensible' he still found there were

times when you are downing Red Bulls or taking Pro Plus and things like that and you are shaking and you have to work the most ridiculous hours and you're in a terrible state, which you shouldn't really be in.

(Interview 29)

Some workers of course spread the risk by working in multiple sites to supplement income. Nell, a producer of arts programmes, described how reductions in the commissioning of arts programmes have made it necessary for her to take on freelance work as a production manager for factual and children's television companies despite having her own arts-based production company (Interview 53). Jazz musician Keith explained that because it is hard to get regular work as a musician he had to take on teaching to supplement an income (a familiar necessity for many musicians):

The reality is you're not earning your living from gigs ... I can think off the top of my head of one person who doesn't teach on the circuit, in Oxford.[3] But of course he takes every single gig going. I suppose on the more positive side of my relationship between doing other types of work in music, was always that sense of I didn't really want to be doing every rubbish gig, and [without the teaching] I'd be forced to do that.

(Interview 62)

---

3 To clarify, this musician is saying that only one musician he knows in Oxford does not teach – a city with a sizeable community of musicians, many of whom Keith knows.

5.2.3 Unions

What role can unions play in countering these problems of pay and working hours? One trade union official has pointed out that 'freelances arguably have more need of union support than do permanently employed workers' (quoted in Saundry et al. 2007: 182). Though this may be the case, the uncertain nature of freelance work and worries about where the next short-term contract will come from means unions are not on the radar of many creative workers. As Saundry et al. put it, 'inexperienced workers [in the television industry], desperate for employment and keen to build their reputation, are unlikely to insist on [union] rates' (2007: 182). This was borne out in our research. Lorne, a junior camera operator working in the factual entertainment genre, who had been on sequential, rolling short-term contracts with a regional factual company found his position frustrating because 'although I'm kind of treated as staff … I'm just not paid like staff' (Interview 25). He worked on a daily rate which didn't specify the length of the day and although he knew BECTU set out different wage brackets relating to hours worked he said he found it 'difficult to go up to a production manager and say I want that amount of money'. Lorne's concern was that by asking for the BECTU rate 'you quickly price yourself out of the market' and the company would find themselves a new camera operator who wouldn't charge the BECTU rate for the 90-hour week. He believed that it wouldn't be for another 20 years of working in the industry as a camera operator that his 'self-worth' would have risen to the extent that he would have the confidence to negotiate his pay with production managers. No wonder then that Gary, a young documentary freelance director, remarked 'if there's one place that should be unionised it's the TV industry. The exploitation is pretty severe' (Interview 24). Yet it was recently estimated that only one-third of UK television freelances are members of the broadcasting union BECTU (Carlyon 2006: 22).

Similar stories come from the magazine industry which, like the audio-visual industries, was once heavily unionised. In a discussion of the impact of union de-recognition in magazine publishing companies Gregor Gall (1997: 157–8) claims that there is a distinct correlation between de-recognition and increasing incidence of 'lower starting rates, longer working weeks, the removal of overtime pay and various allowances, and reduction in holiday pay and redundancy pay'. Those most affected have been 'newly recruited full-time permanent staff, freelances and casuals … because their terms are far easier to vary and worsen because of their relatively greater insecurity' (Gall 1997: 158). One issue for freelance writers is their rate of pay-per-word. Like BECTU, the NUJ (National Union of Journalists) promotes minimum rates but some of the freelancers we spoke to were not aware what these were, such as freelance men's magazine writer Thomas:

> There's a NUJ rate, but I can't remember what it is. It's a minimum rate and it's really miniscule. It's something like £240 for 1,000 words.

Not much. Unless it's £340. These are the sorts of things I should know as a freelancer but I don't.

(Interview 32)

In many ways the rate is a moot point because this writer foresees a similar problem to that faced by junior camera operator Lorne: asking for the union rate could jeopardise getting future work by associating him with 'trouble'. In an industry where individuals have to sell their reputation, there are real limits on the ability of individuals to use unions to negotiate rates. 'The problem', Thomas told us, is that 'say I'd had a dispute with *The Guardian*' – who had recently only paid him one-third of what he thought the minimum rate was – 'it could be that I would get the union in, they'll be embarrassed, they'll pay me an extra 50 pounds for the money they should have paid, and then *The Guardian* would just never use me again.' 'He's a trouble-making bastard', are the words Thomas puts into their mouths, and so 'It's not worth my while for 50 pounds.'

This is a view supported by another freelance writer for men's magazines, Erik, who had never been a member of a union. Whilst unions may, as he said, 'look after your interests if you are being underpaid or stuff like that', in his experience 'editors just don't want to be bothered with that sort of stuff. They just say "okay, fine, we'll pay you more", and then you never get any more work from them because it's just a freelance gig' (Interview 28).

Lyndon, a senior music writer, described how one way to overcome being underpaid was by forming a freelance collective. He talked extensively about the time he, along with other freelance music writers, lobbied a large publishing house where the union wasn't recognised in order to improve pay conditions. This 'was almost unique in the British media. A bunch of freelancers get together in a house where the union is not recognised and negotiating pay agreements for freelancers when there's no negotiation for staff' (Interview 36). But even this optimistic organiser notes that although the agreement regarding rates-per-word is currently in place it is at the whim of the company and 'can be cracked, and when we get a nasty manager it will all end'.[4]

For the most part though, freelancers negotiate rates individually and as Dex et al. (2000: 285) note, while on the one hand established workers have a strong position from which to negotiate their worth, on the other newcomers are 'weak players' chasing jobs on 'unviable terms'. The established freelancers we interviewed seemed more able and willing to negotiate rates. Note for example the assertive use of the first person in this quotation from Shaun, a senior factual/documentary editor, who told us:

---

4 See Section 10.2 for more discussion of such networks in relation to unions.

if people haggle about what they pay you, and people do, they say 'I am this company and I want this, this and this', I just say 'well, I am me and ... I charge what I charge for what I do'.

(Interview 14)

So, says Shaun, 'I am quite straight in saying I am worth what I do.'

However, for those still in the early stages of a freelance career, their negotiating stance was more likely to be dramatised in terms of a portrayal of the self as desperately needy. Take for example Yasmin, an assistant producer in factual:

The higher up you get the easier it gets because you've got more contacts, you've got people who regularly ask for you and the higher they get they generally get to pick their programme. ... .But early on in your career you are thinking 'anything – now!' because I've got to pay rent.

(Interview 31)

And it is not just rent that has to be paid. For as Ekinsmyth (2002: 239) reminds us 'freelances are responsible for their own development and training, pensions and social security; and home-working freelances are additionally responsible for their capital equipment, their accommodation, lighting and heating'.

5.3 Security and risk

Annette, a jazz musician, told us that 'if you don't mind a bit of risk in your life you do a certain kind of job and if you like a very stable regular life you do another kind of job' (Interview 10). But the 'risk' she refers to is not always sustainable. In television, for example, factual producer Samuel reported that 'quite a few people have left because they found it ... just too uncertain' (Interview 21). And as entertainment producer Harry suggested 'with telly it's never a job for life, so you have always got to be thinking about what else you might do' (Interview 52). We explore these dynamics here (and we examine the implications for understanding questions of self-realisation in Section 6.4).

According to Murdock (2003: 31), moves in the cultural industries 'toward outsourcing production, relying more on freelance labour, and assembling teams on a project-by-project basis, have combined to make careers in the cultural industries less secure and predictable'. Researchers have noted how in television, for example, changes in regulation and developments in technology have 'increased uncertainty' for television workers since the 1980s and that these workers 'find uncertainty a problem; they dislike it and it causes stress for the majority' (Dex et al. 2000: 283). Much of this uncertainty centres on concerns about gaps in employment. Given the short-term nature of most contracts, new work is constantly being sought. Job seeking is relentless, even during times of employment, 'in order to sustain sufficient employment and to maintain career progress' (Paterson 2001: 497). For Neff et al. (2005: 319), the cultural industries are 'built upon workers being motivated by the promise of one Big Job being right around the corner' and also their 'willingness to take the periodic risk of being out of work along with the continual risk of investing in their careers'.

In this section, we again concentrate on the mental and emotional states produced by the uncertainty facing many creative workers, across all three of the industries we studied. Many spoke of nervousness, anxiety and even panic as a regular part of their working lives. Junior camera operator Lorne told us of his worries about extended gaps of unemployment between contracts and said that whilst he enjoyed being freelance it 'is really insecure because you know it [a big gap in employment] could happen at any point and it's quite a nervous thing to be' (Interview 25). He looked ahead: 'I don't know when this contract ends in November whether I'm going to get another one. I just keep thinking if I work hard then it will happen again and I'll get something else.' Established freelance camera operators, like Simon and Nigel, face the same uncertainty. As Nigel explained:

> not all of us are working all the time. For example, I didn't work for the first 3 months of this year, or I had very little work. But then again, the second half of the year was very busy.
>
> (Interview 33)

Freelancers in magazines reported spending a lot of time 'chasing up things that you should be paid for' and spoke of how approaching people for work meant 'you are constantly living sort of on the edge' (Interview 32). Music writer Norman described how a sudden change in the amount of work coming in, precipitated by a drop in regular work for a single title, has resulted in some months without work, sending him to 'that dark place where I panic – "I'm never going to work again and it's impossible to earn a living and I should go and get a [proper] job really – working at a bank or something"' (Interview 46). Despite having been a freelance writer for almost ten years Norman reported that he had 'never got used to the fact that I don't have work ... I don't think you get used to not earning a wage'. Or take for example senior freelance music journalist Lyndon who described a fall off in the amount of work that had gone his way.

> I haven't got significant work at the moment. It's quite weird. 'Superb' [as an editor described his last major feature article] leads to no commissions in the last month. No substantial leads I mean. I've had loads of bits and pieces.
>
> (Interview 36)

However Lyndon found this piecemeal work frustrating and unsatisfying: 'What you like is to have one big feature you're working on and then the bits and pieces.' He told us that he was always worrying that 'I'm not going to work again'. Few workers we interviewed, even those with salaried staff positions, seemed immune from such feelings of insecurity.

5.4 Esteem and self-esteem

5.4.1 Self-doubt

Feelings of insecurity were often combined with personal experiences of vulnerability and self-doubt. Actor Bob, for example, claimed that all actors that he worked with experienced high levels of uncertainty about their status and potential longevity in the industry. Here Bob, who was also a budding script writer, enacts a dialogue with an authoritarian internalised self who tells him that he isn't good enough:

> I was overjoyed when I got a job and I got an agent and all those kind of things, but I don't know. I never felt really happy about being an actor and I don't know why that is. The same thing with being a writer, even saying it, you know, 'I'm a writer', it's like 'no you're not, you're just pretending'.
>
> (Interview 16)

He considered these feelings to be widely shared, suggesting this is as much a structural issue as a subjective one.

> Every actor I've ever met has said that you finish a job and you go 'phew, I didn't get the finger on the shoulder' and you turn around and somebody goes 'you're not an actor, go on, get off, get away with you'. 'All right, I'm found out', and it's the same as a writer. Everyone I have worked with has had that fear of the tap on the shoulder, 'hey, you're not an actor, what are you doing in here, go on, get off, go and get yourself a proper job!'
>
> (Interview 16)

We asked one magazine journalist, Larry, what it felt like to do his job, and his answer echoed Bob's emphasis on the uncertainty, almost helplessness of creative work:

> You feel very vulnerable because I suppose you just really care about what you're doing and you really put a lot of thought into it and a lot of emotion into it and then to have somebody just go through it, it's just very frustrating.
>
> (Interview 9)

But Larry also admitted that this sense of 'rejection' and 'annoyance' was something that he had to inflict on others: 'at the same time when I'm doing that to other people, I do feel very guilty and I feel nervous when copy comes in because I've commissioned it and it's shit'. This led to unstable emotions concerning work:

> There's pride if it goes well and you think that's great, vulnerability, fear, and also when you're handing copy in and you've put a lot of work into it, you're just worried that it's going to come back. You turn into a needy child half the time. You're desperate for approval. Was it any good? You find people doing that a lot in magazines.
>
> (Interview 9)

Of course creative workers find ways of dealing with that vulnerability. Confidence is vital – but there are situations in which confidence, if not naturally present, has to be forced. Pop/rock musicians Niamh and Robert, a couple, discussed issues of pride and confidence (Interviews 2 and 3). Niamh told us that feelings of pride come only in 'a snippet of a moment ... I am always so unsure a lot of the time'. Robert responded about the need for confidence: 'The more confident you are, the more proud you are.' Such feelings were transient however: 'One day you can think it's absolute rubbish and then the next day, if you're feeling confident about it, then it's incredible.'

> And I've seen that with any number of artists. Even like million selling writers. It's all based on, it all revolves around confidence. And then when the record is finished then you'd better be confident in it. And you'd better make yourself confident. Otherwise you can never sell it. You can never expect anybody to buy it, unless you're confident and proud of it. And I've seen that with someone that I know. Because they're not happy with it, but they force themselves to be, to make it work.
>
> (Interview 3)

5.4.2 Cool and glamorous

An aspect of their work that many of our interviewees found pleasurable or satisfying was that the work they did was recognised as interesting or desirable by others. It is worth considering this aspect in relation to the experiences of self-doubt just reported, because recognition *may*, in some cases, feasibly act as compensation for more difficult and troubling aspects of creative work. As Neff et al (2005: 310) found in their research with workers in the fashion and new media industries, work in such cultural industries has particular 'cultural value: the industry is "hot," and the jobs are "cool"' and these factors play a part in workers' internalisation of the risks of creative labour. Also looking at the new media industry, Rosalind Gill noted that its workers are popularly regarded as 'artistic, young and "cool"' (2002: 70). Camera operator Lorne described to us how people reacted to being told of his occupation:

> You say 'oh, I work on documentaries as the cameraman', and they kind of go 'wow, that sounds really interesting', and you kind of say 'yes, it's

really interesting', you meet lots of people and you do pretty fantastic things I guess.

(Interview 25)

This reaction was commonly shared, perhaps especially among television workers. Assistant producer Yasmin, quoted in Section 5.2, revelled in the interest that other people showed in her work, compared with the interest they might show in other occupations: 'You know if you meet someone and you say "what do you do?" and they say "IT" [i.e., information technology], you don't really want to find out anything more about them?' By contrast, Yasmin found that 'the first question people normally ask is "what programmes have you worked on? Have you met many celebrities?" People are quite interested'. This interest derived, in Yasmin's view, from the special status of enjoyment and shared public culture involved in television: 'This is something that people go home to relax to or do in their leisure time, so to work in something that people enjoy and everyone is talking about the next day or people can relate to' is, for Yasmin, very pleasing. 'You're working in something that people have seen' (Interview 31).

The music industry too was felt by Jerry, a music PR company director, to be an object of envy on the part of others. Asked what he liked about his job, he replied, 'doing a job that I know a lot of people would love to do' (Interview 54). What's more, in Jerry's particular case, he felt he had achieved this position of working in music through his own determination and drive. 'This isn't being lordy [*sic*] or egotistical', he was keen to tell us.

> I made the decision to work for myself. I was the traditional non-achiever at school. Further down than non-achiever. I just had so much ability but I wasted it. Traditionally the music industry is full of people like that, but I couldn't play an instrument but I still wanted to work with music. So I created something that I could do and that I love. I love being around music, I love collecting records, I love being around a specific sort of music, and I do it.[5]
>
> (Interview 54)

Magazine work was also understood by workers as something that could be perceived by others as interesting, glamorous or cool, though this of course depended to some degree on genre. William reflected on this and on the associated pleasures of seeing his authorship recognised in the form of by-lines. When he worked for a construction magazine before moving to the men's genre, 'people would say "never mind, no one reads it" because they

---

5 There is a strong sense in this quotation of the exhilaration associated with entrepreneurialism, the sense of having achieved success through one's own means.

think it's really crap'. This was wrong: 'It's not, it's a great publication'. But since moving to a prominent men's magazine, William was conscious that people saw his new publication 'as this cool magazine and they've got these ideas of the magazine world, and they love that. So it's quite nice that people would like your job'. But in magazine writing also comes the satisfaction of having one's authorship publicly displayed in the form of the byline: 'You can pick up a magazine and you can say "I wrote that and there's my name". That is the reward for me' (Interview 12).

We will discuss career paths more in the next chapter but the sense of creative work as being good work because of its unconventional nature was conveyed to us by workers who told us about the period in their lives when they 'chose' their occupation. Television researcher Margie told us, 'I thought maybe law would be a career for me, and then I decided actually "no, it's not what I want to do".' Rightly or wrongly, she associated professional legal work with repetition and routine: 'All I knew was that I didn't want to be doing a nine till five. I didn't want to sit in an office Monday to Friday and doing the same repetitive thing over and over again.' Significantly though, she had a way into television: 'All my friends are in TV and I used to hear what they used to say about their job, and it sounded really interesting and so diverse and doing different things day to day.' This was not all though:

> being totally honest, I thought it's probably really glamorous as well. The glamour of it all. I thought I'm sure it's great fun and there's lots of glamour and I'd meet lots of celebrities, because I'm a bit of a celebrity person.
>
> (Interview 35)

This sense of being on the inside of an industry that most of us are outside was cited by Giles, a music journalist and, like the journalists discussed earlier, he mentioned the pleasure of freebies, and of being ahead of others (c.f. McRobbie 2002b on club culture sociality). 'I get to hear new music up to three months ahead of anybody else hearing it. And if I'm honest I then get to sell the promos on eBay and make some additional income' (Interview 4). And Giles had discovered something while working as a journalist: 'There's no such thing as a sold out show ... I can get into pretty much any show I want to get into. I failed on Live 8! But that's my only significant failure of late.'

Of course, the glamour or kudos of working in the media does not necessarily lead to good products, in the terms we define them in the book (see Chapter 2). Nor does it necessarily lead to genuinely life-enhancing experiences. After all, this desirability may be based on external and arguably superficial notions of the good such as contact with famous people. So some were keen to stress that their attachment to their work went beyond such trivial attractions, such as freelance director Gary:

I'm not in it for the kudos of working in TV. I really don't care about that. I'm in it to make interesting programmes and have that freedom to look at different subjects. It's a great freedom and a great job.

(Interview 24)

5.5 Challenge, interest and involvement

A number of our respondents found substantial rewards in the complexity and challenge of their work. It was difficult, faced by these seemingly genuine and often effusive declarations of enjoyment and enrichment from creative work, for us to come away from our interviews feeling that such experiences could be best understood as mere compensations for the insecurity and lower wages they face.

Men's magazine writer William told us: 'I love my job and I think about it all the time. It's not like you go home and stop thinking about it. I'm always thinking about it' (Interview 12). He linked this directly to the strong component of challenge in his work: 'I think loads of my personality is to do with that, like the confrontation, defending your stuff. Everything you write you are judged on constantly, so I quite like that, that it's a constant challenge.' This directly contributed to a very strong identification of his self with his work: 'I think of myself as a writer. It's not a job.' William's enjoyment of this sense of challenge seemed to us individualistic and rather gendered. Perhaps William's ability to thrive on confrontation reflected the very masculine culture of the men's magazine world where he found employment.

Another reward frequently cited by our interviewees was being able to learn as part of the job. Those involved in documentary and factual entertainment tended particularly to emphasise this as did journalists. Irene, a journalist for a trade publication specialising in building and architecture, for example, talked about how journalism allowed her to exercise her curiosity. She had

> always wanted to be a journalist. It's one of those boring things where I just realised that journalism would suit me. I'm not sure if your personality makes you become a journalist, or your journalistic instincts come out with your personality.
>
> (Interview 44)

Its pleasures were that it was 'a passport to do what I want to do', allowing Irene to meet people, to 'have access to things I shouldn't have access to' and exercise 'a licence to be nosy'.

This sense of satisfaction from the pursuit of information is echoed by Aggie, a journalist for a construction publication, who also describes her enjoyment of the variety in her work; in particular, its potential to provide her with an understanding of different aspects of the world, including policy, but also the work that goes into buildings themselves. 'You never go into this business for the money, but I would say journalism is hugely rewarding. Certainly I find feature writing rewarding' (Interview 18). The publication Aggie writes for

> covers a very, very broad range of sectors. Virtually any element of government policy is affected by construction. If they say they're going to build more prisons, you can go and visit a prison. If they are going to build more hospitals you can do that.
>
> (Interview 18)

Aggie conveyed a real sense of excitement at the variety of situations she had to cover, and also their public nature (echoing the discussion of 'glamour' in the previous section). She told us how she had watched 'the Eden Project taking shape down in Cornwall' and had stood on top of the Gherkin, a notable London landmark tower, and 'watched them put the glass on top of the roof while they were abseiling'. She also revelled in the varied sociality of her job: 'you work with people from all walks of life, from the top chief executives right down to the guy that is basically the signaller telling the crane where to go'.

There is a strong sense of self-realisation in these journalists' way of talking about the rewards they gain from their work.[6] Malcolm, an experienced documentary producer, talked in a similar way to Aggie of the wide variety of experiences that his work had opened up, and boasted of how it had helped him to see history in the making:

> I've had an amazing life. I've watched democracy come to Argentina, witnessed the most violent riots they had in the country for 50 years. I was there when the gates of Gaza were opened. I've been attacked by the KGB. I've filmed with the Contras in Nicaragua, all kinds of places and amazing experiences from plane crashes to sharing terrible tragic moments to moments of great elation. I've seen so much of the world and I've been paid to do that. So it's been a very intense life with great experiences and I'm glad I had it.
>
> (Interview 37)

But he immediately noted, reflecting on the declining possibilities for documentary-making in the UK, and his own shift into film-making: 'I'm also glad I'm moving on from where it's going now.'

Similarly, freelance director Gary discussed the way that television documentary allowed him to learn about a wide variety of different topics. 'It really suits me to be able to go from one subject to another, because I get

---

6 We discuss workers' attitudes, values and experiences as they bear on self-realisation in Chapter 6.

really interested in lots of different things' (Interview 24). He gave the example of 'studying the afterlife for six months' for a programme he had recently been involved in making, but then being able to move on to something different. But a thread of self-realisation was provided between these different subjects: his enjoyment at the aesthetic component in the transmission of knowledge.

> So from my point of view it's studying the real world, but at the same time it's fulfilling something else for me which is creative and I love framing shots, pictures and adding music. I mean it's a fantastic feeling. I love doing that as well.
>
> (Interview 24)

Men's magazine journalist, Erik, told us that there were 'loads' of rewarding aspects of his job. 'It's a great job', he claimed. 'I get to learn about all sorts of really exciting stuff, really interesting stuff. I am never bored at work.' Part of this interest derived from having 'to research all the quirky little stories you see in the papers, that is my job', but part of it was that it allowed him 'to keep in with music and magazines and popular culture'. Part of it was, as for the other journalists quoted above, meeting 'really interesting people' (though it takes a while perhaps to get to this stage; 'I do really good interviews now', Erik said). Also significant for Erik and for numerous other creative workers were freebies, 'I get sent away to New York or for skiing holidays ... I get sent free books and CDs and DVDs'. 'It's lovely' was Erik's overall verdict on his job (Interview 28).

If for younger creative workers such as these, there is an excitement about creative work, for some older workers, the sense of new challenges was something that allowed them to retain a sense of intellectual vigour. Shaun, a film editor, talked about former colleagues: 'There have been a whole generation of people I've worked with in TV who have either retired or they've stopped making things or they've gone into writing or education' (Interview 14). But Shaun found that he was still 'intrigued by new things'. Being an editor allowed him, like freelance director Gary, to learn on the job. Editors do not need to be particularly knowledgeable about the subject of the films they are editing, Shaun said, so 'part of the fun of doing it' was that he was 'intrigued by new ideas and new things and new people'. This included the challenge of working on new genres and sub-genres as well as editing films and programmes covering a wide range of topics.

The varied nature of work and the rewards to be gained from it provided great pleasure for some people. Keith, a jazz drummer who, when asked about the rewards he got from his work, said that 'it would be easy to say "well, that feeling of a job well done", or X, Y and Z, but I think it's less tangible than that'. Explaining what he meant, Keith told us of an old adage in jazz that 'you either learn, you earn, or you enjoy it', and when seeking and accepting work he categorised jobs according to which of these three rewards they provided; and 'hopefully all three'. Such learning experiences could be painful: 'You learn from the experience because the other musicians might be slightly roasting you, and you can take that away with you and work with it', or alternatively 'you are earning a lot of money' and best of all, 'you are just simply having a really nice time with the other players' (Interview 62).

These pleasures could be fused, so that at times Keith found it hard to distinguish 'whether a gig was good because I just simply liked the people I was with ... rather than it being great, objectively great playing'. The most rewarding experiences were those where he felt that he could have 'a nice easy time of it with the other players', combined with

> maybe just a bit of an edge. So it's not so comfortable that the experience is bland, but just somewhere on the top of that there's a bit of an edge. That's where I feel it's a really nice gig.
>
> (Interview 62)

What's more, this mixture of pleasure and challenge was a regular feature of this drummer's working life.

Some workers emphasised the pleasure of working with ideas. Yasmin, an assistant producer in factual, told us that her work in television was 'ideas all the time' (Interview 31). This was not only 'quite satisfying' but it exceeded her expectation of television work, and her reasons suggest the value of the autonomy structured into some forms of cultural production in allowing some workers to combine conception and execution (c.f. the discussion by Murphy 1993 of Aristotelian notions of good work). Yasmin had thought that she would be 'a little cog in the wheel and they send you off and say "find it" and you come back with answers' – like an exam, as she put it. But instead

> you are given an area, whether it be finding a certain person or finding a location or setting up a shoot, and then you will look after that entirely and you will deliver the goods in a certain amount of time, and then you know that when it's all worked out and you see it on camera, it works in a certain way or it was shot in a certain place or it involved that person because you found it, you chose it or you decided that is the best way to go with it.
>
> (Interview 31)

This autonomy, Yasmin told us, was 'very satisfying'.

For others, this sense of a lack of routine, and of constant variety in the work, was closely linked to ideas of glamour and even 'cool', which we explored above. For others, the emphasis was more on pleasure and 'fun' and was contrasted with the repetitive nature of other jobs and occupations that could easily descend into staleness. Izzy, a music industry marketing manager, highlighted this enjoyable aspect of work in the music business, and, like many others in that industry, talked about the pleasures of being associated with music. 'The plus side is if you love music it's a great job to be in and there is a lot of fun to be had, and it's a fun environment.' Music's ability to attract 'big characters' meant that there was no sense of her workplace being 'a really stale office to go and work in, it's very lively'. And this produced the variety she valued, along with the changing nature of the acts that she publicised: 'No week is ever the same, no act is ever the same, so it's really varied, and that's what's good' (Interview 49).

We should not forget though that such proclamations of enjoyment were rarely without qualification. 'The downside of it', said Izzy 'is the long hours, which does eat into your social life a lot.' But even this part of the job involved sociability (see Chapter 6): 'you actually become friends with lots of people that you work with, and also you become friends with lots of people at other labels. You might see them at a gig or out beforehand as well.'

Margie, the BBC factual researcher, told us that the most rewarding aspects of her work came 'when you are working on something which is quite testing or challenging'. On one programme, Margie had to set up an event where a minor celebrity had to arrive to be greeted by crowds. The location fell through at the last minute. This was traumatic but pulling through it was immensely satisfying:

> when things fall through and you do your best and things transform and your effort pays off and the event went really well, and it could have been the total opposite. ... It's the fact that the people on your team and together you did something.
>
> (Interview 35)

This sense of working with others to overcome challenges, widely prevalent in the 'project team' ethos of television production, is something that we treat separately in Section 6.5, but the pleasures of sociality are bound up in the rewards of involvement. Margie gave another example of the satisfaction she gained from her work, and set this against days where it felt as though no progress was being made: 'When I am struggling to find a contributor and then I get a call or I make one phone call and I manage to find the person I'm looking for', that produces a real feeling of achievement. She contrasted this with days where 'you can just sit in the office all day and feel like you've not got anywhere'. There was a 'real buzz when you know things are all coming together'. Of course, this raises the Oppenheimer problem discussed in Chapter 2.4: the satisfactions of creative process can sometimes get detached from any reflection on the value of what is being produced. We return to this issue of how creative workers discuss value in Chapter 8.

5.5.1 Pleasurable absorption

The challenge and interest that many creative workers seem to find in their work allows them, at least some of the time, to achieve states of pleasurable absorption in their work that are the opposite of the alienated clock-watching that many of us dread in labour. Elliot, a jazz saxophonist, reflected on a state of relaxed concentration that on occasion he felt able to achieve. This involved a certain amount of internal conversation:

> you come back and you say 'oh, this is going all right now' and you can just relax and play. That's when it's really enjoyable I think, when you get on that plane where whatever happens, nothing goes wrong. You are just playing and not trying too hard.
>
> (Interview 34)

In Elliot's perspective, this involves a 'move from the stage where you are thinking about the music, trying to think of it before playing it, and then you come to the stage where you play it and then you think about it'. At such moments, Elliot tells himself 'oh, that was all right' – the satisfaction of doing something well that we come back to. But musicians performing live are in the unusual position of doing work while being watched and heard doing it. Jazz improvisers, like Elliot, are – even more than most musicians – in a position of not wanting to think too hard about the success of this work: 'You know, just let it happen, let it flow. It's surprising how that works, but I don't know how it works.' There is conscious thought: 'you're thinking about what key it is and you're trying to work it out and all that sort of thing', but that seems to recede in moments of pleasurable absorption, of what Mihaly Csikszentmihalyi (1990, 1997) calls 'flow experiences'. In this state, Elliot finds, 'all of that' conscious thought 'is floating along now and everything is happening without having to worry and think about what you are doing'.

Of course work can not always be as pleasurable or as absorbing as this. Elliot commented that at times it was difficult to achieve this relaxed state of successful playing. 'I think on improvising you go through different phases. Maybe not in one gig, these phases can depend on the people you're with and other circumstances.' But the difficult times tend to come for Elliot when he is pushing too hard: 'the worst phase is when you are trying and you think "oh, I've got to try this and this" ' – the wrong kind of interior conversation.

It is not just musicians who can achieve this kind of pleasurable absorption. Bob, an actor, spoke of the pleasure in comedy acting when actors can be 'in the moment': 'You do something on set, you are working with one person, and you close in on them.' Whether there is 'six inches or 42 feet' between two actors in this closed-in state, it is possible to feel the 'power of what's going on between you'. There is a pleasure in this, specific to television work, said Bob, involving knowing that it's being captured by a camera a few feet away ... but you don't have to transmit like you do in a theatre. You don't have to communicate to the back row, you just make it as real as possible between the two of you. That is the most important thing for me, and I love that, I love that feeling of just being completely in that moment.

(Interview 16)

The consequence of this absorption can be a great sense of satisfaction: 'at the end of it you come out of there and go "wow, that was great, I was really in there, I was really in that moment".' This seems to be made possible, in Bob's view, by a sense of connection with the words and character, and although this is to anticipate the pleasures of communicating to audiences and peers addressed in Chapter 9, Bob also discussed the way that the success of that moment of absorption might be confirmed, almost at the edge of consciousness, by an awareness of the response of others:

> By being deadpan, you deliver your line and it's not for anybody's benefit, it's because you completely 100 per cent believe in what you have to say at that time. The words are coming out of you because you connect to it, and if you connect to it and you sell it, then it gets a laugh. The crew have got their hands on their mouths or they've turned away and you can see people shaking out of your peripheral vision and then they shout 'cut' and everybody laughs. That is such a great rush.

(Interview 16)

It is perhaps musicians though who are most involved in that sense of 'timeless time' (see Frith 1996: 145–57). Jazz drummer Keith, quoted in the previous section, talked about the 'huge part' that 'groove' played in jazz. Groove is partly a rhythmic element of the music, but Keith also used the term to refer to 'that feeling when it's sort of effortless almost, the music is just going and you are absorbed in it, fully absorbed in it. I think those are the moments that you long for really'. Yet Keith acknowledged the limitations on being able to reflect on all this

> because by definition those moments are quite resistant to thought, and you aren't thinking about them. But I think it might happen briefly on every gig at certain points, and on really good gigs you probably get into that state more.

(Interview 62)

Journalists too can experience something like this sensation of groove or flow. Lakshman told us of the satisfaction 'when you just kind of write and you're actually enjoying it, when you're feeling inspired and you write something and you're working your way through it'. In fact, Lakshman went so far as to say that this 'pretty much makes up for any of the bad pay', and he used the same term that Bob used for the thrill of having been 'in the moment' while acting: 'it's a bit of a rush'. However, Lakshman was also a little nervous about talking about his work in this way: 'It sounds a bit corny, but it's a bit of a rush I suppose' (Interview 41).

We quoted earlier television researcher Margie on the satisfactions of things 'coming together'. In creative labour, with its strong emphasis on rehearsal, planning, composition and so on, leading to a final performance or broadcast, or publication, there is a strong notion of temporality, of effort sustained and expended, with the satisfaction of completion to follow. In Raymond Williams's words (1965/1961: 44) the 'excitement and pain of the effort are followed by the delight and rest of completion'.

This is often linked to the experience of communicating to an audience – the issue that we shall discuss in some detail in Chapter 9 – but here we focus more on this sense of 'things coming together'. Hannah, an experienced artist manager, observed this process in a highly successful rock-pop act she had managed.

> The highs for them I think are when they know they've kind of got it in the studio and they know they are onto something really good and it's really exciting and they are really enjoying making music and they have people down at the studio play it and they are proud of it.
>
> (Interview 42)

Further highs could follow in the live setting, 'when they play it for the first time and to see that kind of feedback from somebody'. The emotional investment involved in this process of conception, execution and performance was likened by Hannah to childbirth: 'It's almost like delivering a baby. I think the emotion that comes before a release is anticipation and fear of how something is going to be received.' Unlike most parents expecting babies, though, creative workers may have to be ready to have their work condemned: 'you are very proud of the body of work that you've done and you've got no idea how people are actually going to criticise it and be critical of it'. It's striking that Hannah here says 'how' rather than 'whether'; some criticism seems almost to be expected. This perhaps stokes the vulnerability and self-doubt discussed above.

Creative work often demands long, sustained periods of effort, especially when work is near completion. Lachlan, a freelance documentary sound recordist, said 'I love doing a good job and sometimes I go into a shoot knowing they're going to go into a really tough bit of work. It could be for four or five days and quite sustained' (Interview 23). If the work goes well, then there is not only the satisfaction of doing a job competently, there is also the sociality involved in sharing that satisfaction:

> It's a fantastic feeling when you come out the other side and it's all gone well. If it's a trip away or something, it might even be just the last couple

of days, having some nice meals out or even doing a little bit of shopping before you go to the airport and being totally relaxed and chilled and knowing that you've got some great stuff.

(Interview 23)

Although we are deliberately focusing in this section on the positive aspects of our interviewees' experiences of creative labour, it is important not to lose sight of the fact that such rewards are only possible for some of the time, and in some jobs. As Lachlan remarked

The other side of it is if you are working on something where you are having to rush and you know what you are doing is not good, not good technically and you are compromised. That leaves you very unsatisfied.

(Interview 23)

What is more, some people's commitment to a good quality of product is so high that it can lead to difficult working relations (which we discuss further in Chapter 6). As Lachlan observes, 'I'm a pretty friendly person, and I like to work hard … but I like to have a life as well. I absolutely don't mind working hard all through the day, having a sandwich at lunchtime' rather than taking a break. But he also talks of how some people do not allow team members to unwind: 'Sometimes you find yourself working with people that don't take that on board and it's pretty relentless actually.' And ultimately if this is a director or a producer, 'that is something that just has to be endured' (Interview 23).

Other television workers also discussed their deep pleasure in the sense of reward and satisfaction they gained from completing high-quality work. For Simon, a freelance camera operator, the greatest satisfactions derived from pacing himself in such a way that he could 'focus myself on doing the best job I can for the people I'm working for' (Interview 29). The reward for this though was best experienced in private, a moment of peace 'when I'm on my way back in my car', preferably alone, and with a sense of 'having done a good job of work'.

For Samuel, a freelance television producer, the greatest satisfaction came 'when you see the film'. The satisfactions associated with completion rely on certain rhythms of conception, execution and finishing, and a sense of order emerging from chaos: 'It's a bit like a building site for most of it, and it's quite funny because I think you're only really satisfied when you've finished it.' Television programmes, he found, are 'huge, woolly, difficult to pin down when you're in the middle of it', and a programme only becomes 'more satisfying as you start editing it and it comes into some shape'. The satisfaction of completion does not make the process ultimately any the less testing:

then when you start the next one you remember the satisfaction of finishing the last one and then you realise how frustrating the process is to get to the endpoint. ... It does require a lot of being able to see through to what it is that you want.

(Interview 21)

Samuel went on to discuss the great frustration he was experiencing on a project he was currently working on, where the nature of the final product would not be clear for many months ahead, because of a protracted period of filming: 'it's frustrating because it's such a long production period and we won't really start editing it until we've spent four months filming it'. This deferral of the satisfaction of completion was difficult, and was made worse by budget constraints: 'it feels like we're making a documentary each week with a new set of characters, and yet we know that we don't have enough time in the film to be able to make each of these people'. If our interviewees were able to reflect with a certain satisfaction on the process of meeting the challenge of doing difficult and interesting work, it should not be forgotten that, when in the middle of the creative process, this can feel anxious, uncertain and chaotic. People's sense of whether their work is good or bad of course changes over time.

5.6 The experience of autonomy

In spite of the problems of insecurity and uncertainty reported above, some workers value highly the relative autonomy that creative work gives them, especially in terms of their working and leisure time. 'I can go and have a round of golf on a Monday morning and I couldn't do that if I was five days a week with a regular income' said Gary, a freelance documentary director, and he set such freedom against the grinding routine of other jobs: 'I know a lot of people who are really unhappy in their nine to five work' (Interview 24).

Ingrid, a managing director of a large independent production company, explained that what she enjoyed most about her work was 'the fact that you make the job up as you go along. I don't have anyone telling me what to do, and I don't do anything about timekeeping here'. This was based on a strong sense of motivation derived from the nature of the work:

People are so keen to do creative work. I suppose what allows you to do work you are proud of is that there's an environment here where we're proud of what we do and what goes out of this building, I would not want to see anything go that isn't something I think is good.

(Interview 11)

Banks (2007: 55), drawing on the Foucauldian perspectives (such as 'governmentality theory') discussed in Chapters 2 and 3, comments that 'to be (or appear to be) in control of one's destiny is what encourages workers to endorse the systems put in place to expedite flexible production'; autonomy becomes a mechanism to encourage self-exploitation or acceptance of poor conditions. Citing the work of Knights and McCabe (2003: 1588) who claim that 'employees welcome a sense of self-organization; for when individuals organize their (our) own work it becomes more meaningful', Banks argues that the offer of autonomy 'is sufficiently powerful to override any misgivings, constraints or disadvantages that might emerge in the everyday reproduction of this highly competitive and uncertain domain' (2007: 55).[7] This is apparent in the above quotation from Ingrid.

It is useful to think of the experience of the autonomy of creative labour as a pleasure or satisfaction that can very easily be compromised. This ambivalence was nicely captured by Giles, a music journalist, who, like Gary above, contrasted his work with 'normal' work:

> While ideally I would like to work less hours, I think the quality of my life within a lot of those hours is probably higher than people who have to commute or work in an open plan office or you know deal with moody colleagues or any of those sort of things. … It's a very complicated version of freedom in that I often don't feel very free in that I am free in what music I like, I can have a good coffee whenever I want to, I can write my copy in my pants [underwear] if I want to but at the same time it often feels like I don't get very far away from my computer for days at a stretch and that something as simple as getting a paper from the corner shop can just not happen for up to a week. And I literally will not leave this flat for three days.
>
> (Interview 4)

The refreshing contrast with 'ordinary' work can tip over into obsessiveness and a sense of alienation from everyday life.

5.7 Ambivalent experiences

Our research suggests that worker experiences of creative labour are highly ambivalent, across all three of the industries we studied. (We found no clear evidence that particular industries or genres produced significantly more positive or negative experiences than others.) The high levels of casualisation to be found in all three industries led to expressions of victimisation and anger on the part of many workers, a sense of being on the receiving end of harsh and aggressive treatment. Long working hours were combined with a sense of responsibility for agreeing to take on such hours. The great army of freelancers sustaining the cultural industries have little access to the financial and psychological benefits accruing from strong union representation.

---

7 Though, as we saw in Chapter 3, Banks takes a different perspective later in his book, in order to balance such neo-Foucauldian perspectives.

These conditions manifested themselves in the form of considerable anxiety on the part of creative workers. Nevertheless, on the basis of our interviews, it can hardly be claimed that the cultural industries fail to offer elements of good work to many creative workers. Numerous interviewees reported pleasure in autonomy and freedom, that their work was complex, challenging, interesting and varied. It may be demanding, but it offers considerable opportunity for a sense of completion, and of having done a job well. There was widespread appreciation of the fact that this is work socially recognised as interesting, even glamorous. In the next chapter, we explore these ambivalences and contradictions with regard to two crucial aspects of creative work, indeed of any good work: the degree to which it offers experiences of sociality and teamwork; and possibilities for self-realisation.

6 Creative careers, self-realisation and sociality

6.1 Decline of the career?

Once upon a time, the story goes, occupations and the organisations associated with them offered relatively predictable, secure and clear career routes to their employees if they worked hard enough. But there was another side to this predictability and security. William Whyte's (1956) concern about *Organisation Man* was that he represented a widespread tendency for people to give up their individuality for the sake of the enterprises that employed them. Organisational, management and business studies have engaged in much discussion of the decline or otherwise of the traditional organisational career, and whether or not this is a good thing. Usefully surveying a wide range of empirical evidence, Edwards and Wajcman (2005: 84) conclude that the bureaucratic career has not disappeared in an era of outsourcing and downsizing, but 'the rungs on the ladder may be fewer and further apart' and the influx of women into many labour markets has made competition for access to careers more intense. The emphasis on the development of 'organisational cultures' in 1980s and 1990s management discourse was interpreted by many analysts as an attempt to get employees to internalise the values of the firm (see Kunda 1992). Under these regimes, employees were increasingly required to monitor and improve their own work performance. They do so though 'in relation to ideals that serve the interests of the organization, but are framed in terms of an abstract "good" person unconnected to any particular firm' (Edwards and Wajcman 2005: 73).

This suggests that it may make more sense to think of developments in middle-class managerial and professional careers as a matter of *individualisation*. Employees come to view their own firm 'more instrumentally, as providing the right opportunities for them at the time. The organization may be viewed as offering resources and scope for self-development, rather than the basis for allegiance and identity formation' (Edwards and Wajcman 2005: 74). Certainly, many creative workers conform to this picture, shifting from project to project, in an attempt to develop a portfolio of achievements and, crucially, reputation. But how might we evaluate the shift towards this way of living?[1]

Management analysts have discussed the rise of the 'portfolio career' or 'boundaryless career' (Arthur and Rousseau 1996) and at times seem to stress the way it provides new freedoms for (managerial and professional) workers. Such concepts have been applied to creative work (Jones 1996; Peiperl et al. 2002) and this is not surprising, for the the cultural industries, especially non-commercial artistic professions, seem to offer archetypal examples of such careers (see Menger 1999, 2006). Because a great deal of creative labour has traditionally been conducted beyond the organisation, by freelancers and short-term contracted staff, the cultural industries have been celebrated in some quarters as a place where employees might be free to achieve self-realisation away from the confining spaces of the organisation. We illustrated the tendency for creative industries discourse, and its attendant academic cheerleaders, to indulge in some of this kind of thinking in Chapter 1.

Others have reacted against the celebration of portfolio or individualised careers by arguing that 'flexible capitalism' is detrimental to self-realisation. Flexibility, wrote Richard Sennett (1998: 9), is bringing back the original medieval meaning of the word 'job' – a lump or piece of something that could be carried around. People now do 'lumps of labour'. This has potentially damaging impacts on *character*, 'the long-term aspect of our emotional experience', expressed by loyalty and mutual commitment, the pursuit of long-term goals and the practice of delayed gratification for the sake of a future end (Sennett 1998: 10). These are surely important aspects of people's lives, and values that are worth considering carefully. But such robust statements of the value of self-realisation should not blind us to the attendant danger of self-exploitation pointed to by some of the critics of modern work we discussed in Chapter 2, and of creative labour, as discussed in Chapter 3.

This chapter explores two further aspects of workers' experiences of creative labour in the cultural industries. In the first half of the chapter, we consider the extent to which the cultural industries provide possibilities for self-realisation that are, we claimed in Chapter 2, fundamental to any definition of good work. Self-realisation in relation to labour involves a sustained sense of good work, so that work may contribute to a sense that a person might have – and other people might also share – that they are developing, flourishing, achieving excellence in forms of work activity that are valuable. The concept of the career has been fundamental to discussions of this aspect of good work, along with related concepts of the vocation or the calling. In Section 6.2, we

---

1 It is also worth noting that these two different models of the career – the possibly mythical notion of the organisational career, on the one hand, and the individualised model on the other – are both highly gendered, in that the structure of professional and managerial careers is 'at odds with women's life-cycle patterns of work and childbearing' and the 'developmental trajectory of a career is still designed to fit men's life course' (Edwards and Wajcman 2005: 77). We discuss the gendered aspects of careers below.

show that creative labour, at least according to creative workers, offers genuine possibilities for self-realisation. Creative workers find in their occupations ways of fulfilling potential and developing talents that give them a sense of purpose and meaning in their lives. For others the particular challenges of creative work helped build their self-esteem, confidence and sense of recognition by others. Yet there are at least two problems with creative careers. One is that they are 'fragile', difficult to sustain over an entire life, especially for women (Section 6.3). Another is that the very lure of self-realisation brings about an over-identification of the self with work (Section 6.4). This can be true in any form of the modern work ethic (see Heelas 2002). But there are specific forms this kind of attachment takes in creative labour.

In the second part of the chapter, we examine the sociality or otherwise of creative work. Workers of all kinds experience work as a burden, but it can also be a source of pleasurable social interaction, friendship and even love. Creative labour is often highly collaborative, but equally it can be carried out by a single person working from home as a freelancer. Both these aspects of labour carry with them benefits and problems, and we explore them here. In Section 6.5 we examine an aspect of creative labour that many of our interviewees presented as positive: the high degree of sociality, friendship and teamwork to be found in much creative labour. Then in Section 6.6 we outline experiences of isolation, and of a kind of forced sociability, here building on the discussion of the 'obligation to network' in Section 4.8 – though there the emphasis was on the effects of that obligation on autonomy, rather than, as here, on experiences of creative work.

6.2 Finding the right creative occupation

A number of our interviewees indicated a high degree of self-realisation through work by indicating that their occupation involved talents or enthusiasms from their childhood. Wayne, a music magazine editor, half-joked that 'my wife thinks I'm a total magazine boy. She is absolutely right, but we did meet at a magazine. She works in magazines so she can't really complain' (Interview 5). This relationship with magazines began when he was a child. 'I've always loved doing magazines since I was a little kid', Wayne recalled. 'When I was a little kid I used to get given those things called "Make your own newspaper" and "Make your own magazine" kits and you would get a little Letraset and blank pages. I was six or seven.' As an adult, he felt 'lucky in that I have been able to keep doing that as a pretty successful career' but he had developed facility with contemporary technologies. 'I am not necessarily a natural but I am pretty attuned to Mac computing for instance, which is extremely important, and to having a rough eye for design, which helps when you are an editor.' This is a story of self-realisation from Letraset to the Mac. His wife's teasing that Wayne is overly dedicated to the job provides self-deprecation. But then there is a sense of adaptation and personal growth, underpinned by a love of what he does.

Other creative workers told us of a similar life-long commitment to a particular form of creative work. Tim, an improvising jazz pianist, started playing at 8 and by the time he was at secondary school, 'there was no question'. At the time Tim didn't know what music he was going to do. 'I was probably thinking of going into classical and then maybe going on to pop. At the time I didn't know anything about jazz', and he added ruefully, deciding to be a jazz musician in terms of finances, probably 'wasn't the greatest thing'. Comparing musicians with other occupations, Tim went on to discuss how the desire simply to play music means that musicians eschew the ambition to achieve greater status.

> So you do have this sort of reverse status, where everybody else can't wait to move up. Musicians would rather be on any old gig if it means as long as they can stay a musician. I haven't got to that stage yet, fortunately. I know a lot of musicians who, once they've started making a living, the lifestyle, they can't imagine doing anything else, especially the ones that do the session leg. They'd rather do that than not play.
>
> (Interview 61)

This presents Tim as one of a community of people who forgo material rewards for dedication to the activity that enchants them, fascinates them. It would be wrong to equate this with romanticism. There is an attempt here to create a distance from harmful consumerism. But there is also a strong sense that the pleasure of what musicians do leads them to act against their material interests. 'You don't worry about a pension. There's no such thing as a pension scheme in this thing', Tim mused. And referring to Lol Coxhill, a prominent UK improviser, 'he's 74 … and until he physically can't play that saxophone, there's no way he's going to stop playing'. In this respect, said Tim,

> it's a very strange profession. It's more like a vocation. It's like a nurse. Someone who is a nurse, especially today, it's definitely not for the money. It's just that's their thing, and there's nothing they can do about it.
>
> (Interview 61)

Tim expressed sympathy for nurses:

> when you see how much we spend on footballers, what a footballer can make a week, is more than a nurse will get for their entire life. It's insane, and then we're wondering why we've got a lack of nurses.
>
> (Interview 61)

Tim also discussed pop musicians as an example of excessive rewards.

> For a musician it's always going to be their thing. It used to get on my nerves a bit when I'd see pop stars and they're on for ten minutes and

they're going to make more money in that two years than you're ever going to make.

(Interview 61)

But Tim suggested that the demands of the musical life, with all its addictive properties, perhaps merit high rewards. 'Then you realise all the side effects they're probably going to have. Like Michael Jackson is the best example' (this was two years before Michael Jackson's sudden death in 2009).

Other creative workers talked about arriving at their occupation somewhat later in their life. For Shaun, a freelance film editor, his job provided the opportunity to combine scientific or technical and artistic interests. At school, he took science subjects at A level – the exams British students typically take at the age of 17 and 18. 'I was brought up on *Horizon*[2] and stuff like that ... *Horizon* fascinated me' (Interview 14). These were his academic choices, but all the time he loved photography. 'I should have done A level Art or something, but I used to go in the art room at lunchtime for Art Club, and I couldn't see the marriage of the two.' But photography and film seemed to Shaun to 'cover both things', science and also 'you could pursue ideas. You weren't designing fuel plants or cars, you weren't designing medicine, the end product was something quite intangible, films, music, whatever'. So for Shaun, 'it just fell into place. It was a marriage of the two, you could say. There is some art in it, but there's a lot of discipline and technique'.

For one men's magazine writer, access to creative work was bound up in a narrative of personal redemption. Erik initially came to writing as a form of catharsis:

> I started writing because I used to hate my jobs and I actually suffer from depression, so I had some really, really black times for months and months and months. So I started writing as a sort of release for that and it was just rubbish, just poetry and prose, and just anything that I wanted to write, but it was really, really helpful so I thought I'd like to do this full time.
>
> (Interview 28)

The initial appeal of magazine writing to Erik was the isolation it offered.

> When I first started I thought it would be fantastic because I won't have to actually speak to anybody, I can just hole myself up in a room, I can just write and hand off stuff, and I don't have to get up in the morning.
>
> (Interview 28)

---

2 *Horizon* is the BBC's flagship science programme, which has been running since 1964, in a variety of formats.

But Erik then discovered that he enjoyed the social contact made possible by his work.

> Now it's very different. I speak to people all day long. You've got to be up at half past seven, you've got to be on the phone, you've got to be doing really good stuff. But that has been like a gradual process and I'm having a ball and really, really enjoying it.
>
> (Interview 28)

Of course lives are rarely this seamless, and depression has a way of recurring. Short of tracking Erik's career, we cannot know whether magazine work continued to offer this kind of pleasurable sociality. But his enjoyment of working as a men's magazine journalist seemed genuine.

Most cases are less dramatic than this, and involve people gradually getting a sense of what their talents and specialisms really are. One assistant producer, Yasmin, told us of how she had realised in a previous job in graphic design that her particular talent was for ideas rather than design: 'I almost wanted help on the design part, I wanted a team of people helping me do the design if I could come up with the idea.' Her sister, who worked in television, recommended that she try to work her way into the development department of an independent.

> Within three months I was in the development department. And realising that it's not just in development where you have ideas, throughout production you are constantly thinking of an angle, or a place to look where you can find a contributor, or a style or what would create a great reaction for people. It's ideas all the time.
>
> (Interview 31)

This sense of working in an ideas-driven occupation felt fulfilling for this young woman.

For others, self-realisation through creative work was apparent in the way that the challenge of a creative job allowed them to develop personal confidence and self-esteem. Having been 'quite shy as a child', Aggie, a features editor in the construction press, felt that journalism

> takes you into places and opens doors, and I think as far as identity went at the beginning, I probably needed something to make me feel I had a right to do those things so journalism gave me that right ... I just got a lot of social confidence and I wasn't scared of strangers and things.
>
> (Interview 18)

In questioning the damaging effects of flexible capitalism, as Sennett (1998) rightly does, it is important not to forget the potentially positive benefits of career or occupational changes in people's lives. Bob, who when we interviewed him was in the process of making a transition from being an actor to being a script writer, felt that the latter 'has got more purpose, for me personally'. This was very much related for him to the experience of becoming a father.

> It's not a slight on anybody, but I think getting to 37 and having a child now who is coming up to 5, I feel as though it's more worthy somehow, that I can go to a room and spend all day writing and I feel it's a more appropriate way to make a living rather than getting on a train and going down to Soho and going to a room for two minutes and pretend to be a chicken or whatever for a commercial and then get on the train and come home again.
>
> (Interview 16)

Pretending to be a chicken for an advert here stands as an example of creative work without dignity, whereas writing, for all its precariousness, allowed this young father a degree of self-control, a sense of 'being in control of your own destiny a bit more'.

6.3 The fragility of creative careers

The previous section shows that many workers, young and old, were able to indicate that creative work had been a source of self-realisation, and we have given some reasons why this might be the case, building on our discussion of work features such as autonomy and challenge from the previous chapter. But more negative aspects of the conditions of creative labour put limits on these possibilities. For Lakshman, a downside of creative work was that 'it can be quite hard to carve out a career'. This freelance urban music journalist recognised that 'there are a lot of people who do make good careers out of it and have a good focused plan and know exactly where they want to go and how they're going to go about it, and do actually manage it' (Interview 41). Nevertheless, he told us, 'most freelancers have another job, a day job, either teaching or working at a label or doing something totally unrelated like working in a library or something like that because there's no real stability in freelancing'. Lakshman claimed that there was a strong sense among magazine workers of a typical career path: 'freelancing, then you get an editorial job at a magazine and then you are basically sorted, you are set'. But the problem is 'that doesn't happen for most people because there just aren't enough jobs. That's why you have to have another job'.

The precariousness of creative careers inevitably favours those who can draw easily on other sources of income, especially from well-off parents. In established areas of journalism, many workers now have degrees. Larry, a features editor on a men's magazine, felt that it was 'depressing' that so many of his colleagues in magazine journalism have had 'expensive educations'. This wealth allowed them to take 'the whole work experience route'. Larry compared the situation with television, notorious for requiring unpaid internship for entry into the profession: 'It's like telly, you need to have been established because otherwise how can you get into it? Even starting off as a freelancer, you are so brave.' 'Magazines are', Larry said, a 'closed world', 'unless you do what I did and do a fanzine and somehow get noticed that way, but it's really hard' (Interview 9).

For some successful creative workers, such as Hannah, the artist manager of a very successful rock act, the problem was not so much finding a career path, as in gaining any satisfaction from any particular phase of achievement. 'During the lifecycle of a record', she recalled, 'there's never time to actually take stock and give yourself a pat on the back, because it's always about pushing it to the next level and the next level.' So she had never really felt fulfilment because whenever she achieved a new level, 'it's always been "right, next step". Once you get UK domination it's then worldwide domination, and you can always do better' (Interview 42).

But career anxieties were generally more oriented towards the future, to life beyond the thirties. Larry, the men's magazine writer quoted above, saw few prospects for himself.

> I don't have enough ability to be a successful author, financially, so what happens? ... I'm not obsessed with magazines so I wouldn't be a good editor. The only way you're really going to get a job until you retire is if you move above editor and become a publisher and work in the kind of suit area. That's never going to happen for me, and I'm 31 now, so what happens? When I am 38, 39 I'm going to be bored shitless with [the magazine he wrote for], obviously, but also too old to be relevant. So what happens? Fuck knows. It's a real worry and I know a lot of people worry about it too because it's a young industry and if you don't make it by the time you're in your late 30s, you're fucked.
>
> (Interview 9)

One young TV researcher, Margie, discussed her career uncertainty in similar terms. 'I really don't know what to do to be honest.' Reporting that she was regularly asked 'where do you see yourself, are you going to go onto directing?' her sense was that she didn't think she was creative enough to make the 'normal progression' from researcher to director.

> I'm a creative person but I'm not [so] creative to become a director because they are really telling the story. The director really pieces things together and I don't think I could do that. I don't think I've got the brain power to do that, but at the same time I don't want to be sitting as a researcher for ever.
>
> (Interview 35)

Such career uncertainties of course are not unique to the cultural industries. But the cultural industries seem particularly prone to 'a substantial outflow in mid career' (Tunstall 2001: 5). Because of the mismatch between traditional career trajectories and the life cycle of many women, this is a particularly difficult problem for women.

Adele, who had worked as a director and series producer in the entertainment genre before an injury forced her to take an 'office' job in a television 'headhunting' agency, claimed that 'gender is a big issue' in the television industry. Adele observed that there are very few women in production who are over the age of 34 because 'you cannot have a family and live the life TV production involves' – namely working long hours travelling all over the country for shoots. She believed the demands of television production, with its bleeding of working into all other aspects of life, were less of an issue for men in the industry because 'they are rarely the primary carers of children' (Interview 27). Participant observation at the independent production company in London, as well as visits to other production houses over the course of our interviews with television workers, revealed a distinct absence of women in their mid-thirties to late forties in these companies. Women were either very young and working at junior grades – runners, researchers, assistant producers and also production secretaries – or otherwise were much older and in senior, executive positions.

A study by Willis and Dex (2003) of 13 women who took maternity leave from their television production jobs in the early 1990s found that:

> career ambitions at the time of their maternity breaks were marked by caution: a consideration of the constraints imposed by family responsibilities and partner's work, by a reckoning of the realities of the work options available, and by reflections on their own skills, experience and marketability.
>
> (Willis and Dex 2003: 126)

All of these women had delayed having children until their thirties 'after a fairly substantial period of establishing a career', having observed women who had babies at lower grades in production teams struggle to progress their careers when they returned to work (Willis and Dex 2003: 124, 127). One of the issues raised by the women in Willis and Dex's study was the culture of long working hours, attributed to men who are often single and with no family to attend to. With these hours normalised, the women in the study found 'senior working mothers', who had adopted the lengthened working hours, put pressure on mothers at lower grades on the career ladder to stay at the office and work late with little regard to their childcare issues (Willis and Dex 2003: 129). This caused anxiety, with the women expressing 'difficulty in resolving their former total commitment to their occupational work with their new commitments to the demands of household and family, and then with the increasingly competitive and casualised work environment to which they were returning' (Willis and Dex 2003: 131).

Ingrid, a managing director of an independent production company, took up some of these issues in a discussion of the impact of gender on careers in television. She pointed to television news production as being the most difficult area of television work for women with families:

> I think if you want to have a life outside of television – and women are people that have children – you have to think carefully about which jobs you take, and a man wouldn't necessarily. So the news jobs are really hard I think for women, because they are punishing hours and the ethos is still male.
>
> (Interview 11)

As a manager, and as a mother, Ingrid described how she attempts to make home/work balance more possible for the women who work for her:

> I mean I am married and I've got two teenagers, and that's always been very, very important to me. I have been really lucky though because I've been able to invent how I work and been able to have a nice home life. I do try to do that for other people, that's why I say I don't like people staying late to prove that they're working. ... I have my Execs, I have seen about four of them through having all their children and going part time and coming back three days a week, that sort of thing. I've got several people who do four days a week now. In a way, television can do that because its project based. It's not like running a shop, it's not always open, so you can make it work. I think you can make it work for women.
>
> (Interview 11)

This may be so, but it would also seem that having a partner who can support part-time employment is important in such situations. Evelyn, one of the freelance assistant producers in the factual development department at IPC TV where we conducted our participant observation, was six months pregnant with her second child at the start of the fieldwork. Evelyn hoped her contract, which was almost at an end, would be extended up until the birth of the baby, though this was looking unlikely. In discussing freelance work and contracts she said that 'contracts can be as short as one week' and it would 'be a great contract if it was for three months'. She explained that 'it is lucky my husband can support me' because 'television really is a man's world'. It is, Evelyn said, 'a cut-throat, knife-in-the-back business with no honesty'. Then reflecting on this she added, 'with all the negatives in TV sometimes I wonder if it's time to get a real job' (field notes, 6 February 2007).

6.4 Defining yourself too much through creative work

The possibilities of self-realisation through creative work, then, are limited, and there are significant age and gender aspects to the limitations surrounding them. The career uncertainty discussed above is made all the more difficult by the fact that creative labour seems, in a great many cases, to demand a high degree of personal, emotional investment on the part of workers. This partly derives from the fact that the products can be both very public and at the same time closely associated with particular individuals. We explore further the satisfactions and drawbacks associated with the public nature of creative work in Chapters 8 and 9, but here we concentrate on the implications for workers' self-realisation of these high levels of personal investment, and also the implications for work–life balance. We asked nearly all our interviewees about the degree to which their identity was bound up in their occupation or job. Larry, the men's magazine features editor, replied that it was, and he discussed a colleague:

> That's kind of what I see in people like [my colleague] as well, winning these awards and having people read your stuff. It's sort of good and bad for the ego and a lot of your self-esteem does begin to rest on your image that you have of yourself as a writer.
>
> (Interview 9)

But inevitably, when one's work is so publicly disseminated, there would be criticism.

> Of course, as always happens, you find that other people don't like what you do and you can go through a real rollercoaster. It's like any kind of creative thing, I suppose it does affect people in probably quite negative ways and you end up using whatever you do as the basis of all your self-esteem … and it's very dangerous because your bubble bursts and you could come down with a bit of a crash. You see it a lot, all the time actually in magazines. It's such a precarious business as well. You can be a golden boy the one minute and nothing the next.
>
> (Interview 9)

Camera operator Simon provided some detail of what a profound personal investment in creative work might imply. 'I am a bit defined by my work', he admitted.

> I don't take it quite as seriously right now as I have done, and it has been a bit upsetting and you do get kind of punch drunk with situations at work. I think I'm a bit damaged in some ways.
>
> (Interview 29)

Though not as damaged as 'people who shoot in war zones', he compared the cumulative effect of shooting many documentaries to being 'like a boxer in a ring'.

> I think in my 50s I was cracking up a bit from it and wondering what life was about. It can creep up on you and it certainly can get to you.

There were some films, I was filming in hospitals and I was in tears filming things. I was not quite having a breakdown, but it was kind of the cumulative effects of having shot so many documentaries and shot a lot in hospitals.

(Interview 29)

Yet this very masculine tale of heroic devotion to documentary had a reasonably happy ending, according to Simon: 'But I've got through that and I'm pretty robust from that point of view.'

To be done well, creative work sometimes requires intense engagement with subject matter, and this appears to be true of much documentary work. While Simon suggested that he had got through a difficult stage of vulnerability, it is striking that this was not an early career experience; it happened to him in his fifties. Few people of course would wish to present themselves as unable to achieve any kind of work–life balance. A number of our respondents admitted that much of their personal identity derived from their work, but made strong statements about other aspects of their lives. We asked Elizabeth, a music reviews editor, whether her job was a big part of her identity. 'Yes and no', was the reply. 'It takes up a lot of my life, I love doing it, I'm always listening to music and my social life is related to it.' Equally though,

I can easily go home, go out with my friends and not talk about it at all. If tomorrow I was told 'you can't do this anymore, you've got to do something else', I'd be sad about it but I'd just move on really.

(Interview 30)

Investment may be higher though when people have set up their own businesses or developed their own projects over many years. Lionel, a hip hop record label owner we interviewed, had recently begun work on a novel and had gained a significant advance. Lionel's answer to our question about the degree to which his job defined his identity suggested an ambivalence about his core job – excited by music, but not always enjoying the business aspects of it. 'Obviously if you set something up then it's more than just a job. I am emotionally invested in it or whatever.' Like other interviewees, he hesitated about sounding pretentious about his feelings about his work, and like others too, he used a baby metaphor to convey his investment. 'That sounds a bit psychoanalytic or something, but it's my baby basically and so in that sense I'm still very bound up in it. I love music; I just don't particularly enjoy selling music.' But Lionel claimed to be relaxed about this ambivalence. 'These things happen, don't they? You take a path and that's where you end up, and I'm still excited by the music side of it, definitely.' Nevertheless, his high degree of personal investment meant that also devoting considerable time to another creative project (writing a novel, eventually published to some success) resulted in a divided state of mind: 'I guess I am slightly schizophrenic at the moment in that I also have this other thing going on' (Interview 45).

Documentary producer Lilith told us that 'sometimes' her work and the rest of her life were hard to disentangle. At work, she shared with colleagues discussions about 'kids and family'. But when she travelled away and was immersed in a festival with her peers

> then you are in that bubble again. Everyone talking about documentaries, it's the most important thing in everybody's minds for days and days and days, and then you come back and you get that jolt back into doing maths homework and clearing up sick, whatever a mum has to do.
>
> (Interview 43)

So the demands of domestic life helped Lilith to put work in perspective. Yet there may be some ambivalence here too: 'doing maths homework' and 'clearing up sick' are grounding, but they may also be tedious and unpleasant compared with immersion in a festival atmosphere. 'I think it's the same with any working parent really, isn't it?' Lilith asked us. 'I don't see it as a glamorous thing, but I do see it as more than a job, much more than a job. I live and breathe it a lot of the time.'

Others resisted the idea that they were defined by work. This was so for trade press reporter Irene:

> I like writing and I like the news. So those sorts of things do come out in my personality anyway. So I'll go to a party and I will be happy to go up to a stranger and say hello and make friends.
>
> (Interview 44)

But Irene found that her observations of journalists who cannot switch off from the inquisitive aspects of their work had made it clear to her that she wanted to keep some separation between professional and personal aspects of her life.

> I have been at someone's wedding where someone I sat next to happened to be a journalist and they were talking to someone who worked in the NHS, and she was very much being a journalist and she was firing questions at them. The thought did occur to me, "you can switch it off now. You can still be inquisitive and you can still do your journalism things in your head, but don't let being a journalist define you that much".
>
> (Interview 44)

Self-realisation through creative work is precariously linked to work–life balance. Workers, it seems, must constantly engage in a difficult and anxious process of self-monitoring to ensure that their good fortune, in doing work that they find challenging and rewarding, does not topple over into an excessive level of identification with their occupation.

6.5 Teamwork, socialising, networking

We turn now to issues of sociality and isolation with regard to creative work. In his fieldwork with IT professionals, Andreas Wittel (2001) found that the social relationships among these workers were commodified, and yet this commodification was hidden 'by creating a frame ... that makes people feel comfortable, that suggests a somehow "authentic" interest in meeting people' (Wittel 2001: 56). His picture is of a working world where instrumental sociality rules, and yet where that instrumentality is denied. Is this bleak vision characteristic of the cultural industries?

Certainly, many creative workers seemed to believe that they gained a great deal of satisfaction from working in project teams with other creative workers. 'I love working with the filmmakers', Lilith told us.

> They are people I really like and I get on with, it's just fantastic and you just feel really inside the loop creatively. You feel privileged to know what's going on in their brains and how they're doing things, and I love being part of the process.
>
> (Interview 43)

Similarly, in a different industry, music-making provided a great deal of pleasurable sociality for the musicians we interviewed. Some of the most satisfying aspects came from unspoken moments of affirmation. 'People will compliment you and that's important, not just audiences but other musicians will compliment you on what you have done', jazz singer Annette reflected. 'But it's actually those moments during a song when you just catch another musician's eye because you know that they just heard something that you've done that's been really interesting or exciting.' Or it might be when an entire band 'has had a moment, wonderful improvisation where something has gone really right'; and in such moments, 'you can just see how other people in the band have reacted to that' (Interview 10).

What is more, experiences of cultural production could lead to real friendships. 'People you work with can be real friends and real mates', said Simon, the traumatised camera operator quoted above. 'They can be really close and it can be really good because you spend quite a lot of time together on planes and you see some amazing things together and there is a lot of camaraderie.' This relationship could be 'almost therapeutic. Sometimes I almost feel like I'm a therapist when I'm with other people, but then other people have helped me in fact. Other people have talked me through things'. Simon immediately followed this with a rather poignant, if semi-humorous, complaint that the love of his work was something that may have caused problems at home (reflecting Hochschild's (1989) analysis of American working lives): 'Here at home I'm not really supposed to talk about my work, even though I think it's really interesting, but my other half doesn't like me talking about my work' (Interview 29).

In many companies there was a ritual of going to the pub on a Friday night after work. There is a particularly strong tradition in the magazine industry – the celebration of going to press. Nixon and Crewe (2004: 137–9) describe a culture of hedonism in magazine publishing and the advertising industry noting that 'it was drinking with colleagues after work in the local pub on Friday nights, as well as frequently in the week, that formed a more regular social ritual for both sets of media practitioners'. Elizabeth, a music reviews editor, told us 'after we go to press we go out for a pint and to me and to the art director that's really important ... because the last week is all stress and panic and adrenaline going' (Interview 30). Such social events often bring people together from different parts of the same company, such as creative and marketing personnel. As Neville, a men's magazine marketer, explained: 'If you are based with the editorial team and they are going to the pub on a Friday night, you are naturally going to go with them because you are part of a team' (Interview 47).

There is another aspect to sociality in the cultural industries too, which we touched upon in the previous chapter. Some creative jobs allow workers to meet a wide variety of people, and this is highly valued by some workers. In television, researcher Margie said, 'you have to be a people person, which I think I am, and you have to communicate with people, and I just love it. I love meeting people. I've met so many people, it's mad' (Interview 35).

For those who are less inclined to such forms of sociability, however, this emphasis on post-work bonding and meeting people can be difficult. Many workers, such as drama producer Ally, described themselves as 'not a sociali-ser' (Interview 59) and while recognising the importance of networking and socialising with industry colleagues preferred not to engage in the pub culture. But not identifying as a 'pub person' can be a problem, as expressed by camera operator Nigel (and given that pubs are very racialised spaces, it is significant that he is black):

> You see, I'm not a pub man, and I think there are lots of cameramen or lots of crew who are pub people, and I've never been into that pub cul-ture. So the problem I have is that even when you are out on location, as soon as you finish everybody wants to go to the pub and get drunk, and I've never been into that so that's probably put me as a bit of an outsider in that sense.
>
> (Interview 33)

Freelance producer Samuel described his lack of interest in the drinking cul-ture of production crews as a 'downfall' and said 'maybe I'd get a lot more work if I was a pub person' (Interview 21).

The music industry is, as one might expect from the close links of its products with contemporary hedonistic lifestyles, particularly prone to such a mingling of work and hedonistic leisure. For some in the music industry, including music journalists, socialising is a compulsory element of a job

(Gregg 2010) which still has a focus on collective experience, such as live gigs, launches and so on. Izzy, a marketing manager at a large record company, felt there was simply no choice about whether or not to go out:

> Probably two or three nights a week we are out at gigs, wherever that might be. It might be in London. Normally if you've got an act that's on tour you will see a gig in London and we always try and encourage everyone to go and see them somewhere else in the country as well. ... So you are out a lot and yes, it is very sociable.
>
> (Interview 49)

The consequences of not participating in such a culture are varied. Ernie, an artist manager, described to us how not being a 'pub person' forces a choice about how to position oneself within the music industry. 'The network is very, very important, but I think personally there are better ways to maintain and build a network than going out and getting pissed at gigs, and I've never really been part of that scene.' This meant that he was 'excluded from a big area of the business', but he had come to accept this: 'that's a choice I've made about how I wanted to be and how I wanted to work' (Interview 63).

By making that choice, though, Ernie felt excluded from certain powerful cliques that had developed around the genre that he worked in, and not belonging to these meant 'you don't get a look in': 'So if I were to take a new band to a label, I wouldn't really know where to begin at this point because I'm not really part of any of those scenes.' But on the other hand Ernie felt that he was not too limited by this exclusion 'because ultimately if they are interested they are going to find you'. There were also questions of work–life balance to be taken into account: 'I'd rather be at home with my wife and kids than out getting drunk with a bunch of people I didn't particularly like, chasing a deal that I didn't believe was right for the band.'

Even in less 'glamorous' occupations such as trade magazine journalism, the expectation to be sociable was strong. Irene, a junior reporter in the building sector, described the visits to the pub as 'an extension of work hours really' and said that often 'talk can revolve around work' which was frustrating on days where 'you want to switch off' but, she said, 'it's actually genuinely fun as well' (Interview 44). Here again we see the blurring of pleasure and obligation, freedom and constraint, characteristic of so much creative work. There was no doubt that the blurring of networking and socialising means it becomes very difficult to maintain a boundary around one's 'working life'. Harry, a series producer of entertainment programmes, said that although he would like to keep his work and 'private life' separate 'the nature of telly normally encourages you actually to bleed your work into your personal life, because that's how you build up contacts, how you get jobs' (Interview 52).

As music reviews editor, Elizabeth, put it, networking is 'important for the freelance part of the job'. But although it tends to happen outside of work hours it isn't necessarily pleasurable because 'lots of people are never off so you can't relax and socialise with them' (Interview 30). 'Never off': all hours become work hours. This also points to anxieties about the authenticity of friendships in this world of work. As Erik, a freelance men's magazine writer, put it: 'I tend to socialise with my editors in London once every two or three weeks, and I pretend that it's me being pally with them, but it's not really, it's me just maintaining relationships' (Interview 28). This kind of 'schmoozing', as music writer Lakshman described it, might not be enjoyable but was regarded as important because part of networking socially is letting people

> know who you are without making it too blatantly obvious that you want them to help you out ... I do sometimes go for drinks with people, but I'm guessing that is pretty much the definition of networking. That is how a lot of people do get work and do get new jobs and things like that.
>
> (Interview 41)

In the magazine industry, said Lakshman, networking is implicit and covert. 'People just being friendly with each other, just having a drink and being casual' is networking masquerading as socialising:

> you are basically being friendly under the guise of networking ... it's like an unspoken thing where people are being friendly and being friends and you all invite each other out to things. At the end of it you are kind of saying 'do you want to do this?' or something.
>
> (Interview 41)

What is more, the project nature of much creative work makes the friendships and relationships built up there difficult to sustain. Amongst a varied set of rewards from creative work, Katie, a production manager at an independent, listed 'working with a really lovely team of people'. 'But basically', she said, 'the thing is you move from one project to the other so quickly, you just go straight onto the next thing usually, if they don't overlap, which they usually do' (Interview 26). We explore the ramifications for friendships and working relations of such short-term project-based television jobs in considerably more detail in the next chapter. But in all the industries we studied, not just television, there was a sense that sociability is essential for professional success.

Wittel then is right to point to the limitations on workplace sociality. But it would be too cynical to discount all the positive experiences of friendship, collegiality and sociality in creative work. And it would certainly be a mistake to think everything is pretence, for certain forms of working solidarity seem to endure. The difficult conditions under which creative work is carried out can also lead to friendships that can enable workers to cope with the insecurity and precariousness of creative work. Take executive producer

Malcolm's description of the friendship he developed with fellow documentary producer, Samuel:

> We're very close friends and we don't get together to talk about work anymore, we usually talk about wine. He's a great wine expert. But I'm very close friends with [him] because we've worked together and we've been driving through the night, we've faced huge difficulties, and it's an interesting thing about this process that when you've been really up against it in a really bad situation, it might be a violent situation, it might be just the plane didn't arrive and you've got to drive 200 miles to the next place and the conditions are cold or difficult, or it might be that you have to turn something around in no time at all. There could be 1001 things but you go through these really, really intense emotional experiences, and if the person you are working with is able to match your energy and actual drive or maybe exceed it, then you develop a bond, you've been through some powerful experience.
>
> (Interview 37)

It cannot be denied that collective experience of production can lead to conflict too – and such conflicts are addressed in Chapter 7 where, drawing on our ethnography of the production of an entertainment show we discuss particular examples of the pressures of television production and how they impact on creative workers' relationships with each other.

6.6 Isolation

Our interviewees, then, reported many ambivalent experiences of the intense sociality of creative work. Many though also reported a strong sense of isolation. For Norman, one of the music journalists we spoke to, one of the hardest things about being a freelancer was the seclusion: 'you don't talk to anyone and you don't see anyone'. This can be 'crippling' as it has an impact on motivation. He found himself

> filling my day sometimes, even when I've got things to do, [with] very random things ... they get me nowhere ... and at the end of the day I have this mild sense of self-loathing that I've done nothing useful today.
>
> (Interview 46)

Norman links this to his personality:

> I am a born worrier, which probably means I'm not the best person to be a freelance. I am concerned about where the work is coming from, I'm concerned about where the work is going, whether my career path has any direction, and it's quite difficult when you are isolated to get

reassurances because you don't see other people. You look at other people and think 'how come you've got all that work, where is mine?'

(Interview 46)

Giles, the music writer we quoted in the previous chapter (5.6), who referred to his work as involving 'a very complicated version of freedom', was referring to the fact that he didn't have to 'commute or work in an open plan office or deal with moody colleagues'. Giles observed that up until a few years ago it was almost expected by magazines that the freelance writers would go to the office fairly regularly. At the time he didn't quite understand the importance of this but now, after spending the last couple of years in isolation, he reflected on the value of regular office visits:

It was beneficial to you because they saw you there, you seemed to get more work, they seemed to remember your existence. But often you'd just think 'what am I going to the [magazine] office for? I have no good reason to be there'.

(Interview 4)

In 'the connexionist world' that Boltanski and Chiapello (2005/1999: 111–12) identify as central to modern work, 'a natural preoccupation of human beings is the desire to connect with others, to make contact, to make connections, so as to not remain isolated'. In an effort to combat the isolating conditions of freelance journalism, Erik, a men's magazine writer, rents a desk in the office of a design agency which is located in a regional 'creative industries' precinct. But whilst locating yourself in an office space, as Erik had done, puts you in contact with other people to reduce that sense of isolation it does not address the isolation from one's profession. As Norman emphasised:

It's the same with all magazines; I've never met anyone who works on them. I wrote for *Esquire* for two years and never met anyone. On and off I wrote maybe five or six pieces for them spread over a two year period, but I never met anyone.

(Interview 46)

Norman said that a positive side of this was that you would avoid a magazine's office politics 'but then on the other hand you don't see the fun and games of office life'. On the basis of our interviews, then, it seems that isolation continues to be a danger for most freelance creative workers.

6.7 Self-realisation and sociality: ambivalent features of modern creative labour

For those workers who are able to sustain a career in the cultural industries, their work can offer a certain degree of rewarding self-realisation. But the nature of creative work places serious restrictions on these possibilities. Multi-jobbing makes it difficult to develop the skills and expertise necessary to thrive. The need to do long periods of unpaid work to get access to rewarding and fulfilling employment means that people from working-class families are unlikely to gain access. There are significant age and gender dimensions to these limitations, with many men and even more women leaving creative jobs in mid-career. But even where people found careers that felt likely to offer some level of self-realisation, a balance between work and life, and an appropriate level of identification with occupation, felt hard to achieve for many. The intense sociality of much creative work was also highly ambivalent. Much creative work involves considerable levels of teamwork. There is a very strong culture of hedonism associated with many creative jobs. This brought with it burdens for those not inclined to the dominant forms of sociality – and this had age, sex and ethnic dimensions. Meanwhile, some of our freelance informants reported feelings of isolation, and a lack of contact with the workplace.

In the next chapter, we explore the issue of sociality in greater detail, drawing on the participant observation fieldwork we undertook, and focusing on the degree to which the teamwork involved in some creative occupations fits with recent theories of 'affective' and 'immaterial' labour.

7   Emotional and affective labour

7.1 Immaterial labour, affective labour and 'precarity'

In recent years, an attractive option for many intellectuals seeking theoretically informed critique of a number of developments in contemporary capitalism has been autonomist Marxism. Autonomist concepts of immaterial labour, affective labour and 'precarity' have been of increasing interest to critical commentators on contemporary work, including labour in the cultural and creative industries.[1] The concept of immaterial labour has its origins in a series of papers in the journal *Futur Antérieur* by Michael Hardt, Maurizio Lazzarato, Antonio Negri and Paolo Virno in the early 1990s. The concept was there defined as 'the labour that produces the information and cultural content of the commodity' (Lazzarato 1996: 133). It was to come under serious attack from other autonomist Marxists (notably Caffentzis 1998) for its excessive optimism, lack of attention to gender and failure to recognise the continuing significance of highly *material* forms of exploitation and oppression. Consequently, by the time of their widely read book *Empire*, Hardt and Negri (2000: 290) had developed a more expansive definition: 'labor that produces an immaterial good, such as a service, a cultural product, knowledge, or communication'. This now incorporated 'affective labour', involving human contact and interaction, and including the kind of heavily gendered caring and health work to which the critiques of Caffentzis and others had drawn attention. In autonomist discussions of both immaterial and affective labour, there was a focus on labour and the production of culture, knowledge and communication – and a reaching for a critical conception of the place of such labour in modern societies. This clearly makes the concepts of potential relevance in a book about creative work in the cultural industries, in relation to questions of equality, freedom and social justice.

However, when it comes to understanding creative labour, these autonomist Marxist concepts have some conspicuous shortcomings. The idea of immaterial

---

1 Ros Gill and Andy C. Pratt (2008) provide a survey of relevant writing in their introduction to a special section of the journal *Theory, Culture and Society* on 'Precarity and Cultural Work', where a version of this chapter originally appeared (see Acknowledgements).

labour is not really based on any adequate theoretical or empirical engagement with the specificity of culture, or of cultural production (see Chapter 3). For one thing, the notoriously vague categories of information and culture are not adequately specified in accounts of immaterial labour. Take the discussion in *Empire*: Hardt and Negri begin from a discussion of how the introduction of the computer has radically transformed work. Even where direct contact with computers is not involved, they say, the manipulation of symbols and information 'along the model of computer operation' (Hardt and Negri 2000: 291) is extremely widespread. Workers used to act like machines, now they increasingly think like computers. They modify their operations through use, and this continual interactivity characterises a wide range of contemporary production. The computer and communication revolution of production has supposedly transformed labouring practices in such a way that they all tend toward the model of information and communication technologies, and this means a homogenisation of labouring processes. In this respect, Hardt and Negri are pessimistic about the 'informationalization' of the economy. But they are much more optimistic about 'affective labour' (see above), which, they claim, produces social networks and communities; and, for Hardt and Negri, cooperation is immanent to such labouring activity. In a typical moment of incoherence, this networked cooperative aspect of affective labour is then transferred to other more computer-driven and 'symbolic-analytical' forms of immaterial labour, as if nurses and computer programmers were doing the same kind of work. The next leap is to see all such workers as therefore equally imbued with the same capacity to struggle against capital. Because wealth creation takes place through such cooperative interactivity, Hardt and Negri believe, 'immaterial labor thus seems to provide the potential for a kind of spontaneous and elementary communism' (2000: 294).

This combination of rampantly optimistic Marxism, combined with a post-structuralist concern with questions of subjectivity and affect, has helped to make Hardt and Negri's work popular amongst some contemporary radical intellectuals. But where would the kinds of symbolic, expressive and journalistic work characteristic of the cultural industries fit into this model? This is not clear. It is true that Hardt and Negri (2000: 293) make reference to 'the immaterial labor of analytical and symbolic tasks', including 'creative and intelligent manipulation'. But they are explicitly referring here to the writings of Robert Reich, US Labour Secretary during Bill Clinton's first term as US President (1993–97), who sees 'symbolic-analytic' work primarily as 'problem-solving, problem-identifying and strategic brokering activities' (Reich, quoted by Hardt and Negri 2000: 291). Reich (1991) means this set of activities to cover a very broad sweep of professional work (lawyers, scientists, academics, engineers and so on) rather than the kind of artistic-expressive creative work that is central to the cultural industries (journalists, musicians, designers, actors). Of course it is interesting to think about what these different 'symbolic analysts' have in common with each other. But as we stressed in Part One of this book, at some point in an account of the labour undertaken in a particular sector, such as the cultural industries, it will be necessary also to consider what is specific to them too. At no point do Hardt and Negri offer even a hint of assistance in this respect. This is perhaps not surprising; they are, after all, offering a very general account. Yet, even in the terms of their own argument, the notion of immaterial labour in *Empire*, as the most eloquent and lucid of all the autonomist Marxist writers puts it, 'covers up chiasmic differences, fault lines of segmentation, veritable continental rifts that present the most formidable barriers for the organization of counterpower' (Dyer-Witheford 2005: 152).

Another potentially valuable concept associated with autonomist Marxism is *precarité*, which unfortunately has been translated into the Engish neologism 'precarity', rather than the perfectly good existing word precariousness. Enda Brophy and Greig de Peuter (2007: 180) refer to precarity as 'a collectively created conceptual tool, the practical purpose of which is to aid in naming, understanding and ultimately transforming the conditions of labor under post-Fordism'. The term is used to refer to many different forms of 'flexible exploitation', including illegal, seasonal and temporary employment; homeworking, subcontracting and freelancing; and so-called self-employment (Neilsen and Rossiter 2005). In some formulations, the sense of the term extends beyond work to encompass other aspects of life including housing, debt and social relations. But some of its most vigorous applications have been to knowledge and creative work. The overall objective is undoubtedly a good one: to counter celebrations of knowledge work in contemporary capitalism, and to point to the increasing insecurity faced by many, in contrast with the social guarantees of the 'Fordist' era. Brophy and de Peuter's advocacy of the concept makes important points about contemporary labour, some of which are significant for the cultural industries. They claim that 'precarization' – another neologism – is not necessarily imposed from above but involves the *internalisation* of certain techniques and practices, and that the 'democratic-sounding discourses surrounding precarity are particularly insidious' (Brophy and de Peuter 2007: 183), pointing to the way that the term 'flexibility' connotes freedom, nomadism and lack of rigidity.

We are not convinced that the concept of precarity as such brings real added value as a conceptual tool rather than as essentially a synonym for the insecurity and exploitation recognised and analysed in other theoretical and activist traditions. What is more, like immaterial labour in the work of Hardt and Negri, the idea seems to be linked to accounts which distort and exaggerate the nature and extent of transformation in contemporary labour. However, Brophy and de Peuter are surely right to draw attention to the insidiousness of the connotations of flexibility surrounding these terms.

7.2 Emotional labour

The autonomist concept of affective labour seems to owe a great deal to the concept of emotional labour. This is defined in Arlie Hochschild's (1983) seminal discussion as 'the management of feeling to create a publicly observable facial and bodily display', sold for a wage. Such labour requires the worker 'to induce or suppress feeling in order to sustain the outward countenance that produces the proper state of mind in others' (both quotations from Hochschild 1983: 7).[2] Hochschild explored this kind of labour, prevalent in service occupations, using the case of flight attendants. As important as their manual skills, such as how they handled food trays, was their ability to handle emotions. In order for airline passengers to feel cared for and looked after, flight attendants had to disguise feelings of irritation and fatigue, and to make their work look effortless. The companies that employ such flight attendants laid claim not only to the physical effort of their workers but to their emotional actions as well. For Hochschild, a major problem with such labour was its personal cost or even damage to the worker. Emotional labour drew heavily on 'a source of self that we honor as deep and integral to our individuality' (1983: 7), risking a sense of alienation of the worker from an important aspect of her or his being. All this was intended to draw attention to problems in service work and mental labour, moving beyond the emphasis on the alienation of manual labour in the Marxist tradition. In terms of the framework for evaluating labour that we developed in Chapter 2, emotional labour draws attention to ways in which work can act as a threat to autonomy and positive self-realisation among workers.

Hochschild's ideas have aroused huge interest. Numerous later studies applied or tested the concept of emotional labour in a whole range of occupations, including nurses, barristers and call-centre workers.[3] More generally, Hochschild helped to spark an explosion of interest in the role of emotions in work organisations (e.g., Fineman 1993) and in the particular nature of interactive service work (Taylor et al. 2002). Because 'the range of emotion most often captured in research on emotional labor is stereotypically associated with femininity, emotional labor has typically been identified with historically female jobs' (Steinberg and Figart 1999: 10) and this has aroused particular interest in the concept from feminists (see, for example, Sharma and Black 2001 on beauty therapists, and Weeks 2007, discussed below). Perhaps inevitably, given this level of engagement, there have been numerous criticisms of Hochschild's approach. In particular, some have argued that Hochschild neglects the potential for workers to gain satisfaction from contact with customers and clients, and to feel genuine warmth, humour or compassion in dealing with others at work (see Korczynski 2002:77; Edwards

---

2 Many later uses of the term miss the fact that Hochschild distinguished this emotional labour, sold for a wage, from 'emotion work' and 'emotion management', both of which were terms she used to refer to the management of feeling to create a facial and bodily display, but in private settings.

3 See Steinberg and Figart (1999) and Bolton (2005: 45–65) for surveys of the research. Bolton even refers to an 'emotional labour bandwagon' (p. 53).

and Wajcman 2005: 35; Bolton 2005: 60–2).[4] Others have pointed to the way that the concept of emotional labour downplays the embodied presentational aspects of service work, and have advocated the concept of 'aesthetic labour' (Witz et al. 2003).

For now, though, our main concern is to compare emotional labour with the autonomist Marxist concept of affective labour. Both affect and emotion can be contrasted with the cognitive realm of knowing, perceiving and conceiving. 'Affect' potentially refers to a broader domain of such non-cognitive experiences, not just emotions, which are usually thought of as having objects (we are angry with someone, or angry about something). 'Affect' then can include feelings that are not necessarily emotional in this way, but are still non-cognitive, such as pleasure and pain. The concept of affect rather than emotion is therefore potentially useful. But it is hard to escape the sense that in many cases the preference for the use of the former over the latter is mostly motivated by a fear that the idea of emotion is somehow tainted by liberal humanist individualism.[5] As with the post-structuralist rejection of concepts such as autonomy and self-realisation, this is to throw the analytical baby out with the liberal humanist bathwater.

Explicit comparisons of affective and emotional labour are rare, but Kathi Weeks (2007) provides a useful one, and she also engages valuably with the ideas of C. Wright Mills (1951) whose writing on how white collar workers sold their 'personality' influenced Hochschild and provided a seminal account of the problems of twentieth-century work. Weeks sees Mills's interest in creativity and craftsmanship as foundations of meaningful work as a futile exercise in nostalgia. She finds Hochschild guilty of setting up a false evaluative contrast, finding in the private realm 'practices, subjectivities and relations that she suggests are not subject … to the same degree to the strictures of capitalist valorization' (Weeks 2007: 243). Hochschild then supposedly contradicts herself by recognising the gendered hierarchies of private relations. Both Mills and Hochschild are, Weeks finds, reliant on 'essentialist models of the self', in that they set up 'a certain model of the labouring self from which we are estranged to which we should be restored' (Weeks 2007: 244).

---

4 Brook (2009) defends Hochschild against Bolton and other critics, but he too recognises problems in Hochschild's thesis. It is, he says, 'over-simplistic in its dichotomizing of private and public sphere emotions; inadequately captures the complex and contradictory nature of emotion work; and over-focuses on individual experiences at the cost of workplace social relations' (Brook 2009: 533).

5 See Clough (2008) for example. Clough praises the 'affective turn' in social theory for moving beyond the excessive constructionism of deconstructionist-influenced approaches, and directing attention to the distinctive properties of bodies, and the embodied nature of human beings. But then she seems to object to analyses of affect that deal with subjectively felt states of emotion, because they 'return to the subject as the subject of emotion' (Clough 2008: 2). While we agree that a focus on emotions can risk methodological individualism, this does not have to be the case, and the 'affective turn' seems to run the greater danger of marginalising questions of subjective emotion in social theory and sociology.

While we too have reservations about the value of alienation as a critical concept (see Chapter 2), we do not agree that there is a problem of misplaced essentialism in Mills and Hochschild. Rather, Mills is suggesting that some sources of meaningfulness may exist in the exercise of skilful work; and Hochschild is suggesting that there may be areas of life that are more open to negotiation than others and that, with the many sensible qualifications she makes (see Hochschild 1983: 85), this may apply to private relations between human beings more than to workplaces. Hochschild may downplay, in her 1983 study, the way in which unpaid domestic and paid work are bound together in modern economies, but there are still differences between the relations between employers and employees, on the one hand, and private relations between lovers or families or friends, on the other; in our view, Weeks's argument implies that such differences are, in evaluative terms, non-existent or trivial.

The only *detailed* discussion of the autonomist concept of affective labour as opposed to Hochschild's more sociological notion of emotional labour that we have been able to find from within the autonomist Marxist tradition is a fine piece by Dowling (2007) on her own experiences of waitressing. Dowling shows convincingly that the two main claims that autonomists tend to make in relation to immaterial and affective labour – that they are 'beyond measure' (thereby undermining both mainstream economics and 'classical' Marxian political economy, because of their supposed reliance on notions of measurable value) and that they are the basis of 'elementary communism' – do not hold up when examined in the light of the *experience* of such affective work. However, why Dowling would therefore want to hold on to these autonomist conceptions of immaterial and affective labour in the light of her powerful critique of them is not made clear in her piece.

7.3 Media labour and symbolic power

Our discussion has recognised that autonomist concepts of immaterial labour, affective labour and precarity are evocative metaphors, but we have been explaining our doubts about whether they are theoretical-political constructs with real analytical force.

In what follows, we seek to engage with the complexity of actual networks of cultural production, against the bland generalisations of much creative industries policy (see Chapter 1) but also against autonomist Marxism's lack of empirical engagement with the specifics of those forms of labour that supposedly comprise its wide-ranging categories. We are aware that the goal of autonomist Marxism is not sociology, but analysis and intervention. The generalisations of Lazzarato, Hardt, Negri and so forth are often stimulating and there are limits to the value of close studies of particular working environments. But this chapter is not intended as an empiricist call for sociological studies to displace political speculation. Rather it is an attempt to counter the failure adequately to theorise culture and the media in theories of 'precarity' and 'immaterial labour' that put culture (and therefore the media) at the centre of social change. Good theory needs to be founded on careful definitions and on sensitivity to specifics, without falling into the empiricist trap of producing data for their own sake. Given that 'immaterial labour' is linked to the precariousness of cultural and informational work, and given that our interest here is in creative work in the cultural industries, then we need to recall our discussion of definitions in Part One, where we explained that the term 'culture' refers to primarily symbolic, expressive and informational production, and where we claimed that the main locus of artistic-creative work in modern societies is *the media*. The media industries are the most important disseminators of culture, when culture is understood as symbolic, expressive and informational communication. What is more, the media industries *are* the core creative or cultural industries in that they provide most of the employment and revenue that, by any reasonable analysis, fits with these more circumscribed definitions. To emphasise the point, the alternative to such definitions is to operate a definition of cultural and creative that includes so much activity as to render the terms effectively meaningless or at least incapable of dealing with specificity.

So, in this chapter, we break down the overly generalised debates about immaterial, precarious and affective labour by looking at artistic, creative work in the media – and in what is still the most important media (and therefore cultural) industry of all: television. This also involves, in contrast to Hardt and Negri's heady optimism about immaterial labour, incorporating into our analysis a conception of *symbolic power*. Underpinning our analysis is a view that the media involve a particular type of power-laden interaction, which John Thompson has called 'mediated quasi-interaction' (Thompson 1995: 82–7). This is a quite different kind of interaction from face-to-face interaction or mediated interaction such as a telephone call or a letter. Mediated quasi-interaction has a primarily monological rather than a dialogical character, and is oriented not towards specific others but to an indefinite range of potential recipients. Crucially it involves a fundamental asymmetry between producers and receivers. Whatever claims are made about the power of networked communication or the Internet to change this model to a more dialogical form of mediated quasi-interaction (see, for example, Benkler 2006) – and we think there is good reason to be sceptical about many of these claims – it is this form of monological, asymmetrical communication that still characterises the contemporary media. It follows then that cultural producers are, from one point of view, very powerful. They constitute a relatively small number of people who have the capacity to communicate to many others; in some cases, literally to millions of people. Combined with the prestige attached to artistry and knowledge, this gives creative workers influence, recognition and often prestige and glamour, at least relative to nearly all other workers getting similar wages. Even relatively unsuccessful creative workers confess to the appeal of this potential influence and recognition in interviews, though of course some disavow it. However, there is an important qualification to be made. Such power and prestige are of course distributed very unequally, both *between* different media organisations, and between different creative workers *within* the same media organisation.[6]

In what follows, then, we analyse how the power to provide exposure or not to individuals in the talent show genre in contemporary television (a feature that derives from the symbolic power of producers to make texts distributed to massive numbers of people) and disputes between commissioners and independent producers about how best to go about doing so (an organisational issue) are registered in the form of stress, anxiety and sometimes poor working relations among project teams of young television researchers (a matter of working conditions and experiences). Against Hardt and Negri's blithe assertions about cooperation in immaterial and affective labour, we discuss how additional pressures are borne by these workers because of the particularly strong need to maintain good working relations in short-term project work, a need generated by the importance of maintaining contacts in order to secure future employment. Our conclusions, based on participant observation in a medium-sized independent television production company in London in 2007, are not optimistic ones. While recognising the pleasures of creative work, we provide evidence of the real difficulties faced by young workers in modern creative labour markets. Ultimately, then, we support the view that creative work is 'precarious' – but we go beyond the generalisations involved in concepts such as immaterial labour to show the specific ways in which precariousness is registered and negotiated in the lives of young workers in one media industry, including their handling of 'emotional labour'. We also want to make clear at this point that working conditions at the production company that forms the basis of this case study are relatively good compared with many other areas of independent cultural production, and that the difficulties we report below are by no means particular to this organisation.

7.4 The talent show: budget, commissioners and independents

One reason to study talent shows is that they provide a particularly vivid example of the power of television to make the ordinary extraordinary. This has its magical dimensions – the transition from anonymity and marginality to wealth and fame can be extremely rapid. But behind this is a more mundane form of influence. In talent shows television producers have the power to decide which 'ordinary people' will gain television exposure and which ones will not. As we shall see, this is demanding work for junior employees working on such programmes.

---

6 This helps explain why Bourdieu's concept of the 'dominated fraction of the dominant class' (see, for example, Bourdieu 1996) is a suggestive way to describe media workers, but also why ultimately it is an unsatisfactory one: it underestimates the inequality within this fraction.

The talent show we studied, *Show Us Your Talent*, was broadcast by the BBC in mid-2007 and was produced by an independent television production company, which we are calling IPC TV.[7] The essence of the programme's format is as follows: amateur and semi-professional entertainers perform before a live studio audience. Each member of the audience can push a button when they no longer want to watch the act. When 50 per cent of the audience have pressed their buttons, a klaxon ends the performance. If anyone lasts three minutes, they go through to a weekly final ('heats' take place from Monday to Thursday). Winners of the weekly finals go through to a live 'grand final' at the end of the run.

According to Marcus, the IPC TV executive producer who devised the format, the main feature distinguishing *Show Us Your Talent* from the talent shows that have dominated UK television prime-time ratings in the noughties was that it had a 'warmer', more 'democratic' feel:

> the key thing for us always was to try and create a show with warmth, because that 'gong' format can seem quite cruel, and we didn't want that to be the case at all. We wanted the premise of our show to be anyone can come on.
>
> (Interview 55)

This meant that no judges dispensed cruel put-downs, and there were no tortuously delayed revelations of phone-in votes deciding who would stay and who would go. Similarly, there was a much wider range of acts than the singing and dancing that dominated the talent show genre as a whole. Jugglers, magicians and novelty acts featured alongside boy tenors, dance troupes and singer-songwriters. In spite of the 'warmer' tone, and the democratic feel, not just anyone could get on *Show Us Your Talent*. Junior workers must select from a very wide range of people – many of whom would be extremely disappointed not to be chosen.

Show Us Your Talent was commissioned and scheduled as a 'daytime' rather than as a 'prime-time' programme and therefore operated on a lower budget, reflecting the lower audiences that daytime programmes gain. Nevertheless, the programme was shown in the early evening from 6.30 to 7 p.m. (The first series was scheduled at the earlier time of 4.45–5.30 p.m.; our fieldwork was conducted on the second series.) This made it officially daytime but there was a strong stress on achieving a prime-time feel, partly because of its proximity to prime-time viewing, but also because, as Dennis, a company director, suggested, IPC TV wanted to show themselves to be potentially

---

7 The names of the television programme, the company and all individuals concerned have been changed to protect anonymity. We are very grateful to the company for the chance to carry out participant observation fieldwork. The participant observation was carried out by Sarah Baker from February to June 2007.

capable of making a prime-time entertainment show in this genre – namely a family "shiny floor" show that could be scheduled on a Saturday night (Interview 56). This entailed particular pressures on the production team in terms of 'upping the production value' – in effect, making the programme look like it was prime-time but on a daytime budget. Various elements were involved: increasing the size of the studio audience; changing the set design to make it look more like a dance club, with an evening feel; and requesting that the studio audience and contributors dress accordingly. This desire to appear more prime-time also brought with it the pressure to find acts of a higher quality than had appeared on the first series whilst also ensuring these acts represented a variety of genres and, in line with BBC guidelines, maintained a good gender, age, ethnic and social mix. All these factors meant greater demands on junior workers. We shall see in due course how these pressures were registered, alongside pressures that derived from the nature of the talent show itself, oriented as it was to the production of fame. First though, we briefly discuss a further set of pressures, involving the different visions of the programme on the part of the two main organisations involved in its making: the commissioning 'network' (the BBC) and the production company (IPC TV).

For a long time the 'in-house' departments of the two great British television networks, the BBC and ITV (Independent Television) monopolised the entertainment genre on British television. But one of the great transformations of European television since the 1980s has been the rise of independent production companies and in the talent show genre no less than in others, such as drama and documentary, indies have become increasingly important.[8] In parallel, a considerable commissioning apparatus has developed in British television, one which often involves a tug-of-war relationship between production teams and commissioning editors over who has creative control in the production process (see also Born 2004). Indies rely on commissioners for the survival of their businesses. Like many people in dependent relationships, indie executives express ambivalence about the object of their dependence. They express strong feelings of admiration and respect about particular editors, and deep mistrust about commissioners in general. Malcolm, an executive producer from another TV indie (not IPC TV), for example, told us that commissioning editors 'are by and large more interested in power, deep down, than they are interested in programmes' (Interview 37).

Show Us Your Talent had already run for one season in the autumn of 2006 and performed fairly well in terms of audience ratings for the BBC. How does such a show fit in with the BBC's public service ethos? Iris, the

---

8 The most notable entertainment indies are SyCo (the company partly owned by the international celebrity talent show judge and former music industry executive Simon Cowell), TalkbackThames, Celador and Gallowgate. The overall turnover of TalkbackThames in 2006 was £146m (*Broadcast*, 9 March 2007) compared to IPC TV's £19.7m.

show's Commissioning Editor, explained that *Show Us Your Talent* fitted with the Corporation's intention 'to offer a huge variety of programming' (Interview 57), in order to compete with commercial channels in the multi-channel era. The public service justification was the idea of supporting and developing talent – enabled by a group of three celebrity experts, or mentors, who ran workshops at the auditions and with the grand finalists and who also dispensed advice to chosen performers during each episode. Iris described this as 'trying to give something back'. The re-commissioning of the second series was linked to 'Think Big', a BBC initiative to fund what Iris described as 'ideas that are multi-platform and also appeal to a younger audience' enabling the programme to become 'more interactive'. By incorporating other BBC programmes (notably the BBC's long-running flagship children's programme *Blue Peter*), other arms of the BBC (BBC New Talent), and a web-based element to the competition, *Show Us Your Talent* could become a 'bigger concept as a whole' for the BBC (Iris, Interview 57). In practice, however, being a 'bigger project' brought with it additional editorial constraints on IPC TV as it involved working not only to the BBC commissioning remit but also juggling the additional agendas of these other arms and programmes of the BBC. Added to this, IPC TV were very keen to make *Show Us Your Talent* into a longer-running series, and to format it. Again, as we shall see, this only added greater stress to the work of the production team.

Further pressures came from the production team's tenuous control of editorial matters in the face of the commissioner's power. As Martha, a Commissioning Editor from another broadcaster, told us, power is 'something that commissioning editors take for granted' (Interview 6). An example of this came the day before filming was to begin on *Show Us Your Talent* when the production team received a phone call from Harry, the Series Producer, to say that Iris had decided that, although she had previously signed off all the shows as having a satisfactory balance of contributors, she now thought that the first week needed 'more variety' (field notes, 11 April 2007). This created panic amongst the team and incited disgruntled comments questioning how the BBC could make such a decision only 24 hours before the first show was to be recorded. Two assistant producers and one researcher told us independently that commissioning editors very often do this just before filming is to begin.

Iris later described her role in the casting process of *Show Us Your Talent* as raising issues that the production company had 'probably not thought about'. She portrayed a democratic relationship in which both parties tended to agree on casting choices and where 'we just sit down and we just all then sign off together'. Iris acknowledged that:

> There will be some points when the execs say 'actually, I really think this person should go in that show', and I might disagree, but then we might go 'actually, let's work it out', 'no, we're right'. To be honest we tended to agree.
>
> (Interview 57)

Yet on this occasion, despite having produced entertainment programmes before she became a commissioner, Iris's actions showed little sense of the stress engendered amongst the production team when last-minute alterations were requested for the next day's work.

The tensions here derived from the balancing act that is involved in delivering a show to the BBC remit and at the same time producing a show that at least approximates to what the production team wants to make. Series producer Harry told us how he saw the relationship with the BBC:

> You are working with Execs or Heads of Entertainment, and with the BBC remit of what they want for that. So there are always people around who are steering you to different directions. … Obviously you take into consideration other people's point of views along the way but at the same time also have a clear vision of what you want when you first start because I think that's when programmes get a bit muddy.
>
> (Interview 52)

As the series producer, Harry was responsible for developing his vision with the production team. But sometimes this vision was quite different from that required by the BBC, and this could lead to real confusion amongst junior staff. ('I don't even know what this show is about anymore', as assistant producer Ruth put it.) This balancing act has consequences in terms of the final product, and also in terms of the stress and anxiety experienced by individual team members, as we shall now show.

7.5 Emotional labour and the anxieties of star-making

How were the textual and organisational conditions discussed above registered in the experiences of television workers? The producers of television talent shows are involved in the production of success and failure. In sifting through numerous applications the researchers on *Show Us Your Talent* had to use their judgement to decide which acts were immediately discarded in the 'no' boxes and which acts looked interesting enough to be called for an audition. During and after the auditions the casting team then had the power to decide which of the acts would be provided with the opportunity to perform for up to three minutes on television and which ones would not. But the power of star-making brought with it particular responsibilities and pressures for the production team. In particular, it involved a form of the emotional labour we discussed in Section 7.2 above. Laura Grindstaff (2002) has applied this concept to the labour of workers on confessional talk shows in their effort to elicit appropriate and sometimes powerful emotional responses from ordinary guests. Such responses provide the talk show's all-important 'money shot', a term Grindstaff of course borrows from the importance in pornography of the filmed male climax: the display of strong emotion, such as weeping or anger, on screen. Managing the emotional responses of others is a key task of the confessional talk show producer (see Grindstaff 2002: 129–41). It is also integral to the production of talent shows. Television workers are instructed by the series producer to elicit the strongest possible versions of the emotions that the contestant is feeling. This applies not only to the performance itself but also to the contributor's walk on to the stage (trepidation, nervousness, excitement) and the post-performance chat in the green room (joy, disappointment, frustration, anger).

The talent show's potential for taking an ordinary person and making them a star adds to the emotional labour of the TV talent show producer. While there is potential for celebrity to come to the 'ordinary' talk show guest those programmes offer a very different promise of fame to that provided by talent shows. Shows such as the *Idol* franchise, *The X Factor* and *Britain* or *America* or *Wherever's Got Talent* present contestants with an opportunity to establish a career in their chosen field of performance. There is a considerable amount to be gained – and lost – in terms of establishing a career in entertainment. Contributors therefore have a great deal invested in doing well on these programmes. Even on a daytime show like *Show Us Your Talent* in which prizes are no more than £1,000 in value, television workers were aware that the show could make a huge difference to the lives of those participating.

In their phone and email correspondence with contributors these pressures were dealt with by the *Show Us Your Talent* production team largely by maintaining a degree of emotional distance. Throughout the production cycle the researchers received correspondence from rejected applicants and acts that failed to make it beyond the auditions. Rejected parties were often upset and sometimes angry. Baker for example received a phone call from one mother who held her personally responsible for her child not being invited to audition. When Baker asked the assistant producers on *Show Us Your Talent* how they dealt with these calls and emails, Dora commented 'we don't have to give reasons for our selection process'; and Ruth said 'it's the producer's prerogative to change their mind about casting'. By tying their responses to production conventions, workers were able to maintain an emotional distance whilst simultaneously managing the caller's emotional response to the situation. But when the contributors – or their parents – highlighted the producer's power of star-making in their accusations, they challenged this distancing. During a crisis at the studio when a scheduled contributor could not make it to the recording due to missing a flight the production team called a number of standby acts to check their availability for that day's show. Such a call obviously raised the hopes of the performers contacted. Despite having been previously rejected they were, quite unexpectedly, told they might be appearing on the show. However, for all but one of the standbys a second call was later received to say they would not be needed after all. In a moment of crisis the only objective of the production team was to find a contributor who could get to the studio in very little time with an act that complemented the other four. It was later that the junior workers received the emails from parents accusing them of 'shattering children's dreams' (field notes, 2 May 2007).

Dealing with the contributors who have been cast to appear on talent shows presents other emotional challenges. The flight attendants of Hochschild's (1983) study suppressed their negative feelings towards difficult passengers by generating an atmosphere filled with care and concern. Television producers deal similarly with difficult contributors. As Grindstaff (2002: 132) says of daytime talk shows, the regulation of guests' emotional performance is achieved through the production staff managing their own emotions by 'either pretending to care about guests or trying not to care too much'. In talent shows it is sometimes very hard for a junior worker not to care too much. Distance is difficult to achieve when they feel an investment in a performer after having discovered them in the applications or through targeting, after encouraging them in the auditions, championing them in the casting process, producing them at the studio and cheering for them during their performance on stage. Many hours are invested by the assistant producers, and particularly the researchers, on the acts which have been cast in the episodes for which they have responsibility. With grand final contributors for example the researchers spent approximately five full days of close contact with them in the auditions, at the studio, at the grand final workshop, and filming VT footage with them at the contributors' homes and workplaces with additional hours of phone and email contact over a period of three months. When the performers then failed either to reach three minutes, or to make it through to the weekly final or live grand final, the struggle to manage emotion became extremely difficult for the assistant producers involved in such work. Take for example a singer who, as the best runner-up in a weekly final, had the opportunity to perform for a third time in the show's penultimate episode. Again, she failed to reach three minutes and was bitterly disappointed. After filming she was weeping in the main studio corridor. In the production room one assistant producer, Danny, who was needed in a room off that corridor said to the team 'I can't walk past her, I'll have to go the long way around because I was her closest friend on the show and feel like I've let her down' (field notes, 25 April 2007). Danny felt something like a sense of personal responsibility for the contributor's failure to reach the live grand final. Similarly a researcher, Brady, was visibly shaken, on the verge of tears and said he was 'upset and angry' when a performer he had championed failed to reach three minutes in a weekly final. Like Hochschild's airline crew and Grindstaff's talk show producers, workers 'find themselves performing emotional labor while simultaneously struggling to distance themselves from its emotional effects, to make it just another aspect of the job' (Grindstaff 2002: 133). This is especially the case when a producer has some sense of the possibility that a performer's appearance on the show perhaps may be their last chance of making it in a tough industry – particularly the musicians and singers.

Other variants of emotional labour abounded. Although it did not have the status of prime-time talent shows such as *The X Factor* or *Britain's Got Talent*, *Show Us Your Talent* was still seen by some contributors as 'the chance of a lifetime'. With so much at stake contributors were often keen to be portrayed in ways which were not in line with the production team's editorial vision. Contributors' grievances at the studio about their (usually impending) performance were frequently met with (sometimes feigned) concern by production staff in their effort to diffuse a difficult situation and enable the production to continue. When contributors were upset or angry about proceedings they often directed these feelings at the runners and researchers – the junior workers with whom they had the most contact – even though the aspects of the production they were unhappy with was usually a result of decisions made further up the production hierarchy. In most cases a compromise could be agreed upon by both parties but in some instances this did not come about easily. One example of this from *Show Us Your Talent* involved the mother of a child contributor whose demands put such strain on the production team that some of the workers stopped caring, or even feigning to care, altogether. Demands were being made about song choice and costume and whilst they were perhaps reasonable demands for a mother to be making they were unfortunately done in a way that created a negative response in the production team leading to exclamations of 'I want her off'. This in turn led to negative production values where this contributor was concerned – in other words the team were no longer trying to make this contributor a 'star', not caring that the performer looked uncomfortable in the outfit the team had selected for her to wear. Assistant producer Ruth, when reflecting after the filming of the episode on contributors who try and override the production team's editorial decisions, said 'if people have an attitude I don't think they should be given a platform – that mother took the piss' (field notes, 21 April 2007).

Such responses are both an understandable reaction to pressure and at the same time a severing of emotional connection. As Hochschild (1983: 21) observed many years ago, the management of emotions involved in emotional labour 'affects the degree to which we listen to feeling and sometimes our very capacity to feel'. Breaking the emotional rules of production – after all, in the above example there was very little of the 'warmth' sought by the executive producer who developed the format – had a negative impact on the contributor, the programme and on the workers themselves. One worker said of the incident 'this is the lowest point of my career'.

7.6 Pleasure and sociality on the production team

Up to now, we have concentrated on some of the most difficult aspects of working on *Show Us Your Talent*. We have emphasised how junior workers have to bear the burden of the emotional labour necessary to sustain a television programme of this kind. We have also discussed how the short-term project nature of the work increases the pressure on these junior workers. All this suggests that this particular type of creative labour is not good work. There are real limits on workplace and creative autonomy, and, against the claims of autonomist Marxists, it appears that substantial conflict can be generated among co-workers. The short-term nature of the work makes the prospect of a rewarding career in television a distant prospect for most though one to which many workers cling. Researcher Edward, for example, spoke of his longer-term aspirations to develop a strong researcher profile which would then put him in good stead to be given a (relatively secure) Assistant Producer or Producer role in the Children's department of the BBC in Manchester (field notes, 20 June 2007). But for assistant producer Danny the end of the contract with IPC TV was followed by two months of no television contracts leading him to take on temp work as a receptionist. Dora, another of the *Show Us Your Talent* assistant producers, told Harry, the series producer, that Danny was 'thinking about chucking in television because he can't get a job' (field notes, 20 June 2007). Such disillusionment about the nature of television contracts led Dora to leave television shortly after finishing with *Show Us Your Talent*, taking on a permanent position with a small interactive gaming company for which she would be producing an interactive game show that would be screened on pods in pubs. She told us that with a permanent position and a regular income she could finally consider getting a mortgage (field notes, 22 June 2007). Dora later returned to working in the television industry as an associate producer for a quiz show and at the time of writing Danny had secured a permanent position as a production manager for an independent production company specialising in live music. As Danny once passionately said in response to the series producer's comments to Baker that 'there's no stability in television, stick with a proper job': 'people who work in television are there because they love it and while short contracts are a pain you wouldn't be in TV if you didn't have a passion for it' (field notes, 28 March 2007).

Here we need to return to some of the criticisms of Hochschild's seminal work that we mentioned in Section 7.2, and indeed of work on emotions and feelings in work organisations. Sharon Bolton (2005: 2) has complained of a neglect of contradiction in many accounts of organisational life, and a one-dimensional picture of normative control. 'One begins to ask', she says, 'where is the laughter, where is the compassion, where is the day-to-day interaction?' Discussing Hochschild specifically, Bolton questions the degree to which normative control strategies really succeed in co-opting workers. The concept of emotional labour 'undervalues the vitality and independence of outlook that participants bring to organisations' (Bolton 2005: 62), including their ability to resist management imperatives. This echoes the notion of immaterial and affective labour celebrated by the autonomist Marxists, and their hopes in the 'possibilities of resistance' (Weeks 2007: 237) that such work might enable. In this section, we discuss more positive dimensions to work at IPC TV, as part of a more balanced assessment of the possibilities of good work in television.

There is a great deal of camaraderie and fun involved in working together on a television show – pub lunches, shared jokes, team drinks after work, dancing in Soho bars, discussing the sexual merits of good-looking contributors. These very sociable, friendly aspects of television production (which Baker herself experienced in her role as participant observer) are undoubtedly important; they contribute to an experience of the production process as highly collaborative and exhilarating in its intensity. The independent production company strove to create a benign environment in which to carry out such work, through the open-plan design of the production office, a subsidised canteen to encourage staff interaction over lunch and scheduled company social events such as quiz nights (c.f. Ross 2003 on attempts by IT companies to create a 'humane workplace'). In many respects, these efforts bore fruit. Researchers had a friendly working relationship, eating lunch together on a daily basis in the staff canteen, and providing an atmosphere in which new workers, regularly joining the company because of its high use of short-term project work, could be made to feel comfortable. Conversations were sometimes work-related, but often mundane, trivial, easy-going, friendly. Workers regularly shared 'chocolate runs'. One person bought chocolate from the corner store, another made the tea.

A similar pattern could be observed with the *Show Us Your Talent* team. Danny and Alice explained to Baker how during the first series the team would spend many lunches together in the garden of a local pub watching the fish in the pond.[9] These lunches continued regularly during the production of series two. As well as lunches and regular quiz nights for the company as a whole, there were numerous social occasions for the *Show Us Your Talent* team, including a drinks night at a pub a few miles from the IPC TV office. Series producer Harry gave researcher Brady the task of organising the evening. Members of the team would also socialise together in smaller groups with Danny and Alice going to gigs and Edward and Brady frequenting West End gay bars. The social finale of the production, the wrap party, was described by assistant producer Ruth as 'always long and fun-filled – a bodily release from the pressures of the studio' (field notes, 25 April 2007). These social events were enjoyed, but their significance was limited by the short-term nature of the contract work, as the following extract from Baker's field notes suggests.

> I ask Evelyn, in factual development, if she will be attending the company quiz night on Shrove Tuesday. She responds that she might not be with the company by then as her contract runs out 'a week Monday'. But she adds 'I'll go if I'm here. They're usually quite fun. It's quite social here with summer parties and things'. On the walls of the

---

9 However, such autonomy was monitored and was vulnerable to being revoked at times of deadline pressure. 'Remember last series when we started getting emails saying we can't go out to lunch?' asked one colleague of another. Workers were asked to eat in and preferably at their desks (field notes, 13 February 2007).

canteen there are photos from a previous company event – the masked party.

(field notes, 9 February 2007)

The fragility of the situation is also highlighted by comments made by Shanene, the production secretary, who, two and a half weeks after the live grand final, was the only member of the production team to still have a contract with IPC TV as she finalised the production paperwork. She said how lonely it was with everyone gone, looking around the much emptier office to make her point, and that she now ate lunch alone at her desk (field notes, 10 July 2007).

Genuine friendships can and did develop in this working environment, and these friendships persisted between projects. The relationship between Harry, the series producer, and researcher Edward is a case in point. They were already well acquainted before working on *Show Us Your Talent* through mutual contacts but the trust that then developed between them eventually led Harry to make sure Edward was hired as a researcher on a later show he produced. Edward described Harry as having 'become like a mentor' (field notes, 11 May 2007), providing him with advice on how to further his career. On the final day of production, for example, Edward raised with Harry over after-show drinks the issue of his future employment. He had been offered three researcher positions: one would involve moving to Glasgow, another was a two-week contract casting contestants for a high rating reality TV show, and also a six-week contract for a talent show. The two latter contracts interested him more and he expressed a desire to take on both but their timeframes overlapped. Harry told Edward that the reality TV show would look great on his CV and would increase his 'hireability' in future. Indeed Harry had told Baker on an earlier occasion that because Edward was such a good worker he would be bound to impress the right people and have that contract extended (field notes, 20 June 2007). But Edward argued that the talent show would hire him as a 'shooting researcher' meaning that he would have an opportunity to 'strengthen my weaknesses' – camera work – 'and not many people give someone the opportunity to do that'. He wondered aloud if he could take the talent show job but then take a week off during that contract to do the casting researcher job on the reality TV show. Harry thought this was a good idea and suggested Edward correspond with the production manager by email 'because too many people do it over the phone and get screwed over' (field notes, 22 June 2007). This reflects the positive side of affective labour, as outlined by some autonomists.

7.7 Affective labour and immanent cooperation?

We saw earlier that a key part of Hardt and Negri's analysis of work is that cooperation is immanent to immaterial labour, especially its affective labour variant. They make the important political claim that 'immaterial labour thus seems to provide the potential for a kind of spontaneous and elementary communism' (Hardt and Negri 2000: 294). Given the pressures and pleasures outlined above, how might we assess working relations among junior workers at IPC TV?

In a highly competitive and precarious industry, and with tight production schedules producing high levels of stress and anxiety, it was very difficult to maintain good working relations. Kris, one of the researchers on *Show Us Your Talent*, told us that there comes a point in every production 'where everyone hates each other' (field notes, 19 March 2007). Of course, difficult working relations are a problem in many workplaces. However, in television, such teamwork may be particularly important – not only because the final product will be shown to millions of people, but also because working well together on short-term projects is important in the longer term for developing contacts and a reputation that will lead to further contracts. As assistant producer Danny told us, 'you get jobs on the basis of who you have worked with before' (field notes, 13 February 2007). Developing contacts and building a reputation does not result simply from being a member of a project team but by being seen to do 'good work' and if not actually liked by colleagues, at least respected by them. As recommendations for work often come by way of friends and colleagues, good working relations play an important role in television careers. This means that there were further emotional implications in television work, besides those involved in handling the emotions of contributors and their families – namely the suppression of anger and frustration in the name of good working relations.

At times, the strain of such suppression became too much for junior workers. One researcher, Alice, had strong feelings concerning the allocation of members of the project team to positions within it. Back in the production company office following a five-day auditioning process, Alice suggested to Baker that it would be good to take a walk outside to 'get some fresh air' but once outside and away from the rest of the team revealed 'it's time to offload' (field notes, 19 March 2007). Alice believed the series producer was 'favouring certain members of the team' and in particular a researcher who was put on the casting team (so elevated to a position of power relative to the tasks of the other researchers) and who already knew the series producer through a joint acquaintance. They have a 'history', she said. Alice shrugged off their closeness saying it was 'fine' (an attempt perhaps momentarily to deny her own feelings of frustration for the sake of the team) but that she thought there should have been a second assistant producer on the casting team, not a more junior researcher. Alice compared how hard it was being a researcher on the 'frontline' at the auditions managing the disgruntled and tired contributors as opposed to being a member of the casting team which, she argued, spent 'five days sitting on their arses being fed biscuits' – being fed biscuits by the other researchers. She said that being put on the casting team had caused this other researcher to become 'patronising'.

It is hard work to contain such feelings of envy and resentment; not to betray one's emotional responses to workplace situations in one's outward countenance. In the days that followed this conversation Alice's unhappiness was noticed by the rest of the team. On a number of occasions the series producer asked others on the team if they knew what was troubling Alice. He noted that 'she doesn't seem her usual cheery self this week, isn't responsive and looks like she's about to cry' (field notes, 21 March 2007). Reflecting on the situation another researcher, Edward, said that 'if someone is overly bubbly for much of the time it becomes immediately obvious when they are down'. Edward is commenting here on the difficulties of managing emotions in a very sociable working environment and one that carries the responsibility of star-making. Significantly, Alice was expressing anxieties that were heightened during the period of production where the contributors were being auditioned and cast – the time where decisions were being made about who gets to appear on television and who does not.

Edward also struggled with managing emotions when dealing with other members of the production team, particularly where assistant producer Danny was concerned. Once contributors had been cast and allotted to an episode the Series Producer paired each Assistant Producer with a Researcher giving them the responsibility for producing individual episodes. In the days leading up to the recording of the show Edward didn't feel that Danny, the Assistant Producer he had been assigned to, was working productively. He suspected that Danny was spending much of the day on the social networking site MySpace instead of focusing on the production. Edward told Baker that being paired with such a 'useless' Assistant Producer was 'embarrassing' (field notes, 11 April 2007). He was concerned they would arrive at the team briefing on the morning of their first episode and Danny 'won't have done anything' (field notes, 12 April 2007).

On the first day of recording Edward took Baker aside to say it would be a miracle if he got to the end of the following day without 'yelling at' Danny (field notes, 12 April 2007). When Danny forgot to take the production mobile phone home at the end of the day Edward became even more annoyed. This meant Edward would have to make the early morning calls to contributors to check they were on their way to the studio – a task he believed was the responsibility of the Assistant Producer. Edward felt it to be an insult that Danny held a more senior position than he did. He also wondered if Danny was at all embarrassed that a researcher had been put on the casting team instead of them. After a day of more ineptitude at the studio, Edward took Baker aside to say 'I officially hate Danny' (field notes, 14 April 2007). He wondered if he should 'have a word' to the series producer about Danny's work (field notes, 14 April 2007).

Edward's concern was that the Assistant Producer's ineptitude would reflect badly on him. While it is difficult for workers in any job to be paired with colleagues who they feel to be less than competent, there is particular stress and anxiety for these television workers deriving from the weight placed on 'reputation and familiarity' (Ursell 2000: 811) in the television industry. In television and film reputations are 'painstakingly built' yet easily damaged by '[p]oor performance' (Jones 1996: 65) and so need to be safeguarded for the sake of future contracts. There is a general belief in film and television that 'you're only as good as your last job' (Blair 2001; Jones 1996) and it is perhaps because of the centrality of reputation in the industry that there are such high levels of stress and anxiety in the team. This centrality of reputation in part derives from the features of cultural and media production noted earlier – the very public nature of the products, transmitted or circulated to audiences of at least hundreds and sometimes (as with *Show Us Your Talent*) millions.

The pressure to deliver work that will help build one's reputation has a strong impact on the individual's ability to carry out emotional labour. Yet building one's reputation hinges upon the successful management of emotions. Emotional labour is also involved in developing working relations with team members that will lead to those very important enduring contacts – contacts that lead to further contracts. The cooperation which Hardt and Negri see as 'immanent' to immaterial – especially affective – labour is something which is extremely challenging to achieve in the contemporary television environment.

7.8 Conclusions

Our findings here support those autonomists and critical sociologists who find evidence of precariousness and insecurity in modern creative work. However, we have also been wary of some of the concepts developed and articulated by the autonomist Marxist tradition. In particular, like some of the political economy analysis we discussed in Chapter 3, the generality of their concepts fails to capture the specifically symbolic nature of cultural products, or the fact that the core institutions of symbolic production in modern societies are the media, with their own distinctive power dynamics. We have sought to draw attention to important issues regarding the specific nature of the end product of the cultural industries, and how this is articulated with the particular forms of precariousness and insecurity faced by creative workers in a particular industry (television) and genre (the talent show). We have also, though, drawn attention to some of the pleasures and bonds created in creative labour, lending some support to autonomist assertions.

We began from the fact that it is the job of television workers to produce television programmes of specific kinds. One of the reasons that a programme like *Show Us Your Talent* is interesting is that it involves the power to change people's lives – choices are made about who gets to appear on TV and who does not. This is a particularly strong example of the symbolic power accorded to media producers in modern societies. We went on to discuss how this symbolic power is unevenly distributed, residing mainly in the commissioning organisation (here, the BBC) and the independent production company

(IPC TV) – creating tensions between the two. We then showed how these issues were manifested in the lives of junior workers further down the production hierarchy, exacerbated by demands to produce a show with prime-time aspirations on a daytime budget. Such pressures add to the already considerable responsibilities involved in producing goods which are then released to such a wide public – transmitted to nearly two million people in the case of the second series. This means that junior workers have to deal with people who, even in a relatively low-budget, low-audience talent show such as *Show Us Your Talent*, have a huge amount at stake in appearing on, and succeeding on, such shows. The responsibility of star-making gets passed on to workers down the chain. The working relations produced were felt particularly keenly by workers who, if they were to stay in the UK television industry, needed to remain on good terms with their colleagues. In all this, we found Hochschild's concept of emotional labour more compelling and useful than the autonomist concepts of immaterial labour and affective labour. Like Ross (2003: 32) and Grindstaff (2002: 38–9, 244–6) we see this concept as potentially an important one for understanding the socio-psychological dynamics of creative work valuably opened up for consideration by themselves and other writers such as McRobbie and Ursell. All this is a contribution to our larger project of understanding the possibilities of good work in the cultural industries, including the possibility for projects of meaningful (rather than ideological) self-realisation. This chapter investigated in greater detail the insecurity and anxiety outlined in Chapter 5. Our participant observation found levels of anxiety and conflict that were likely to be highly disruptive to people's sense of personal reward and life-progress.

8 Creative products, good and bad

8.1 Questions of quality

Marx's concept of alienation draws attention to a crucial ethical problem – the majority of people may not greatly care about what they produce. '[T]he worker', as Marx (1959/1844) puts it, 'is related to the product of labour as to an alien object.' However, creative artistic production is often assumed to lack this alienation, and some have even claimed that 'Marx's vision of the truly human society under Communism … is the vision of a society of artists, engaged in creative production' (Kamenka 1972: 110). Ideally at least, artists work for internal rather than external rewards, even 'for the sake of the activity itself' (Kamenka 1972: 110) and the same is sometimes said of scientists and others who ideally pursue 'disinterested enquiry' (Kamenka 1972: 111). For the critics we discussed in Chapter 3, especially those associated with cultural studies, these facets of creative labour only end up leading to self-exploitation on the part of creative workers.

This suggests that the question of the relationships of creative workers to their products has considerable political significance in the present conjuncture. In this chapter, we begin to focus on how the workers we interviewed talk about the cultural products they help to make and disseminate; the next chapter extends this analysis by paying particular attention to the closely related issue of audiences. As in all our previous chapters, our primary emphasis is on worker experience and subjectivity. But here, more than in previous chapters, we also engage with the specific nature of the products of the cultural industries, as clarified in Chapter 3: symbolic, aesthetic, expressive and informational. This is to shift attention to those aspects of good work that, in the model we presented in Chapter 2 (Table 2.1), concern product rather than process. Our assumption is that most workers, given the choice, prefer to make high-quality rather than low-quality products, and products that contribute to the well-being of others rather than fail to do so.

We begin by examining how workers discussed the pleasures, rewards and satisfactions involved in making good products (Section 8.2). The next section then analyses some of the ways in which workers conceived of high quality (8.3). These conceptions include not only well-crafted products, but also work that has a powerful social and cultural impact, and that contributes to the common good. Just as high-quality work can be satisfying and rewarding to workers, involvement in mediocre products can be frustrating and disappointing (8.4). And it is as important to understand what constitutes poor quality as what constitutes outstanding products (8.5). Analysing these experiences and interpretations of good work gives us insight not only into processes of production in the cultural industries, but also the relationship of processes to products. Creative workers tend to care greatly about their products and so without an understanding of good and bad work in the sense of good and bad products, we are unlikely to understand creative labour. But there are exceptions – at times the nature of the product seems almost incidental to the work. Here we might be witnessing something close to what Marx described as alienation.

8.2 Pleasures and satisfactions of making good cultural products

We asked nearly all the workers we interviewed about work they had done of which they were proud. This was our way of eliciting reflection on the emotions involved when a mix of conditions, talents and luck mean that creative workers are involved in what they feel to be good products. We concentrate initially on four examples, across the industries we studied.

The first example comes from Simon, an experienced camera operator, who told us that work he could be proud of involved 'doing really good camerawork that really expresses the situation and expresses it really honestly'. And, although our question had been about 'pride', he immediately reflected on a different element of the experience: 'That is so satisfying.' Among a number of examples, he talked about a documentary he had helped make about air traffic controllers at New York's John F. Kennedy Airport. Filming was taking place in the air traffic control tower, and one of the controllers there was 'quite a plane spotter, and he quite often went out on the runway anyway, so I said "why don't we do some stuff out of the tower?"' Simon's instinct was to get closer to the planes. Although the sense of planes being 'dots on the screen' was 'part of the story' Simon thought it would be a good idea to get closer to these 'great big lumbering beasts' and to 'actually get down on the runway with this guy because he was a fantastic talker'. Simon told us what then happened:

> We got down there and then this amazing fog came in and it was one of the most extraordinary sequences ever and the guy was amazing. I thought 'that's fantastic', a plane was coming through the mist and taking off when it was almost not supposed to be, and you kept seeing great big jumbos lumbering by about 30, 40 feet away. We were really close, and with this guy, these big, big planes lumbering by, and his dialogue, it was just amazing. I thought 'we've really got this right. We're on a winning streak here. Because we've persevered and because we've tried

so hard and because we cared so much, we're now reaping the rewards and our luck is in'. Just after this happened, there was a cloudburst and it was all [over] in a few hours, and the next thing the planes started taking off again and going up into the sky because the mist eventually cleared with this rainstorm, and I was getting these amazing things called vortices, which is where you get these amazing capes of mist and things surrounding the planes. Although that's been filmed before by people, even the air traffic control people said those shots were really amazing. The planes were taking off with these great capes on them and you could just see the wind flow, like little wind tunnels. We went back to the hotel and we looked at some of it on the monitor and we were just so happy. We thought 'yeah, we really did it; today we really did it. If we don't live another day' ... and we got there, for once we got it right ... Just to occasionally get it really right and to really hit the nail on the head and actually just express something perfectly so you can walk down the street on air and think 'I got that right' ... There's a lot that goes into that to get to that situation, but if you do get there, boy, it's satisfying.

(Interview 29)

There is delight here not only in capturing the planes close up, a matter of unusual access, but also pride in having captured on camera striking and unusual footage. Simon quietly includes reference to the admiration and recognition of the air traffic controllers – perhaps suggesting a proxy for the audience that might eventually see the film – and that of his collaborating peers. Although of course his story involves an element of self-aggrandisement, it also conveys the shared, cooperative pleasures possible when good creative work is achieved.

Simon's story is an almost ecstatic case of involvement in high-quality creative work. Our second example introduces the ambivalence that is generally more associated with such success. A rock musician, Robert, told us that 'the greatest thing' is

when you've written a song and you love it so much, you just can't wait to get into the studio the next day and hear it. Our studio is not very far, it's attached to the house. And you think of any excuse to listen to it again. And that's when I know that I've done something that I think is good.

(Interview 3)

But then Robert immediately followed this by telling us how 'then you send your record to fifty record labels and they all say "no", and then your pride takes a bit of a battering. You still know it's good. But you can't be proud of it, I don't think'. Yet there was a further twist (to the laughter of those in the room with him): 'Well you can, because they're all idiots at labels, let's be honest.' This dismissal of the opinions of others with regard to creative work is an important way in which creative workers defend themselves against the repercussions of their own close personal involvement in their products. We return to some of the problems and disappointments associated with producing goods that one feels closely connected to shortly. Here we see how satisfaction and disappointment are, in reality, often intertwined.

Our third example is a construction features editor, Aggie, who explained why she gained much more pride and satisfaction from writing features than news. Aggie emphasised how it was possible in writing features to gain a deeper understanding of a subject than when writing news:

> I think anybody who really enjoys writing probably is more likely to go into features than people who go into news. We do have more scope to be creative about it and with features I find it more satisfying because you can tell the whole story.
>
> (Interview 18)

But she also emphasised a cooperative relationship with the people she covered. 'There is an endless joy', she said, 'in meeting people and creating something about them, which not only gives them pleasure but tells the rest of the world what's going on.'

> News takes a very hard angle and you are upsetting people. [In] features you can give both sides, you can explore the backgrounds, you can really get into a subject and there are huge rewards. I mean people will phone you up afterwards and they usually say 'I'm surprised at how good that was', which is always insulting, but when they do you are always pleased and you think 'Okay – I've done a good thing'.
>
> (Interview 18)

From one point of view, based on a model of investigative journalism, it would be possible to read this as an abdication of the professional responsibility of journalists to act as an irritant. Good investigative journalism is extremely valuable, but most journalism is considerably more mundane than this, and most journalists are unlikely to be able to find satisfactions in such work. Resources may mean, for example, that news journalism is based on superficially interesting or shocking stories. Aggie suggests that for many journalists good products might instead be exploratory, without necessarily producing the kinds of 'hard angle' that might cause distress to those who are being reported upon, only some of whom may be acting in ways that merit the kind of negative exposure that journalists sometimes seek to provide in news. Perhaps there is a different way to gloss this. There is a vital need for radical, investigative journalism, but it requires huge resources and personal commitment. But there might also be room for another notion of good journalism, which seeks to be well crafted and which explains and illuminates.

These workers, then, suggest some of the strongly positive feelings potentially attached to involvement in the creation of products that they can be proud of: a great day's filming, a song beautifully put together and which demands to be repeatedly heard, a sense that a feature is both well constructed and fair. In the cultural industries, such pleasures seem to be strongly related to the personal nature of the relationship between creative worker and creative product. In fact, those pleasures may even be said to *derive* from that personal relationship. To clarify this, a men's magazine journalist, William, told of his pleasure when funny stories he had written for his magazine appeared on the back page of the magazine unchanged by the intervention of his editor: 'Quite often maybe two or three of them will go through that haven't really been changed at all, and that makes me really proud because I think "that's what I wrote, there it is"' (Interview 12). The pride here is more than a matter of editorial approval. There is a strong sense of something emanating from one's own self and then becoming publicly available.[1] This may well be a crucial element of the satisfaction of much work, but it is particularly prominent in creative work because of the strong expressive and aesthetic elements involved. What is more, creative workers often have their names publicly assigned to their work – in the form of bylines for journalists, production credits for television workers and the listing of musicians' names on information associated with recordings.[2]

This also means, though, that when a worker's name is attached to copy that they themselves did not write, and may not even like, this can be a source of great frustration and disappointment – and for William at least, this is the rule, rather than the exception.

> Other stuff, much bigger stuff, like maybe a few pages travel thing that goes at the back, that will get changed loads and I'm not particularly proud of it. I'm glad that I wrote some of it and my name is going to be next to it, but I'm not particularly proud of it because it's not what

---

1 A pleasure or drive that may have its roots in primitive impulses of a kind best understood through a psychoanalytical conception of creativity that is outside our purview here, but which a more fully synthesised notion of subjective experience would need to incorporate. Kleinians tend to see creative activity as attempts to make reparation for destructive phantasies; Winnicott (1982) discussed the links between creativity and play. As in sociological accounts, there are tensions about the degree to which creativity is a general aptitude (cf. Williams on creativity as 'ordinary'), and available to everyone, or a special gift, in which case psychoanalysis would need to account for why some people translate their drives towards reparation or play into creative work; See Rycroft (1995: 29–30).
2 See Ryan (1992: 45), as discussed in Chapter 4, on the concrete and named aspect of much creative work, which he contrasts with the abstract nature of work in many other industries. 'Every book must have an author, every score a composer, every film a writer, director and cast of actors.' It is true that some commodities appear under a generic name (a newspaper masthead or radio station brand) but '[w]orks which appear unsigned or with false human accreditation have difficulty being accepted as works of art' – or of high quality.

I wrote. So, what allows me to be proud is if nothing has been changed and it's as I wrote it, which is very rare.

(Interview 12)

Margie, a television producer, provided another example of this connection between the quality of the work and its public nature. Reflecting on what initially motivated her to work in television, Margie's initial answer reflects the attraction of producing work that is widely consumed, an issue we return to in the next chapter: 'It's knowing that what we are making people are going to see, and people are going to be watching.' But she followed this immediately with a reflection on her pride in making a programme that is 'great, brilliant'.

> There's more pressure on us to make sure that we film balanced features and a mixed bag of features, because we're the only Asian magazine programme out there.[3] So I don't want people to be thinking 'oh God, that programme was no good'. I want it to be a great, brilliant programme, and knowing I was part of that is just so rewarding.

(Interview 35)

As was the case with so many of the creative workers we interviewed, the notion of satisfying, pleasing, rewarding and purposeful work – good work – as involving the creation of good products is mingled here with the importance of communicating with an audience – the issue discussed in the next chapter. It might be objected that the validity of Margie's claims regarding the quality of the programme might be compromised by pressures on her to promote the product she is involved in making. Pressures on workers, whether in the interview situation or outside it, might, for example, come from the organisations employing workers, in the form of expectations explicitly stated or implicitly conveyed. Or they might be subtly internalised as part of the commitment necessary to devote emotional energy and time to making cultural goods. It should be said in response to such worries about the validity of interview statements that we offered anonymity to all our interviewees, and many of them were frank about problems with quality. We explore these issues further in Section 8.4, but it is worth pointing out now that Margie was able to distinguish this particular programme, as a good product, from other programmes she had been involved in producing which she felt were not so interesting or original. She contrasted the British-Asian magazine programme with property and makeover shows she had worked on, and emphasised its superiority in terms of its flexibility: 'there's no format, it's not rigid, it's not structured', whereas in those other programmes, 'you do A, B, and C and

---

3 Margie refers here to a BBC-produced programme which deals with British Asian culture, entertainment and art. Margie herself is British Asian.

that's it'. She considered the magazine programme to be 'one of the best programmes in this building to be working on because the rest are just bog standard programmes really'. Not that it was impossible to enjoy being involved in these other texts: 'I've worked on property programmes and house clearance programmes, and they are always the same. I've enjoyed them, I really have.' But eventually the rigid format limited the satisfaction that Margie could experience: 'but there's only so long I can work on a programme like that before I get bored'.

8.3 Conceptions of good texts

Having discussed some of the pleasures and satisfactions experienced by creative workers when they are involved in the making and dissemination of products that they perceive to be of high quality, we now move on to concentrate more explicitly on ways in which workers discuss what constitutes quality. This matters because unless we gain a sense of what kinds of end product workers are oriented towards producing, we can have only a limited sense of political and aesthetic questions concerning how their conditions might enable or prevent good products from being made. This is to shift the emphasis of our discussion further towards product, but we are still concerned primarily with the experience of process.

The most successful creative workers are in the fortunate position of being able to gain great pleasure and satisfaction from seeing their products have a significant impact on society and on the industry that they work in. One executive producer with an impressive track record of television production discussed some of the pressures she faced as head of her own production company, and we asked how she coped. Ally's initial answer was brief and evasive: 'chocolate'. When we probed, she admitted, referring to the quality of the programmes she produces, 'because I believe in it [i.e., quality]. I really believe in those things. Not that every project I make I believe in, but nearly.' The projects that do inspire such commitment, 'I absolutely believe in them and think that they'll be brilliant and I want everyone to see them.' We asked Ally why, and what she wanted people to see. 'I want people to see good stuff', was her reply. 'I want them [her productions] to be slightly provocative and slightly world changing, but also very entertaining', and implying that she was beginning to sound pretentious and wanted to return to basics in her explanation, added, 'I want to make good drama.' Still probing, though, we asked which products Ally was most proud of, in terms of this 'world-changing' aspect. Ally produced a drama about gay men in Manchester (originally shown on Channel 4 in 1999). This she describes as 'world changing' – referring to its explicit and humorous portrayal of gay male sexuality on screen. She also produced a Channel 4 series (2000–03) about the lives of workers in a northern textile factory, which was praised by critics not only for its in-depth portrayal of working relations, but also its innovative form, concentrating on one particular character or set of characters in each of its episodes. This programme, says Ally, 'did change the [drama] landscape a bit'. This ability to feel as though one's work has had a significant effect not only on one's peers, but on attitudes within society as a whole, is potentially a highly desirable characteristic of work in the cultural industries.

An actor, Bob, stressed this social and cultural impact even more strongly. He recalled his involvement in a television drama called *Hillsborough*, first shown in 1996, about the death of 96 Liverpool football fans at the Hillsborough Stadium in Sheffield in 1989. The programme was written by the noted dramatist Jimmy McGovern (and, in fact, Ally was a key member of the production team). It was a furious depiction of the negligence and insensitivity of the police at the football ground and afterwards.

> I had three lines in it and it was like one of my first jobs out of drama school, I think within two years of drama school … It was just such a fantastic experience and it's funny because I can feel myself getting emotional just talking about it … It was brilliant writing, production, everything about it was just … and because it was a real thing as well and it was very important. You felt that.
>
> (Interview 16)

For Bob, this was more than just drama of high production quality, this was work that was 'real' and 'important' – and part of this seems to have derived from the way that the programme dramatised the traumatic effects of the disaster on working-class families, and argued that among the causes of the tragedy were attitudes towards football fans, based in turn on attitudes towards working-class people. *Hillsborough* also criticised the appalling and incompetent coverage of the disaster by *The Sun* newspaper and, again, dramatised the effects of this coverage on the lives of victims. Bob was frank about his limited involvement in the project – only three lines – but his story conveyed the excitement of being involved at all in the production of such a programme.

Quality, then, provides a sense of meaning and purpose in creative work. Some examples from music journalism suggest other positive conceptions, not only of quality of work, but also of this sense of purpose – of a potentially valuable set of uses of the product. Lyndon described to us how most musicians, in his view, 'have a readily available supply of stories and quotes to tap into' but that this could lead to stale, uninteresting material when journalists wrote up interviews in magazines. Instead, music journalists 'need to be somehow getting something fresh'. According to Lyndon, these potentially powerful interview moments, where interviewees go beyond their 'scripts', often involve stories: 'Stories are crucial. Nearly all the best moments that come out of interviews are stories.' Interviews, he admitted, are not entirely about stories: 'Occasionally someone will say something, observational or analytical, that's really good.' But 'mostly the things they say that really matter are stories'. He gave the example of country singer Emmylou Harris, who had told Lyndon about how 'she was standing beside her mother when her mother took the call saying that her father was dead – which he wasn't as they later discovered – in the Korean War.' This led directly on to a discussion by Lyndon of the purpose and value of eliciting such stories:

> The thing that you do as a music writer, I think, is that you are an intermediary between the artist themselves and the people who either like or at least are interested in their art and their work. So your readers, these really interesting readers who actually buy our music magazine, hundreds of thousands of them, but still a small minority of the population, they will probably get more out of that music from knowing about the artist. A lot of artists would disagree with that, but I think it's true. It just is true, regardless of aesthetic theories. We are talking about our people's music here, pop music, and absolutely it's art. It isn't any less an art than Henry Thoreau, it's absolutely not. It's insane to say that.
>
> (Interview 36)

In this conception of good creative work, then, music journalism at its best enhances people's pleasure in and understanding of music – and Lyndon defends the importance of doing this in relation to popular music, through an explicit invocation of popular music as 'people's music'.[4]

Another music journalist, Lakshman, told us in similar terms of how he took pride when 'you have a good interview and you feel you've got good answers from the artist and you feel you've actually uncovered something and not necessarily developed a bond, but got somewhere other than just the basic surface stuff'. But there was another aspect to this, which Lakshman mentioned immediately afterwards: 'If you feel you're writing a piece that is quite honest and says what you actually want to say, then yes, that's quite rewarding and I suppose that does give you pride.' There is a sense here of the importance of autonomy, that there might be occasions when organisational and institutional contexts might prevent a journalist from being able to 'say what you actually want to say', as Lakshman puts it (Interview 41).

A final example from music journalism highlights the craft involved in conveying the feeling of an encounter between people. A freelancer, Norman, told us that he liked interviews 'that put you in the room'. Switching his use of 'you' from meaning 'reader' to the 'interviewed subject', Norman went on: 'So I get your reactions and that is what my job is, to convey the way you do things, the way you say things.' The craft of this was evident in the difference between articles 'describing everything you are wearing', on the one hand,

---

4 Lyndon may well have in mind here a collection of journalism published by the great British music writer Ian MacDonald, *The People's Music* (MacDonald 2003). Lyndon is likely to have known MacDonald personally, given his rock journalism CV.

and on the other, in good journalism, 'describing the way you play with the sleeve of your jacket'. Norman went on:

> I know people who would describe head to toe what someone is wearing and it's boring because it's irrelevant to me, whereas if you are fiddling with a cufflink, you are wearing a formal shirt, that gives me the picture.
>
> (Interview 46)

As another example of a writer conveying the feeling of being 'in the room' with the musician, Norman gave the example of an old interview by another writer with Gaz Coombes from the British indie band Supergrass.

> It was done in his living room and it described everything in the living room. There were socks drying on the radiator and his girlfriend made him and the journalist a cup of coffee, and apparently the room was in absolute chaos and he spent five minutes hunting for coasters.
>
> (Interview 46)

What Norman seems to value here is the conciseness involved in this craft: 'That to me was as good as two pages of quotes because it told you so much about him. You could see him doing it, and I love that.' The enthusiasm conveyed by Norman suggests his own strong drive to produce good texts, having experienced the pleasure of consuming them himself as a reader: 'I really, really love that and I love the drama of a piece.'

We have explored some of the elements that people find satisfying and rewarding in the cultural products that they and colleagues produce. This includes innovation that has an impact on society and on the industry, work that is ground-breaking, or that reveals injustice in the world. But it can also involve craft elements, the skilful and adroit conveying of information or character or feeling. Being involved in the production of these qualities can bring a real sense of purpose and meaning to the lives of creative workers.

8.4 Bad texts: frustration and disappointment

Unfortunately, mediocre, hurried and constrained cultural products are a common feature of cultural production too. Involvement in the production of good texts can produce pleasure, satisfaction, a sense of purpose and, potentially, in the longer term, self-realisation. But playing a part in the production of bad texts can mean frustration, disappointment and a sense of purposelessness.

We begin with Nell, an assistant producer on arts and history television programmes, who described to us what she felt was 'probably the worst' programme she had ever been involved in, but also 'the funniest'. As will be apparent, the humour was unintentional, and although Nell began her story in humorous vein, it became clear that the frustration she felt during the production process was only funny to her in retrospect.

> It was a programme, it actually sounds quite serious, and it was quite serious, about the finding of this Bronze Age village, which was destroyed by Vesuvius, how many thousands of years ago I can't remember, but before Pompeii, so it was 'the first Pompeii'. It was commissioned at the time when there was a real kind of history fever on television and everybody wanted Pompeii films and volcano things. If you've got two things in it, volcanoes and history, fantastic. Disaster – fantastic! So it's the kind of real tabloid disaster history programme, which I have come to despise. We made it and it was for Channel 5 and it was just kind of the thing where you are very aware that you are spinning out a five minute story into a forty-five minute programme, which is actually what most history programmes are. Every few minutes you'd have a kind of sound effect and it was quite melodramatic. You couldn't see anything of the village really, it was just humps of dirt, so what can you see? What can you make of that on TV? It's quite hard to spin it out and you are just aware that you are being given that money to make that programme. Everybody was aware of that and we just had to get on with it, and I don't think anybody felt particularly they had a lot of personal investment in it.
>
> (Interview 15)

Nell describes a situation in which poor product helps to bring about poor process. Here we see a very different dynamic from one we outlined in Chapter 5, where workers can gain considerable reward from being involved in the conception and execution of ideas. Although Nell was involved in pitching the programme, she had no real 'connection' to it, and so when it came to filming it, the inadequacy of the idea resulted in a sense of drudgery and meaninglessness for her and her co-workers: 'we just had to get on with it'. However, the difficulties of the production were made even worse by the presence of an ambitious director, whose investment in the project resulted in conflicts with the much more sceptical staff working with her.

> She'd just come from the BBC and she was trying to drive her career as a director in the independent sector. So I think she was giving it a good stab because it was very important for her career, which meant that she was a bit mad and was quite difficult to work with [laughter]. Especially when you felt a bit lukewarm – because I was feeling quite sarcastic about it. It's difficult when some people feel very lukewarm and cynical about it, which obviously I did, and other people are quite into it. That's difficult.
>
> (Interview 15)

Poor texts can lead then to a sense of 'churning it out' for creative workers, and conflict between those who are committed and those whose professional ambition allows them to commit themselves even to low-quality texts. For another example of this, we turn to the magazine publishing industry, and to the trade press sector. Aggie, a journalist working in the building and construction trade press, told us about the obligation to produce copy to fill the advertising supplements that provide a great deal of the income for trade magazines.

> Often I would say creatively-wise I am so driven by the supplement agenda that often I think you can get quite tired, and constantly coming up with new ideas can be a real pressure. There are certain sectors that our sales team know very well so they sell a lot of adverts, and therefore that means that the supplements are enormous. For example one of our most successful areas is piling and ground engineering. I don't know if you know what piling is. It's putting stabilising rods into the ground. Piling is a form of ground engineering. You might see a rig on site and it looks a bit like a mobile crane and it's forcing concrete or huge steel rods into the ground, which act as foundations for buildings and all sorts of things. It's a huge area, a huge money-making machine. It's not uncommon that that supplement, which the sales team now want us to run twice a year because they can make so much money out of it, is thirty pages each time. So effectively you've got to find fifteen new ideas twice a year in a sector that's quite technical.
>
> (Interview 18)

Aggie ends with a precise cataloguing of how many ideas she has to come up with, indicating the tedious nature of the job: a ticking off of items on a long list that she must work through, year in, year out. Rather than conveying the difficulty of this aspect of her job through the accumulation of negative details (as in Nell's account of the Vesuvius documentary), here the frustrations of the work are conveyed through a matter-of-factness about what Aggie has to create copy about: 'It's putting stabilising rods into the ground' – full stop. The implication is that *little more can be said*.

8.5 Conceptions and explanations of poor quality work

Just as much as the production of good texts, of work that they can be proud of, creative workers are motivated, and given a sense of purpose, by the drive to avoid what they think of as bad products. Unpacking this category, as with good products, therefore helps us to understand experiences of creative labour, and the motivations and drives of workers.

Eli, a hip hop musician and label manager discussed what he felt was a decline of creativity at the level of genre, or sub-genre, or 'scene', in British rap, one that was making his life as a label manager increasingly unsatisfactory.

> What happens is someone comes out with a style, whatever that style might be, and they do really well, and then all the people coming up

under that artist, maybe coming up two years later who were fans of that artist and influenced by that artist, they start doing that style, and then it becomes worthless because everybody is doing it. What you would always get in hip-hop was people would be critical of them and saying *you are copying that, you are biting*,[5] and that was one of the big ethics of hip-hop, is *you never, never bite. You never copy the style of somebody else. Always do your own thing.* Now, that has been lost in the last ten years because there is such a big slice of it. There are probably lots of reasons, but there's such a big cake now to be had, such big amounts of money to be made that people don't care whether somebody says *oh, you are copying so and so.* It's just *yes, so what? I am making two million dollars. I don't really care.* But that's even translated into UK hip-hop now, where people see an artist like Skinnyman come up and all of a sudden all the demo tapes that we get in the office all sound like they're trying to be like Skinnyman.[6] So that waters all of that down, and you have to keep regenerating the whole time. But people are not doing that. That's starting not to happen. It's not regenerating anymore because that ethic of *you've got to be creative, you've got to come out with something new*, that doesn't exist anymore. So we have a more stagnant music scene. In the UK I think that's definitely the case.

(Interview 58)

Eli attributes the decline in hip hop creativity to the erosion, via commercial imperatives, of an ethos prevalent in hip hop as a whole that valued innovation above borrowing and recombination, to the extent that the genre even developed its own negative term for such imitation. That term, 'biting', has strong physical connotations: are the imitators biting into someone else's food or biting their very body – taking a piece of them? This *prohibition on appropriation* might seem to suggest the guarding of property, but as expounded here by Eli, the ethos is based not so much on ownership (though it can be) as on a view of individual creativity within the genre that everyone should, and can, invent their own style. The decline is attributed not to commerce itself, but to an excessive level of commerce, a result of the growing success of hip hop. Eli talks of innovation being lost 'because there is such a big slice of it' and the 'it' here refers to money. Presumably he means to say, perhaps making an unconscious connection between 'bite' and 'cake', that bigger rewards are available for the successful, but without the same levels of innovation.

---

5 We want to draw attention here to how Eli uses personification and reported speech to convey a sense of conflict, and so we use italics to make it easier to identify where such segments are to be found and to avoid littering the text with inverted commas.

6 Skinnyman is a prominent UK hip hop musician, originally from Leeds. He is very skinny.

In order to convey these ideas, Eli uses *personification*: the representation of a thing or abstraction as a person or people. He differentiates two groups:

- 'people in hip hop', who say *you are copying that, you are biting*, and who lay out a set of rules concerning imitation that warns *you never, never bite. You never copy the style of somebody else. Always do your own thing*, and who when they encounter copying, say *oh, you are copying so and so*
- against this group, those who say *yes, so what? I am making two million dollars. I don't really care.*

Personification is used here by Eli to dramatise the conflict between creativity and commerce.[7] It is a presentation of the conflict which strongly favours 'people in hip hop' over another group of people, who are unnamed, but are uncaring and unresponsive (*so what? ... I don't really care*) and concerned primarily with money (*I am making two million dollars*). Hyperbole is used to add to the dramatic effect. It is highly unlikely that Eli knows any musicians who are making two million dollars. This seems to refer to those musicians who have come to dominate hip hop and who had become symbols of the triumph of avarice over originality in some quarters of hip hop in the noughties.[8] But, by extension, it refers to those who aspire to commercial success without creativity. There is some bitterness in this highly polarised presentation of good and bad.

Tensions between creativity and commerce, discussed in Chapter 4, are of course apparent here. But the word 'tensions' does not imply a radical separation between the two. Elsewhere in the interview, Eli spoke at some length about his enjoyment of combining the business side of his hip hop label with his own creative work as a musician.

> The last few years have been more developing the business and more enjoying that side of things and being creative with the business as well, with the structure of it and the finance and so on and so forth. That's the thing I've been really concentrating on.
>
> (Interview 58)

Clearly then Eli was not presenting us in our interview with a naive or utopian polarisation of creativity and commerce. However, he was clearly of the

---

7 By 'use', we do not mean that Eli consciously adopts this figure of speech. It emerges from his 'practical consciousness' (Giddens, 1984: xxx).

8 See Nik Cohn (2006: 190) for an example of this discourse:

> Great rap, almost always, was born of rage. The world had its foot on your throat, and hip-hop was your howl of defiance. ... That, in large part, was why even the best of rappers had a short shelf life. A few triple-platinum albums, a mansion, a Mariah or Beyoncé on your arm, and it was hard to summon up the authentic primal roar.

view that in some cases it is possible for commercial goals to compromise creativity.

What is the significance of these linguistic devices, as used by Eli in this specific context? Such personification, combined with hyperbole, is a way not only of conveying emotion to the interviewer about the putative decline in hip hop creativity, but also as a means for Eli to strengthen his own resolve and that of others. Although the fieldwork interview context is of course a highly specific one, it is not unreasonable to suppose that Eli would present similar opinions in media interviews, and in conversation with collaborators. And, in fact, in a discussion during an interview with an online rap newspaper concerning his final album, Eli says:

> I was really happy with it. The only thing that bugs me is when you talk about politics, some people, mainly reviewers, scoff at it, like *who does he think he is*, like music should be purely superficial bullshit and have no business aspiring to more than that.[9]

In another media interview he described his label as 'just this thing, this vehicle that exists to put records out and promote them, it's all about good music and not trying to find people to put on six album deals and make lots of money out of the publishing, it's just good music and putting records out'. Eli's discourse is part of a wider 'repertoire', as discourse analysts tend to emphasise (see Wetherell et al. 2001). But it also has a potential performative function in that it may serve to reinforce an ethos of individual originality oriented towards collective creativity, against a more imitative, complacent and commercially driven ethos.

A second case study of conceptions of bad texts comes from our interview with a freelance film editor, Shaun, with long experience of working in television documentary, on the experience of making a factual entertainment television film. In this case, the original conception of the programme was, in Shaun's view, a good one. (As in the quotation from Eli above, we use italics to indicate the use of reported speech – see note 5 to this chapter).

> It was about a fireman that wanted to change his life. There were tears in it, there was an argument, and so clearly there was a story about human beings, he needed to change his diet, the young kids wouldn't have it, she [the fireman's partner] wasn't going along with it, there were arguments. It was a snapshot of what I know is happening. It was great. But then *oh no, we've got this expert saying* ... and then it became a different film, and then of course we hadn't got the material to do that. So then you'd get that material, you'd try and force it into *right, expert says "hello Russell, good morning"*, and they have all these sort of clinics where he

goes, and those moments sort of work and they motivate him to change. No, *there must be day two*, and they hadn't shot those things. So, *go away and shoot them.*

(Interview 14)

Shaun begins by listing a number of positive elements of the original conception of the programme: there is real drama, there is a human element, but it was 'real' (note the use of the same word used by Bob in Section 8.3 above). The quick-fire listing conveys the simplicity and elegance of the original conception. The problem was that 'Sky wanted to formulate the thing' – in other words, the commissioners wanted to make the story conform to a reality-TV format or formula rather than provide a depiction of reality, of 'what I know is happening'. Here too, like Eli, Shaun conveys the problems involved in cultural work by personifying different aspects of cultural production. But Shaun also enacts the rapidity of the breakdown of the integrity of the film through his use of clipped narration. *Right, expert says "hello Russell, good morning"* is an imitation of the director's instruction to the 'cast', putting words into their mouths, and this is used by Shaun to put across the inauthenticity of the production: the diet clinics, which the firefighter never in reality attended, are inserted into the narrative to make it seem as though his success in losing weight was the product of expert advice. *There must be day two* is another paraphrase of the attempts by the commissioners to force a new narrative on the production staff. At this point, then, relatively late in the shooting, the decision by Sky, the commissioners of the programme, to make the programme conform more to reality-TV/lifestyle TV narrative conventions, whereby an ordinary member of the public gains advice from an expert on how to achieve a set of goals (whether better dress as in *What Not to Wear*, better interior design as in *Changing Rooms*, or weight loss as in *Biggest Loser*),[10] meant that the project team had to gain material that was necessary to produce this narrative, but which had not been filmed. The effects on Shaun, and by implication his colleagues, are indicated by a peremptory command: *go away and shoot them*. You can almost picture Shaun's colleagues trudging away disconsolately.

This dramatised conflict between creativity and commerce becomes more apparent as Shaun discusses a further development which exacerbated the problems he identified (though it is not possible to discern from the transcript whether this situation was connected to the shift to the reality-TV format) and his account is again marked by paraphrased reporting of peremptory questions and commands, this time from a new member of the team:

> And then the director was sacked, and then they brought this woman in who was the Red Adair of something or other. She had so many series

---

10 See Palmer (2008) for analyses of lifestyle programming in contemporary television.

out and she came in, *right, we need the template, who has got the tem-plate? Well, what do you want to do? [...] Go and shoot some more material.* Basically what they then did, this fellow had lost two or three stone in five or six weeks, and *you can't turn the clock back, you can't go back to day one because this fellow looks much fitter,* and they did. They basically did. They said *you've got to go back to day one and we've got to get the doctor going in and opening his fridge up and trashing all the food.*

(Interview 14)

Whereas Eli, in our first case study, sets up an encounter between a wider creativity-driven group who reasonably lay out the rules of the game, and a rival commerce-driven group who uncaringly break those rules through a blunt reply (*So what?*), Shaun conveys the difficulty of the specific production process here by enacting the irrationality of the production process in his speech and imitating a kind of panicky urgency, indicated by cutting out 'they said' or 'we said' from his account. Red Adair, the semi-mythic firefighter of the 1960s and 1970s, brought in at short notice to tackle oil field disasters, figures as an ironic point of comparison, to criticise the new director. The metaphor evokes the image of a sudden and self-important arrival, accom-panied by rapid-fire questions. The production team, so far voiceless, are now given words by Shaun. Not specifying who is speaking in response to the director and the commissioning channel helps give a sense of a number of discontented ordinary workers. This team, or Shaun, is initially compliant (*well, what do you want to do?*). But their/his response soon becomes horrified: *you can't turn the clock back, you can't go back to day one – because this fellow looks much fitter* (it is not clear whether this was a response spoken by Shaun or a production team member, or thoughts that they kept to them-selves). Shaun's account also suggests that this mock-heroic figure asked for very similar things to the director she replaced: more footage resulting from the dubiously imposed narrative, and here Shaun elaborates on his problems with the project.

First of all that was against the grain a bit for me, and it was totally wrong to ask him to do that because he was so proud of what he did and he had to fill the fridge up with all the crap that he'd junked. So you are then taking someone who has agreed to film, who thinks you are trying to help them [*sic*], *can you sit down Russell and eat egg and chips? What do you mean? I've given it up!* And there's this huge row with the con-tributor and then half the other contributors turned out to be fake girls wanting to promote their business and get on TV. There was a whole layer of that and I just thought – oh, and they asked me to stay on and I had got another job – and I thought *I am so well out of that* because it was a farce. There were all these people running around kicking every-one's bum, you know, *you must do this.*

(Interview 14)

This dialogue captures the conflict between the programme-maker and the contributor (*What do you mean?*), with Shaun as editor clearly taking the side of the contributor. He then moves on to another layer of problems involving other contributors. Finally, he summarises the coercion implicitly involved in the production (*can you sit down Russell and eat egg and chips?*) by perso-nifying – possibly hyperbolically – the commissioner as barking commands (*you must do this*). Shaun's response is a moment of interior monologue as he leaves the production: *I am so well out of that.* He strongly emphasises that all this is an inorganic and inauthentic way of creating narratives about human subjects. The fireman featured in the film objects to being made to eat egg and chips when he has given them up. It might be tempting to think that this involves a naive view that documentary-makers would film reality 'as it hap-pens'. But in fact this is a way of protesting against the sense of manipulation in the production, involving the introduction of experts into the narrative, and the consequent erasure of the fireman's own achievement, his determination and willpower in dealing with his own appetites. As with Eli above, the dramatisation of creativity (here linked to order and authenticity) against commerce (linked with chaos and falsehood) potentially serves as a way of expressing and articulating an ethics that values excellence, here associated, in the particular genre context of documentary, with truthfulness and authenticity.

In this respect, it might be worth comparing Shaun's account with this quotation from Simon, a camera operator who had worked on documentaries:

> It's recording something that's really happening and that's what I'm there for, to try and express and show something that really is happening. A lot of the time people don't want you to do that. Everybody is saying things they are being told to say, it is kind of awful. It's a bit like *can you both have a conversation now in your own words?* and then the conversa-tion starts and the director says *hold on a minute, that's not what I want you to say, can you actually say this or say that?* A lot of things are manipulated.
>
> (Interview 29)

All documentary is a construction, of course. But there is a great deal of difference between a naive realism that believes that documentary can 'reflect the world as it is', and a more thoughtful realism that accepts the intervention of the film-makers, but questions when the boundaries of appropriate inter-vention might have been overstepped.

8.6 Negative and positive experiences of quality

The contemporary cultural industries provide opportunities for workers to do work that they consider to be of social, cultural and political significance, or to be involved in making cultural products that bear the mark of high levels of care and skill. Many of the workers we spoke to were deeply concerned about the aesthetic quality of the goods they produced, and about their ethical implications. But cultural production is by no means protected from the worst aspects of what Marx and others called alienation, and which we are preferring simply to call bad work (in order to cover a greater variety of ills). We have shown that workers can experience deep frustration and disappointment, as a result of careless, meaningless ideas, and the distortion or perceived hijacking of good ones. Some of these problems seem to emanate from the kinds of structural pressure we discussed in Part One and in our discussion of organisational forms in Chapter 4. Workers have their own way of framing these forces. These positive and negative experiences of the quality of creative work are intensified by the fact that cultural products are highly visible and audible in public, and workers' names are often displayed in association with those products. This brings us firmly to the question of the relationship of *audiences* to the experience of creative work, and the next chapter considers that relationship.

9 Audiences, quality and the meaning of creative work

9.1 Creative workers thinking about what audiences think

In his study of the Hollywood television industry, Todd Gitlin encountered Arnold Becker, the vice-president for television research at the CBS Network. 'I'm not interested in culture', Becker told Gitlin. 'I'm not interested in pro-social values. I have only one interest. That's whether people watch the program. That's my definition of good, that's my definition of bad' (Gitlin 1994: 31).

In Chapter 2, we argued for the need to develop normative conceptions of work, including creative work, and we introduced our own model of good and bad work. This included two different, sometimes complementary, notions of good *product*, as opposed to process: the first comprising good work in the sense of producing work of high quality or excellence (in the context of the cultural industries, 'culture' in Becker's terms); the second consisting in products that contributed to the common good ('pro-social values' for Becker). In the cultural industries, as the quotation above from Arnold Becker suggests, an issue that haunts nearly all discussions of quality is *the audience*. Products and services in any industry tend ultimately to be for someone. But the cultural industries are oriented towards consumption in particular ways, for they are centred on *acts of communication* more than any other set of organisations. What is more, this is communication more often than not intended to produce some kind of emotional or affective relationship, whether a singer moving an audience to sadness and even tears, or a journalist trying to report or explain a phenomenon or process as clearly and as accurately as possible. Yet the problem is that in the modern media industries, this often consists of communication with groups of people with whom the creative worker is likely to have little interaction. This is quite unlike the situation of the traditional artisan, but it is also unlike the labour of many modern service workers, such as retail workers or flight attendants. Creative workers are rarely co-present with their audiences, except in live performances. The often deeply affective and emotional nature of the response sought by creative workers in these distant, mediated audiences produces anxiety, ambivalence and even distrust, as we shall see. Some creative workers deal with these feelings by professing not to care what their audiences think. But there is often a sense that this might be a disavowal – and there may be something of this in Becker's gruff proclamation that all he really cares about is ratings, the size of the audience. (Becker, as a senior executive oriented towards the commercial pole of cultural production, is necessarily concerned with a quantitative measure of audience engagement, one that can be easily translated into financial benefit – and we return to the issue of ratings, circulation figures and sales below.) Equally, when creative workers care very greatly about the size of their audiences and try very hard to anticipate what audiences might think, there might be a danger of workers losing contact with their own sense of excellence, with standards internal to their chosen form of cultural activity.

Attitudes towards audiences, then, are deeply bound up with questions concerning the quality of texts, and the quality of workers' experiences of production. As we also saw in the previous chapter, the creative workers we spoke to presented more complex notions of what constitutes good and bad work in their industries than that offered by Arnold Becker above. And crucially in terms of our interests in this book, how workers conceive of 'what the audience thinks' (Schlesinger 1992: 109) – or what they might think – can have a strong impact on their experience of the production process, including the sense of meaningfulness and purpose they get from their work. In Section 9.2, we explore this issue by examining different conceptions of readers among magazine workers; and in Section 9.3 by analysing how various musicians and creative managers discuss audiences for music, whether live or mediated. The issue of what audiences can 'handle' is an issue which, across different cultural industries, can generate conflicts among those involved in creative work, and we explore this in Section 9.4. In Section 9.5, we discuss the way in which the very large audiences still gained by television affects the sense that creative workers have of the meaning and purpose of their working lives, and how workers experience the importance of audience statistics ('ratings') in the television industry. The stress throughout is on how the conflicting pulls of creativity and commerce produce great ambivalence towards audiences, which in turn has ambivalent effects on the experience of creative work.

9.2 Magazines: is the reader everything?

Larry, a men's magazine writer, told us that when he worked for *Zoo*, a men's weekly, one of the few things he learned was that 'your reader is everything'. Yet, he says, 'readers figure very surprisingly little in terms of making magazines'. Finding out what readers think of a magazine is difficult because, as Larry puts it: 'we don't get feedback from readers, apart from sales figures'. When sales figures drop, insecurity sets in among the workers because 'no one really knows what's going on'. This recalls screenwriter William Goldman's famous axiom concerning the film industry's knowledge of what happens and why in the world of film production: 'nobody knows' (cited among many others by Richard Caves, 2000: 3). And the biggest unknown for creative workers, and the primary source for the particular uncertainty that afflicts the cultural industries, is what its audience will think. Larry provided a recent example:

> I was talking to [editor] yesterday about this because we've taken a hit over the last two or three months and we don't know why, and because I'm quite new I was saying, 'it's nothing to do with the features is it, or anything I'm doing?'. He said 'It's not. Because if it's editorial you don't feel the readership hit for the first six months because people don't suddenly go "it's shit now" and stop reading it.' They notice very slowly and for some reason one month they'll just stop buying it. So you just can't tell what it is that stops people buying your magazine.
>
> (Interview 9)

It is the role of marketers in the magazine industry to try to understand what works for audiences and what does not. Ellen, a marketer for leading magazine conglomerate EMAP, told us of her company's emphasis on half-yearly 'brand tracking' to gauge people's awareness of titles, large-scale questionnaire-based research which contributes to 'shaping what the magazine does', followed by 'focus groups about what people wanted to see' and more 'informal pub groups of people and that kind of thing' (Interview 7). However, Larry was sceptical about the extent to which marketers like Ellen really have an understanding of the audience. He felt, for example, that the focus groups run by EMAP's marketing people did not help him understand his readers:

> It's really difficult because when we were at *Zoo* we used to have very regular pub groups where they'd get six readers to look through the magazine and say what they thought, and it was always a waste of time because the company that did it just wait outside building sites and get the first six people, they'd be in a pub for 50 pounds and they just want to go, they're not really interested. They're meant to read the magazine before they turn up but they haven't really and they're not really paying attention and you're expected to make serious decisions on the basis of what these six blokes said. They're not representative and they're not going to give you the truth, they're not going to put any thought into it, and they're pissed [drunk] by the end of it anyway.
>
> (Interview 9)

Whether this portrayal of marketing focus groups is accurate or not, it reflects creativity–commerce tensions in the form of a deep distrust of marketing data on the part of creative workers. This no doubt in turn derives from a desire on the part of workers to protect their own creative autonomy.

For writers such as Thomas, another men's magazine journalist, the solution is not to bother thinking about the audience or the marketers' perspective when writing copy at all: 'I mean, I just work on the premise that "would I want to read it?", and I know what I like to read and I have written things that I would laugh at and that I would find interesting' (Interview 32).

Frustration with what audiences might actually want leads to situations where some creative workers detect in their colleagues, and in themselves, a contempt for their audiences that reduces the quality of the texts, and therefore the value of their work. William, a junior writer at a monthly men's magazine, told us:

> I mean [the magazine he works for] is written for blokes who have got loads of money. If you become a writer you hate those kinds of people and you sort of want to be cynical about it all and you just don't like that kind of thing. You don't like suits and stuff like that, you want to be a bit more bohemian and 'I'm a writer and get drunk' and all this sort of stuff.
>
> (Interview 12)

Other creative workers though find greater evidence of contempt in attitudes that seek to please audiences too easily, but in so doing, underestimate their capacities for enjoying richer, more interesting, more meaningful products. Larry, commenting on the standard of humour in men's magazines, makes a distinction between 'talking' to readers and 'talking down' to them. 'If you look at *Nuts*,' he said, 'it's all about boobs and in *Nuts* they actually had a guy with those glasses with eyeballs on springs. That is the level they are dealing with. If you look at *Loaded* and *FHM*, it's similar stuff. It's so shit.' He praised *Loaded*, which transformed the men's magazine market on its launch in 1994, for being 'a magazine that talked directly to its readers'. Since then, though, 'I think that magazines have lapsed and they're just talking down to their readers. Every magazine I've ever worked for, I've always heard somebody say at some point "we understand that, we think it's funny, but our readers won't". I just think that's stupid and you hear that all the time' (Interview 9). We discuss this issue of assessing what audiences are capable of dealing with further in Section 9.4 below.

In the construction and building trade press, writers have a very different relationship with their readership than that expressed by the men's magazine journalists. When knowledge of the audience is so uncertain, the maxim that 'the reader is everything', which Larry took away from his time at *Zoo*, can only really be interpreted in terms of sales figures. This is not the case, however, in the trade press, where the professional nature of the readership and the subscription base of income provide a somewhat different challenge: combining accuracy and interest. The audience, of course, still remains central. Irene, a writer for a building publication, told us, 'it was drilled into me at journalism college "write for your audience" '. For Irene, the basis of a good story is that

what I am writing is true, accurate and is in the public interest – so for
my audience. So I basically write a fantastic story that my audience needs
to know and at the same time I want to make it as accurate and as
exciting as it can be.

(Interview 44)

Similarly, Reggie, an editor and writer for a construction magazine, told us
there are three essential elements in communicating to a professional readership, and we were introduced to these in Section 4.3: 'everything we write has
to be useful for our professional readers, it has to be authoritative, and it has
to be adventurous and fun'. Being authoritative and accurate however are the
key elements in his business:

Our readership are very, very active in the way they think, so we have to
be accurate. ... So things like that, on a very basic level calling concrete
concrete and cement cement and not getting the two muddled up. If you
work for *The Times*, you can get away with muddling them up.[1] But
if you work for [a civil engineering publication] you can't muddle up
concrete with cement.

(Interview 50)

A good product, as articulated here, is defined as writing without any factual
errors that will be picked up by the professional reader. Reggie speaks with a
great respect for the audience – perhaps even fear? – and this seems to derive
from his understanding of their position as professionals. Before he became a
journalist Reggie was himself an engineer and perhaps this contributes to his
placing such a high value on accuracy.

A problem for a trade publication such as the one edited by Reggie is that
the professional readership consists of a multitude of engineers engaged in
very different specialisations. This can make the necessary level of accuracy
quite difficult to achieve. For Reggie, and also for Irene, quality of work is not
just about accuracy. The writing in these publications must also be useful to
many other members of the readership, regardless of the area of building or
construction they work in. And so for these writers, the challenge of good
journalism in the construction press is to incorporate stories with a common
theme that will win the interest of all professional readers, regardless of their
specialisation. Reggie continues:

1 This interesting claim suggests a journalist seeking to claim their own specialist territory, in
spite of the generally higher prestige of journalists on national daily 'quality' newspapers.
British journalism has seen some introduction of US journalistic notions of accuracy, including some fact-checking and corrections columns (introduced by *The Guardian* in 1997) but on
nothing like the same scale. This reflects a different model of professionalism within the same
Anglo-American system (see Hallin and Mancini 2004).

Because the audience is big ... this is incredibly widespread. Civil engineering covers a whole range of topics from conception, planning, financing to design, to construction to maintenance to demolition, and it covers a wide range of subjects from water to flooding to structural engineering to nuclear power to roads, bridges and railways, a whole gamut, everything you see around you. Because we write about so many different subjects and so many different topics, we have to write everything so that if you are a structural engineer you understand warps, and if you are a warp engineer you understand how you can get things from a nuclear power source, and it's finding that common civil engineering theme in all the stories we write.

(Interview 50)

However, accuracy and authoritative knowledge are not enough in this genre and this, Reggie points out, is why the magazine is not written by engineers but by journalists:

Basically what we have to do every week is put every one of our 56,000 readers in the story, and make it relevant to each reader. That is the reason for turning people into journalists, rather than having engineers write, because you have to be a journalist to be able to tell that story. I'm not interested in a team of engineers; I want a team of journalists who can tell stories. ... I write for a professional readership, and my whole team and I go about what we do in a professional manner. It matters that we get it right. It matters that we not only give people stuff they want to read, because ultimately my fundamental job is to get them to take it out the Polywrap,[2] and if they don't take it out the Polywrap it doesn't matter what you write on the inside. So I have to make sure that what we do is exciting, but I also have to do that in a way which respects their own profession.

(Interview 50)

Here then is a statement of the craft values of a certain kind of journalism, and implicitly an elaboration of key elements of journalism as a *practice* (see Section 2.4). We can see too that creativity/commerce tensions work differently here than in other magazine genres we examined. Trade press publications are not as directly dependent on sales figures as men's or music magazines. As Sophus, a marketing director of building and construction publications explained, trade magazines are often either free or subscription based which means revenue streams do not rely on circulation but rather recruitment advertising and display advertising (Interview 51). There is still an emphasis on creativity, however. Reggie and others aim to produce a

---

2 A clear polythene film that can be used to 'pack' individual items such as magazines.

magazine that is dynamic in its writing style (exciting; adventurous and fun) and which seeks to develop 'a set of generic possibilities in given conditions' through 'balanc[ing] the enhancement of the entertainment, pleasure and education of the audience' (Born 2000: 406).

9.3 Music: a communicative thing or a private thing?

Music has, in many genres, been marked by particularly strong tensions between creativity and commerce, perhaps because music has come to be associated so strongly with authentic and autonomous subjectivity. These tensions are often projected on to relationships with audiences. The great sociologist Howard Becker (1951) once described relationships between jazz musicians and audiences as fundamentally one of 'conflict and hostility' (p. 136), and he linked this to one version of the commerce–creativity tensions we emphasised in Chapters 3 and 4.

> The most distressing problem in the career of the average musician is the necessity of choosing between conventional success and his [*sic*] "artistic" standards. In order to achieve success he [*sic*] finds it necessary to "go commercial", that is, to play in accord with the wishes of the non-musicians for whom he works; in so doing he sacrifices the respect of other musicians and thus, in most cases, his self-respect.
>
> (Becker 1951: 136)

In this section, we explore how various musicians we interviewed discussed their relationships with audiences, and how those relationships affected the quality of their working lives. We conducted a joint interview with two musicians who had been in a relationship together for some time: Robert, a 'veteran' musician who had been working professionally in the industry for more than thirty years and who had been a member of a high-profile band before embarking on a recent solo career, and Niamh, a newcomer to the industry who was recording her first album, with collaboration from Robert, but who was yet to be signed by a label. Robert talks here of the position of the audience in the recording process during the making of Niamh's album where he says 'there is some element' of thinking 'oh well, people might like this' but that doesn't necessarily steer the album in a parti-cular direction:

> When you're making music, which is very much for entertaining, suppo-sedly to entertain people, it's all about how other people are going to respond to it. And when you're making music in the studio for public consumption which Niamh's definitely was, we were always trying to make a record that would sell, that people will want to listen to.
>
> (Interview 3)

Robert then contrasted this with the making of his own album which he said 'was done very much for my own reasons' with less of a focus on the potential audience. However, even in this situation, one relatively close to 'creativity for creativity's sake', audience recognition can remain important.

> But when you're making a record like that, you can never be fully excited and really, really happy, until you get the response from other people ... You can sit in a studio and think 'this is incredible' but you always think 'well, what are people going to think of it? How is it going to be received? How is it going to be interpreted?'
>
> (Interview 3)

Robert was talking about the studio situation and the way in which thoughts of the audience can intrude on recording sessions and the direction an album takes. But for many musicians it is only in live performance that anxieties about the significance and affect of their work can be resolved. For Robert, these anxieties continue right 'until you get a number one record and you're playing concerts and people are going crazy'. Only then comes real affirmation: 'And then you're like "*yes*".'

Similarly, Hannah, artist manager of a successful rock act, described how the greatest 'highs' for the band were 'when they know they've kind of got it in studio and they know they are onto something really good and it's really exciting and they are really enjoying making music and they have people down at the studio play it and they are proud of it'. This though was followed by 'the next high', when new songs are played live and they get direct feedback from audiences. Again, a central theme here is the great anxiety surrounding the potential reception of creative work, which is unresolved until it reaches an audience. In Section 5.5, Hannah registered the 'anticipation and fear' that musicians and those working with them feel before a release when there is no clear sense of how the product will be received, even though 'you are very proud of the work that you've done'. She went on to say: 'And so there are highs obviously when you've got good reviews and people really love it, so that's a high, and then it's a low when you obviously have negative criticism' (Interview 42).

For 'ordinary' musicians who have not achieved significant success, relationships with audiences are also ambivalent, but the downsides can involve greater levels of alienation[3]. A jazz singer, Annette, told us about a series of gigs she and her band had done for 'a big London international bank', on a boat trip on the Thames, and contrasted this with certain pub gigs.

---

3 Often this relationship is highly mediated – for example, in magazine or television work, where most readers and viewers are never seen. But live performance in the music industry, because performers are co-present with audiences, raises in a particularly acute form the issue of relationships with audiences.

> They were all international bankers and they were totally absorbed
> in networking and we might as well not have been there. Even the
> river might not have been there, the boat might not have been there and
> when we got to the Greenwich Observatory nobody looked at the view,
> nobody looked at the Harrison Clocks, nobody listened to the music.
> They were totally absorbed, and so really we might not as well have
> been there.
>
> (Interview 10)

A quiet dislike of her wealthy and privileged audience comes across in the
accumulation of examples of their lack of interest in 'anything but each
other'. By including the river and the architecture in what the bankers fail to
notice, Annette avoids giving the impression that her music arrogantly
demands to be heard. There is a kind of modesty here: music deserves attention just as rivers and beautiful buildings deserve to be admired. Instead, the
bankers lack any engagement with beauty, but are narcissistically self-absor-
bed, and it is hard to avoid the implication that this might be in the interests
of pursuing their own careers. Bankers are of course almost archetypal figures
of commerce, and rivers, music and architecture here represent the aesthetic.
   Annette then immediately contrasted the banker gigs with pub gigs on
the basis of the level of communication involved between performers and
audience.

> Then there are other ones where you will be in some back room of a
> pub and there will be a really focused audience and you talk to the
> audience ... and sometimes you change your set. You see how they are
> responding and you change your set. I don't know if every jazz musician
> does that, but I do. I sort of think 'oh well, I'm losing them a bit here', so
> I'll put a different kind of song in. So that's at the other extreme, and
> then I'll be singing with different tones in my voice as well, which will get
> people to listen more, or I'll be singing with more expression, maybe a
> different kind of singing. ... Inevitably you don't get paid much for those,
> but the communication level is really high.
>
> (Interview 10)

The commerce versus creativity metaphor is subtly woven into this story as
Annette wryly notes that the first kind of gig tends to earn more money than
ones that involve playing to responsive audiences (often in pubs). In the pub
gig, there is co-present interactivity; the difficulty of the first gig, at the other
extreme, concerns being in the same room, working, and yet still not being
noticed. Invisibility and inaudibility are not always undesirable, but for
musician-performers, who practise and train in order to stand in front of an
audience and communicate with them, this, surely, is bad work. But Annette
made clear that, for her, the banker gigs are a kind of necessary evil, which
remind Annette and her fellow musicians, through their encounter with the

bankers, of the desirability of work founded primarily, though never entirely, on creativity rather than commerce.

Annette's account though is markedly different from the 'conflict and hostility' depicted by Becker (1951) as characterising the relationship between jazz musicians and audiences, as discussed above. For her, 'communicating with audiences is important' and that means responding to what the audience wants to hear, but in a dialogical way made possible by co-presence. This has often meant not playing music that she and her fellow musicians have composed themselves. This is because 'what people want to hear is often what they already know' – jazz standards, show tunes and pop hits. Annette told us: 'I don't mean I'm doing music I don't like, because I do enjoy all those jazz standards and well-known things, but if you want to make a living out of it you have to be more conventional.' And this, she says, is 'not a bad lesson to learn because you don't want to lose your audience. There's no point just playing music that nobody wants to hear, I don't think. It's a communicative thing'.

Annette also wondered though about the extent to which other jazz musicians' experiences of the audience were different from her own. She conjectured that 'some jazz musicians aren't really interested in audiences' and this was because jazz is sometimes conceived of as 'a very private thing'. Other jazz musicians we spoke to described a relationship with the audience which emphasised communication, but stressed that the audience could only matter to a certain degree. Elliot, an improvising pianist, described his orientation to the audience as 'a big failing'. He explained:

> Sometimes I try to pre-judge audiences and you think of what you are going to play and [think] they're not going to be into it, so you try to do things [that are] more approachable, and it's not always the right thing to do. Sometimes they have come to hear you play.
>
> (Interview 34)

Elliot plays improvised jazz and he recognised this is a music style that can be quite confrontational for an unsuspecting audience: 'some people come along and wonder "what the hell is happening?"; they didn't know what they were coming to'. But even for those audience members who know what to expect from improvised jazz, Elliot finds himself often wondering 'how can they sit and listen to this?' Nevertheless, he said, 'it's lovely to have audience contact'. Even in those genres that emphasise producer conceptions of quality, then, communication with audiences remain important sources of validation and reward.

Another musician, Keith, a jazz drummer, echoed Annette's experiences of jazz audiences. He talked of the 'bridge over to the audience', something that needs to be crossed if the communication level between musicians and audience – recalling Annette's discussion – is going to feed into the quality of the live experience. Once you've crossed the bridge and the audience seem to be enjoying the music then 'that has a big effect. Suddenly you begin to think "oh yes, we don't have to worry actually, it's happening. We don't have to try too hard to get something over to these people" '. The pleasure of the musician in the performance is directly linked for Keith to the pleasure experienced by the audience. Yet this can't mean giving up aesthetic autonomy out of a need to please that audience – because trying too hard to please would run the danger of undermining the role of risk and uncertainty as part of the aesthetic experience. Keith discussed the bands that he books for a jazz club he runs:

> There is a sense in which, in the end, it [the audience] can't matter. You've just got to do your bit, and if they happen not to like it, then that's okay. I'm talking about the jazz club here rather than other things. I think I've got to the point ... where we are quite comfortable with people not enjoying the gig. I almost quite like it, because it sort of reaffirms that the nature of the music can't always be good. That's the nature of it. Sometimes it doesn't happen. So I don't define the success of the gig by how the audience reacts.
>
> (Interview 62)

Indeed, Keith finds audience reaction quite difficult to judge both in his role as musician and club organiser. The communication level with the audience, for example, cannot be judged on the amount of applause. Keith explained:

> I think that's another thing I've learnt: don't take too literally the amount of noise you are getting. It's not necessarily an index. Sometimes it's actually the reverse. ... People don't clap because they are so engaged in what's going on, or there is a blurring between solos so there is no obvious point to clap, something like that. It's not that the audience is not responding, it's just that they've changed response really. They have gone in a different direction.
>
> (Interview 62)

9.4 What can audiences handle?

The material above on men's magazines and music suggested that views of what audiences are capable of appreciating or 'dealing with' can form the basis of considerable anxieties and problems in creative work, as well as pleasures and satisfactions. Another aspect to this is the debates and conflicts that can take place among creative workers about audiences. One television arts/history documentary producer, Leon, discussed the reaction of commissioning editors at a major US documentary network to a programme he had produced on the history of sexuality. This involved what Leon refers to as a 'thesis', an angle, involving repression of sexuality down the ages. But the US channel that had commissioned and partly funded the programme said, in

Leon's words, 'we're not showing that' because of overly graphic sexual content. In one scene, the presenter, discussing the supposed identification of the clitoris by a sixteenth-century physician with the same surname as the famous explorer, made a joke about 'an important discovery by Columbus'. 'There's no way we're using the word "clitoris" on American television' was the response of the US channel, according to Leon, who claimed that the reason commissioners give for not being prepared to show such content is 'we're reacting to the audience'. This is reminiscent of Caldwell's (2008: 335–6) observation of film and television executives who 'master the prose of "speaking for the audience" ' and whose 'arguments that the "audience wants this" or "that" trumps all others'. The problem with this attitude on the part of executives is that it ignores the way that the audience itself is constituted by texts and therefore by cultural producers, as Leon points out: 'One of the reasons that they're so prudish is because television always says "we're reacting to the audience". This is my big problem. Television commissioning editors will say "we react to the audience" ', but Leon's view, by contrast, is that 'an audience is partially created by television'. Leon then resists the view that the audience have pre-constituted needs and desires which creative workers must seek to fulfil (Interview 1).

Responding to the refusals of commissioners to screen such programmes meant a shift in the way in which Leon's production company now creates and conceptualises the documentaries it makes. They now rely much less on commissioners and funding than previously. Instead, they start from the premise that 'there is an audience out there interested in cultural programmes or poetry programmes or films about [composers]'. Such programming cannot be ratings-led in Leon's philosophy of television: 'if you just follow the focus groups and the ratings then you would never make any of those kind of things'.

For some creative workers, audiences themselves, rather than creative managers' and executives' projections on to them, provide a powerful limit on the autonomy of creative practice. The case of Matthew, an art director working for a men's magazine, illustrates the frustrations of compromising with audiences, and also how creative workers can come to accept this compromise as necessary. Matthew described his experiences of covers and layout work in the following terms.

> The art desk often wants to make the magazine much more creative and you usually have editors that are pulling you back and sort of saying, 'it's still got to be user friendly, it's still got to be all these things'. So you can start to get carried away. When you first start at magazines you want to try everything out and as you get more experience you realise you've got to be designing for the reader and not necessarily for yourself.
>
> (Interview 13)

The suggestion here is that some kind of compromise between the professional desires of creative workers to fulfil their own internal, professional standards of excellence needs to be balanced with an awareness of the different orientations of readers. We asked Matthew whether, given such constraints, there could be any changes implemented in the industry that would somehow make it easier to do good work as an art director. His reply betrayed frustration at the limitations put on what he was able to do by the tastes of his audiences:

> I wish the mentality of people buying the magazine would change where they would go for much more style-based imagery and a beautifully laid-out magazine. The magazines which are doing really well are the weeklies, which are cheap, quick to read and they're not based around their design and creativity.
>
> (Interview 13)

However, Matthew felt that audiences in France and Italy were more amenable to high standards of design:

> If you look at French *Vogue* compared to English *Vogue*, French *Vogue* is beautifully laid out, very simple, stylish, and British *Vogue* you tend to have lots of colours all over it because I think we have a different market over here. I wish the buying public would change and we could make a stylish magazine really successful.
>
> (Interview 13)

This suggests that Matthew sees differences between workers and audiences as open to change. But he saw little hope of such a change, given the competitiveness of the UK magazine industry:

> My covers are getting less and less stylish and much more commercial. They're still very stylish, but they're becoming much more commercial than they ever have been because they have to be. They have to be like that, you've got to have bright oranges and lots of sells on it and things that are going to catch people's attention because it's in a magazine shop where there are thousands of magazines and you've got to grab people's attention.
>
> (Interview 13)

So how might an art director like Matthew do work he can be proud of?

> You have to adapt your work to your market which you are appealing to. I'm creative but I'm not necessarily an artist: 'this is my vision, it's got to be like this otherwise I'm not going to do it'. I've got to work. If I wanted to do that I could have gone to fine art school and become an artist and done exactly what I wanted and tried to flog it and probably never

flogged anything in my life and be living on the street. So you've got to be realistic. You've got to design something which is successful, but you can still be good within your design. You may have the restraints but you can still do the best job of that and be proud of what you do, because it's still good but it's not exactly how you would necessarily do it if you didn't have to sell any copy.

(Interview 13)

Matthew seemingly reconciles himself to the compromises he rather reluctantly must face as a designer by contrasting his position with that of 'artists' who show an unrealistic disregard for the need to communicate with an audience, and to make money. As an artist, he implies, he would never even have found an audience. As a men's magazine art director, although he is dissatisfied with the audience ('I wish the mentality of people buying the magazine would change'), and not doing the designs he most values, he recognises that within these constraints he can still produce good work ('you can still be good within your design') which is both creative (stylish) and commercial. Though he is an art director located on the art desk of a magazine, then, he is not an artist. This distinction seems to enable Matthew to understand what he does, in the commercial environment, to be good work. He distances himself from the idea of self-indulgent artistic work by invoking the image of destitution ('living on the streets'). There is a 'realistic' acceptance of compromise ('you've got to be realistic') but even within this commercial space Matthew finds possibilities for innovative and creative design if he accepts the generic conditions under which he works. He doesn't want to be one of those 'precious art directors throwing their toys out the pram' and so he is resigned to accepting that the limitations of his audience will necessarily mean limitations on what he designs.

A number of our interviewees alluded to the 'artist' as a persona very much avoided in their conceptualisation of themselves as creative workers. When asked if they would ever use terms like 'creative', 'professional' or 'artist' to describe what they did, sound recordist Lachlan, for example, stated definitively: 'No. I don't call myself an artist [he laughs]. That's just pretentious' (Interview 23), and documentary producer Samuel remarked 'I mean you might sound a bit poncy [*sic*] if you call yourself an artist. I think Picasso would have a few issues with that' (Interview 21).[4] The image of the artist that was drawn by Matthew, above, is very much reflected in a discussion by Aggie of her love of writing and her decision to become a journalist. She began writing poetry in school with the encouragement of teachers and then at

---

4 'Ponce' originally meant 'pimp' but it is more usually used in Britain to denote a mixture of effeteness, effeminacy and pretentiousness. The word 'poncy' is therefore loaded with a homophobic and sexist suspicion of the aesthetic and of adornment. But it can also have an anti-bourgeois edge.

age 15 had a teacher who introduced her to 'the concept of writing funny articles'. She said:

> That's what started me off really and I started going away from poetry and started trying to entertain at that point. That's when I took a decision that if I was going to write I wanted to make money out of it. I didn't want to be an artist dying in a garret, so it was going to have commercial potential. So it had to be something that was quite usable, quite flexible, and maybe not the bleeding heart stuff that I used to write.
>
> (Interview 18)

Whereas Matthew was in a constant process of reconciling his art (stylish design) with commerce (commercial covers), and, while not wanting to be a 'precious art director', clearly felt a sense of being aesthetically compromised by the men's magazine market, Aggie seems to have made a clear choice between art and commerce and the audience were part of this decision – she wanted her work to be 'usable', 'flexible' with 'commercial potential' and this wasn't going to happen with poetry ('the bleeding heart stuff').

> Where I am now I think I come down very heavily on people who are too flowery or too self-indulgent in their journalism writing because this is not the place for it. If you want to do that do it somewhere else and I know that because I've made the decision in my life that if I want to do a novel, it's private and it's elsewhere. This is delivering a service and I feel very passionately about that.
>
> (Interview 18)

In Aggie's tale there is no room for the 'self-indulgent artist' that Matthew alludes to. This is not about being resigned to accepting the limitations imposed on one's work by the audience of that work, as was the case for Matthew. Rather, for Aggie, it is a decision, and a passion that was evident in the way in which she talked about her work in the trade press, about delivering a necessary service to the audience in the most effective way possible – a professional or craft notion of good work that resonates with the positions of other trade journalists we discussed in Section 9.2.

9.5 Television and audience size: ratings tyranny?

In the television industry, as in all cultural industries, communication with audiences is fundamental. But in the modern television industry, there is a central mechanism that has dominated discussion of audiences, as the quotation from Arnold Becker that opens this chapter suggests: *ratings*. At all levels in the television industry ratings figure in some way or other in workers' experience and understanding of the audience, if only because ratings give an indication of the degree to which their work has been experienced by others. Of course, what ratings cannot indicate is the quality of audience experience.

Iris, a commissioner of entertainment programmes described to us the significance of ratings:

> They are always important. You don't ignore them. I'd be lying if I said it doesn't matter what we get, because at the end of the day, you have sweated blood and tears to make a show, and you want people to watch it. If you think it's a good show you want people to watch it and it can be disheartening if they don't. I think it is important from a personal point of view, but I think the main goal is that we want to provide a broad and varied schedule that suits all the audiences. So at one time or another there is something that they really want to watch.
>
> (Interview 57)

Two issues are raised here. One is the central role of ratings in the organisation of content on television. The second is the emotional attachment that workers sometimes have for their programmes and therefore the pain, or pleasure, that can come from seeing the ratings figures. The number of people who watch a programme is an important aspect of the value that creative workers find in their work. As we noted in Section 8.2 when asked about the motivations behind her work, Margie, a researcher in factual entertainment at the BBC, told us 'it's just making features that I think people at home would want to watch. It's knowing that what we are making people are going to see, and people are going to be watching' (Interview 35).

Gary, a freelance director in arts documentary, explained to us that the reason he chose television as a career was because of the audience that can be reached in this industry. He compared the viewing figures for his art programmes to the readership figures of *The Guardian* newspaper:

> The reason why it's television and not anything else for me is you are reaching 500,000 people. I mean *The Guardian*'s circulation, that's low viewing figures [for] a Channel 5 arts programme. That's not the millions. *The Guardian* circulation is 212 [thousand],[5] something like that. ... The programmes I make go out to twice as many people so they touch twice as many people as *The Guardian* does. Even though I might think that the comment piece in *The Guardian* is really fantastic, well, you're only saying it to half the people that watch the programme. That's a great feeling.
>
> (Interview 24)

---

5 In fact, *The Guardian*'s Audit Bureau of Circulation figures for December 2007, when this interview was conducted, were 353,436.

Viewing figures were also mentioned by Lorne, a junior cameraman in factual entertainment, as one of the principal rewards of working in television:

> It's quite nice when you think to yourself 4.5 million people watched something you did. That's buzzing. That's a really nice feeling. But when 500,000 watched it you think 'oh, that's not very good'. But then you've got to put it into perspective and think 'that's still quite a lot of people'.
>
> (Interview 25)

Higher up the production hierarchy, articulations of relationships between work and audiences were sometimes more detailed. For factual entertainment producer and company director Kieran, the audience is central to the way programmes come to be structured. The audience comes to be at the forefront of the creative worker's mind because 'there's enormous pressure on them [broadcasters] to bring in a big audience' and this is even the case for the niche factual programming in which his company specialises. The commissioner of these programmes at Channel 4 is 'under enormous pressure to make sure those films clear two million' and with other channels, such as ITV, 'if a show isn't rating they will pull it'. Ratings pressure finds its way down the hierarchy, as can also be seen in Lorne's comments above: 'We want something that I can see is accessible to different age groups and therefore is going to pull a wide audience. You think also about the demographics of different channels.' For Kieran, as a producer, it has a quite specific impact on content:

> We are quite ruthless when we make films that have commercial breaks in them to make sure that they always, always, always [ensure] you are not going to leave that programme. ... What you fear is when one inherits a high audience, say from *Eastenders* and before, and then falls away, because that is really bad. So we try and structure the programme internally to make sure they keep an audience or build an audience.
>
> (Interview 20)

Another producer Ingrid describes this focus on the audience as being a significant shift in production practice, and this, she says, is a result of a multi-channel environment where the 'viewers hold all the cards' and where, as Shaun, a factual editor, pointed out, 'you can't be complacent about an audience' (Interview 14). The changes, says Ingrid, have been dramatic:

> When I started, at the BBC nobody thought about the viewer. No-one talked about the viewer at all, no-one, absolutely no-one. You made a documentary for your head of department to think you've done well, you know, to admire, and for your peers, and for your friends to watch. So if those people thought it was good and maybe if you are very lucky the controller of BBC1 or 2 would ring you up or send you a memo, that

would be amazing, and you also made it to get a good review. I mean nobody got ratings through really.

(Interview 11)

However, there may be somewhat more going on in this discourse than initially meets the eye. For this is a senior creative manager in a powerful independent production company, and her picture of the 'old' BBC as self-indulgently making programmes for itself, may be driven by a commitment to neo-liberal ideologies of entrepreneurial production. Nevertheless, this producer told us that television production should not be driven by ratings but rather 'what people are interested in has to inform what you make and what you enjoy' and that 'you can only really be driven by the great idea you have and whether you like it'.

But ratings are undoubtedly central to the working lives of many people in broadcasting institutions, whether at network broadcasters or production companies. The publication of ratings figures is a key moment in the working day. Martha, a controller of arts programming at one British broadcaster, explained: 'Every morning at about 10 o'clock, and its true of the whole industry, everyone in every single broadcaster will be getting an email saying "here are the overnights" and they'll be going "oh"' (Interview 6). Martha claimed that in her department there was less emphasis on ratings success and more on 'profile raising' for the channel – though of course to claim otherwise might risk making her channel look overly driven by commercial imperatives. But for Ingrid, who works in a more competitive genre, the arrival of the daily email highlighting 'what's won the slot?' is a critical moment in her working day. We asked Ingrid how she felt when opening the email containing the figures. Did she feel trepidation for example?

> Oh yes, particularly if it's a new thing [show]. We are doing eight one hours [one hour programmes] about the home for BBC2, which will go out this summer, and we are making them now, and until real people watch them, we won't know whether what we have created has a resonance with anyone. It's really exciting when something goes well and you can tell people are finding it. ... But there is trepidation as well because the downside of that is if it doesn't do very well, it's something you love and no-one likes it. It's very vicious now. In the past you made a series for the BBC in the late 80s, they would probably give it three series before axing it, hoping it would find an audience and they would say we're not going to try that again.[6] Now four episodes on ITV1, if it doesn't make it, they pull it.

(Interview 11)

---

6 Again, as above, Ingrid's position as a powerful independent producer may push her in the direction of signalling her sector's superiority to the old broadcasting system they have played

Yet, even in the ratings-focused world of contemporary television, it should not be forgotten that these feelings about ratings are linked to something deeper, concerning the desire to communicate with a public. Both Ingrid and Kieran, for example, talked of the satisfaction that comes from moments when they hear people praising a programme they were involved in producing. Ingrid describes how 'it's very exciting when that happens and you hear people talking about it on the bus or whatever. It really is a very good feeling'. Kieran is even more expansive:

> The best thing in the world is to hear people in a playground[7] chatting about the programme you've made and not knowing that you have made it and hearing what they think about it, and it becoming a talking point. You used to be able to do that a lot with ITV in particular, because if it's on ITV at nine o'clock, four or five or six million people would have seen the programme and they would remember [the characters]. There is no point in making programmes for no one, is there?
>
> (Interview 20)

Our interview with camera operator Nigel suggested that this is very much connected to an understanding of good work:

> when you have your work on television, the rewards for me are people saying they saw the programme, because there's no point in having a programme on television and people saying 'well, your camerawork was shit'. You want people to say 'that was really good, we enjoyed it and we thought it was good'. That way when your peers appreciate you, also it means that other people see your work and then you get a slightly better quality of work as well.
>
> (Interview 33)

So for Nigel, a key aspect of the rewards of his work is the response of peers. For freelance workers, at least in documentary, ratings, even though they are regarded as important, are secondary to the professional opinions of those working in the industry. It is, after all, this professional audience that will provide opportunities for involvement in any future 'good work'. For as Nigel indicates the esteem that comes from peers can translate into offers of 'slightly better quality' jobs to work on. The importance of the professional audience as a judge of 'good work' and as a repository of future work is expanded on by documentary editor Shaun:

---

a key role in replacing, or at least her own toughness in being able to cope with this new more rigorous competitive environment.

7 Kieran is presumably thinking of overheard conversations by other parents when he is picking up a child from school.

That is a joy if that happens, if people watch something you've done, that I think is special. The pilot we did for this garbage worker thing went to [documentary festival] Hot Docs and it was applauded and they'd never had this. People stood up and they applauded, and that made me feel quite good.[8] I mean we've got to see what the film does [once released to a general audience], but I did get a buzz from that. I do get a buzz when people ring me up and they say 'we got your name'. The next offer of a job, the next engagement, is only a measure of what you've just done. I can't rest on what I did five years ago, it's what you did yesterday, and I think 'why should it be any other way?' You know, why should your contribution be less?

(Interview 14)

9.6 Audiences, ambivalence and projection

Audiences are central to experiences of creative work, but their role is highly unstable. In his classic analysis of television news, and the relationship 'newsmen' have with the audience, originally published in 1978, Philip Schlesinger wrote that:

> when pressed, they produce vague ideas about their audiences, based on their view of the kinds of people who listen to or watch particular channels, or from interactions with neighbours or people on trains. Ultimately the newsman is his own audience.
>
> (Schlesinger 1978: 134)

This certainly cannot be said of contemporary creative workers, whether in television or in other industries. The marketised media environment makes media workers more conscious than ever of audiences, and the need to please and attract them. But the continuing drive for autonomy on the part of many creative workers produces a great deal of ambivalence in this relationship. Audiences are the means by which creative workers hope to resolve their anxieties about the quality of their work. But profound uncertainty about what audiences might think and feel means that workers project many different views of human intellectual and emotional capacity on to them, with quite different consequences for autonomy and self-realisation.

---

8 This is intended as understatement – a very British conversational strategy. He means it made him feel *really* good.

10 The politics of good and bad work

10.1 The hardest way to make an easy living?

The main aim of this book has been to contribute to recent debates about the quality of work in the cultural industries by examining experiences of creative work. We saw in Chapter 1 that there has been a tendency in much creative industries policy discourse to celebrate creative labour or simply to ignore the contradictions involved (see Banks and Hesmondhalgh 2009). In response to this, a set of critical approaches, many of them derived from cultural studies, has strongly emphasised the way in which seemingly positive aspects of creative labour become tied to negative ones (Chapter 3). Our claim was that these approaches have not always been able to pay sufficient attention to the normative and ethical assumptions underlying their evaluations. At the heart of this book has been an attempt to conceptualise these assumptions more fully (based on the discussion of normative principles in Chapter 2). In listening to creative workers, and observing them, we have tried to achieve a good balance between a number of factors: the recognition that these workers may not always be fully aware of their own conditions and experiences; the need to analyse the forms of structural causality that influence these conditions and experiences, and which result in profound inequalities of access and reward; and the obligation to take seriously these workers when they recount positive experiences, and not dismiss these as the product of ideology or disciplinary discourses.

We sought to achieve these aims by asking: What kinds of experiences do jobs and occupations in the cultural industries offer their workers? And we have seen that many cultural-industry jobs and occupations are riddled with problems and inequities. Many are offered on a short-term basis, making it difficult to plan ahead with any certainty, and constraining workers' abilities to make their work the basis of meaningful self-realisation. Although many people respect art, learning and knowledge, some see them as mere ornamentation, and creative labour as a kind of social luxury. This limits the degree to which workers in these industries can feel sure of social respect and recognition. Autonomy is always limited, but many creative workers have little control over the products they are involved in, especially in terms of how strategies that can develop a number of positive features of work according to our model: sociality and community, recognition and esteem, and security. But Mosco and McKercher also recognise that craft solidarity can be destructive, and that the ITU, for example, tried the patience of workers as they grew into a more bureaucratic and professional bargaining institution, concerned with 'jurisdiction over the tools of the trade' to the exclusion of protection and promotion of the craft itself. Mosco and McKercher also valuably trace efforts to build 'convergent unions' in North America, including mergers of unions, and consolidation of bargaining efforts in particular workplaces. This is a response to real, predicted and putative 'technological and corporate convergence in the knowledge economy': journalists join with technical workers, media workers unite with telephone operators and cable installers. Perhaps the most notable instance is the Communication Workers of America (CWA), which originally represented telephone workers, but has now incorporated the ITU and other newspaper and broadcasting unions. Yet there have also been numerous failed mergers, and convergence is by no means the main factor in achieving better working conditions – solidarity and the ability to reach public opinion matter too.

One important potential threat to the effectiveness of unions is the individualisation that we discussed in Chapter 6, whereby workers tend to see organisations, and jobs, as opportunities for self-development, rather than as sources of commitment. For the most widely cited theorist of individualisation, Ulrich Beck (2000: 94), this offers some new freedoms in that people become independent of traditional ties, but it also leads to competitiveness and isolation. In the eyes of some commentators, this leads to 'an individualistic and self-centred culture of contentment that sees no virtue in forms of collective association and solidarity' (Taylor 2001, quoted in Saundry et al. 2006: 378). In the cultural industries, this leads to a situation where '[p]ersonal networks are recognized as the central mechanism both for individual career advancement and risk reduction' (Christopherson 2008: 89). Susan Christopherson, in a fine analysis of changes in the US film and television industries, claims that in a context where middling budget productions are being eroded by the huge demand for cheap programming in the era of multichannel television on the one hand, and the blockbuster syndrome in movies on the other, there has been a strengthening of 'defensive exclusionary networks' (ibid.) which dominate access to the best jobs. Her case is convincing, but in a study of various UK freelance networks, Saundry et al. (2006) suggest that networks are not always exclusionary devices. In some cases, they can provide assistance and support for workers as they negotiate their way through freelance labour markets. They lack the knowledge and experience of unions, and members can only to a very limited degree represent the interests of others without fear of punishment from employers. Nevertheless, trade unions need to draw on the sense of collective identity and shared interests that some networks appear to foster. They need to work alongside networks and complement them.

There are other kinds of networks too; for example, networks of political activism beyond trade unions. One of the achievements of the recent autonomist Marxist concern with 'precarity' (about which we made critical comments in Chapter 7) has been its focus on the construction of cross-class alliances based around the shared experience of insecurity (see Neilson and Rossiter 2005). Andrew Ross (2009) has argued that if such alliances are to flourish, 'organizers have to understand, and build on, the experience of precarity as a central element of people's lives, rather than as a temporary state of misfortune that can be remedied by a halfway decent contract' (Ross 2009: 212). This recommendation that activists adjust to new contexts is surely right, as long as it does not mean giving up on struggles for job security. Rather than secure, long-term job contracts, suggests Ross, authentic freedoms may best be delivered by other means. But if the job contract and security are no longer to be key demands for workers, then what alternative arrangements can protect workers and professionals, across the class divide? Ross mentions two possibilities – a social charter and a basic guaranteed income – but he does not have space to explore them at the end of a book that has already covered considerable ground. Our own approach is focused more on questions of well-being and quality of life, but we return to the issue of basic guaranteed income below.

10.3 Work and life: choosing not to self-exploit?

There are areas of the contemporary problem of good work that unions, networks and enlightened employers can only play a part in reaching. As a new work ethic has taken hold of many professional, craft and service workers, new coalitions have formed to argue for much greater consideration to be given to the role of work within life, in public policy and in the lives of individuals. While unions and enlightened employers are an important part of efforts to improve matters (see Bunting 2005: 271–300) they can only be a part of it. Individuals need to make commitments not to prioritise their own self-realisation and self-esteem over the well-being of others.

Many individuals gain considerable autonomy in their work, whether by operating as a freelancer, or through the relative freedom that professional status can afford workers in some occupations. In this position, self-management can turn into self-exploitation, where the worker drives herself or himself harder and harder in order to achieve excellence, further status and perhaps even to maintain the very freedom they have struggled to achieve in the first place. Of course, 'self-exploitation' is a misnomer. The seemingly individual decisions made by such workers are partly the result of structural forces shaping the values that people hold about how best to live their lives. But there remains a crucial difference between workers who are closely supervised and monitored, and those educated professionals who internalise their commitment to hard work. Ultimately, it has to be individuals who have to make ethical choices about the degree to which they commit themselves to work.

'Work–life balance' only partly captures the issue here. In terms of our theoretical and ethical framework, this is part of a wider problem: how we might combine self-realisation through labour with other modes of self-realisation and human flourishing, such as bringing up children, sustaining friendships, contributing to the well-being of those with whom we share local communities, and of those further afield too. Work is a fundamentally important aspect of self-realisation, as Murphy (1993), Elster (1986) and others have argued. Yet, even allowing for people's different dispositions and desires, if we seek to realise our capacities mainly or exclusively through our work, we may end up feeling that we live unbalanced and even miserable lives. Statistics suggest that in contemporary societies, while many struggle to gain and sustain meaningful employment, and this keeps figures on average working hours down, many others work very long hours. The USA is notorious for its long-hours culture and poor protection for workers (Schor 1992). But the UK may be heading the same way. Madeline Bunting (2005: 9) cites figures showing that Britain's full-time workers put in the longest hours in Europe, 43.6 per week versus the EU average of 40.3. According to the UK Office of National Statistics, around six million people in the UK, or 19.1 per cent of people in employment, work more than 45 hours a week (Snowdon 2009). Bunting herself and Hochschild (1997, 2003) have shown that much of this derives from the individual's own sense of responsibility and competitiveness. Hochschild (2003) has captured the effects of the increasing time pressures on families in moving ethnographic research, and asks why there is no culture of resistance to the overwork culture. Only part of it is the struggle to keep up with rising expectations of what consumption might offer. It is also that many people appear to feel more recognised and respected in contemporary work cultures than at home, because some workplaces reward skilled and expert workers with a high degree of quality of work life (Hochschild 2003: 206). Hochschild describes this as an emergent form of 'socialism for the rich, capitalism for the poor' (p. 212). Like Bunting, she helps us to understand that it is not only the worker herself or himself that suffers in that situation, it can also affect spouses, life partners, children, ageing parents and relatives, and others who depend on the person involved. Activist groups, local communities and civic organisations need the input of willing and able people. Self-exploitation leads to reduced well-being for others too.

All this is particularly relevant to the cultural industries. As the sector has expanded, as have cognate areas such as information technology work, the growing creative labour market may be a particularly strong site for self-exploitation. This is partly because of the special bond that many workers may feel for their own talents as actors, singers, musicians, engineers, camera operators and so on. This can lead them to push for success against all the odds in highly competitive marketplaces. It is also because 'the myth of the starving artist' may lead workers to believe that it is quite natural that they should have to make sacrifices to achieve recognition. The historical context is important here. In Chapter 1, we put the increasing focus on questions of creativity (and craft) in late twentieth-century management discourse in the context of 'the crisis of work' and 'the refusal of work' of the mid twentieth century. The French social theorists Luc Boltanski and Eve Chiapello (2005/1999) have argued that in effect capitalism was reinvented from the 1970s to the 1990s, based on a 'third spirit of capitalism' with a new set of legitimating principles. These principles appropriated key elements of the critiques of capitalism prevalent in a previous era, especially what Boltanski and Chiapello call the 'artistic critique' of Taylorist capitalism's rigidity, bureaucracy and stifling of creativity. In particular, states and managers began to recognise demands for autonomy. As a result, in Boltanski and Chiapello's words, '[i]n a political reversal, autonomy was, as it were, exchanged for security' (Boltanski and Chiapello 2005/1999: 190, original emphasis). Self-exploitation is particularly a danger in this new system that seeks to gain the love of a much wider swathe of workers for their work by purporting to value their autonomy and creativity. Boltanski and Chiapello coolly hedge around the normative issues raised – including whether values such as self-realisation, autonomy and creativity might still be viable ethical goals in a system that so effectively appropriates them. As should be clear by now, we believe they still can be – and must be. Rejection seems out of the question. But the pursuit of these values by individuals needs to be balanced against other ethical principles.

10.4 Spreading good and bad work: how intractable is the social division of labour?

We stressed individual choice in the previous section. But such choices are made possible by social conditions and political struggles. Individual choice is a matter of social justice. Equally, social justice entails taking into account the variety of people's motivations and capacities. Some people are highly oriented to self-realisation through work, and some people find work the best way to achieve the esteem and recognition that most of us need. There are of course unhealthy and even psychotic versions of this drive. Yet there are many people for whom the demands of devoting substantial energy to work will always feel hard to bear. And for many people raising families, the demands of combining work and home life can feel close to impossible for much of the time. Societies need to recognise that such differences are always likely to exist, and should not punish or reward these groups disproportionately. But in the winner-take-all labour markets of modern capitalism, the very successful are rewarded out of all proportion to their talents and skills (Frank and Cook 1996). Creative labour markets are perhaps the most notably public example of this dynamic in modern societies, alongside sport. Disproportionate celebrity and financial reward create an aura of charismatic brilliance around the very successful, which makes it look as though their rewards are the natural outcome of their awe-inspiring talent.

In fact, motivation, luck and educational capital play a huge role in success. We need to think about these problems of the quality of life, and the role of work within it, in terms of questions of equality and social justice.

In Chapter 1, we explained our view that some post-structuralist perspectives on work risk suspending a realistic discussion of what might constitute good work, and therefore of how work in modern societies might be made better. This includes fundamental questions concerning how the benefits and burdens associated with work might be more fairly distributed.

A balance we have tried to strike in this book has been to consider the problem of good and bad creative work in the context of the problem of good and bad work as a whole, while still holding on to the specificity of creative labour. This has meant drawing upon an unorthodox combination of political theory, cultural studies, business and management studies, sociology of work, and media studies. Here we return to the productive abstractions of political theory, to provide a basis for thinking through what is desirable in terms of radical social change. We do so because of the efforts by some political philosophers to take seriously the uneven distribution of benefits and burdens across societies, and how questions of freedom, justice and efficiency might be addressed.

This is not to say that political philosophy, which predominantly operates within a liberal framework,[3] is always preferable as a tradition to Marxian and post-structuralist approaches. In fact, the mainstream of political philosophy has on the whole been strangely quiet about the meaning and significance of work in contemporary societies. John Rawls's *Theory of Justice* (1971), the major work of political philosophy in this tradition, for example, barely mentions work (though it does question the degree to which a just society ought to reward citizens based on what they 'deserve', the issue we raised in the previous section). Where political philosophers have addressed the subject of work, the results have often been disappointing. Robert Nozick's *Anarchy, State and Utopia* (1974), often cited as the second major book in modern liberal political philosophy after Rawls's, defended huge rewards for some workers (using the case of the then famous basketball player Wilt Chamberlain) on the grounds that people freely chose to give their money to see him play, and that attempts to control or redistribute inequality were assaults on the freedom and self-ownership of those people.[4] The example is relevant to the cultural industries where, as is evident on a daily

---

3 Liberal in its political–philosophical sense of a concern with the freedom and autonomy of individuals and a concern to protect and/or promote 'the capacity of individuals to frame, revise and pursue a conception of the good' (see Swift 2001: 137, quoting John Rawls). As Adam Swift notes, there are left, egalitarian liberals in this sense and libertarian right-leaning ones; this is not the sense of 'liberal' used in the United States and increasingly in other places to denote the opposite of 'conservative'.

4 For a critique of the self-ownership thesis, and of its continuing influence on Marxism, see Cohen (1995).

basis from the media, the best-paid workers are rewarded hugely and disproportionately. Nozick's basic assumption, influential on the libertarian conservatism that was to dominate government from the 1980s on, is that freedom matters far more than equality. Nozick (1974: 246–50) deals with the problem of the widespread presence of bad work in modern societies by arguing that there is no way of fixing such problems that does not violate freedom. Where it produces greater efficiency, capitalism, seen as a thoroughly rational system operating on principles of perfect information, responds to workers' desires for meaningful work by altering their organisations to make meaningful work more available. Where providing meaningful work is less efficient, workers can simply choose to give up some wages to do more meaningful work which might increase their self-esteem; Nozick gives the example of university teachers, but he might just as easily have cited creative workers.

Some political philosophers though have recognised that markets might not be quite as magically able to combine freedom and entitlement as Nozick suggests. Adina Schwartz (1982), for example, noted the existence of large numbers of routine jobs, which she found degrading to people because they did not allow humans to act as autonomous agents while performing them. This was because they gave people 'almost no opportunities for formulating aims, for deciding on means for achieving their ends, or for adjusting their goals and methods in the light of experience' (p. 634). Schwartz's quasi-Kantian critique of the limitations on freedom in much contemporary work was linked to an egalitarian politics whereby all members of society should be treated as autonomous agents. Under present conditions, inequality of access to meaningful work (that which allowed people to act as autonomous agents) prevented this from happening. Schwartz's solution was a wholesale democratic redesign of work, abolition of the detailed division of labour, and an end to the separation between mental and manual labour.

Such a view has deep roots. In a famous passage from *The German Ideology*, Marx and Engels (1974/1845) provided a beguiling portrait of life in a future communist society.

> For as soon as the division of labour comes into being, each man has a particular, exclusive sphere of activity, which is forced upon him and from which he cannot escape. He is a hunter, a fisherman, a shepherd, or a critic, and must remain so if he does not want to lose his means of livelihood; whereas in communist society, where nobody has one exclusive sphere of activity but each can become accomplished in any branch he wishes, society regulates the general production and thus makes it possible for me to do one thing today and another tomorrow, to hunt in the morning, fish in the afternoon, rear cattle in the evening, criticize after dinner, just as I have a mind, without ever becoming hunter, fisherman, shepherd, or critic.

The danger – one which leftists need to take seriously – is that such moves might so prioritise the fair distribution of meaningful work, or of work potentially offering high levels of self-realisation, that other important notions of the good might suffer. For example, the efficiency losses associated with such a shift might mean a significant reduction in leisure time, or in the range of goods available. For Richard Arneson (1987), approaches such as Schwartz's and Elster's were examples of 'perfectionist' social criticism and this risked systematically promoting the preferences of some over the no less rational preferences of others. In modern society, claimed Arneson, people's conception of their own good, and of their own self-realisation, is too diverse to accommodate in a state-driven plan. Arneson felt that the critique of division of labour relies on an assumption that production is to be valued above consumption. But consumption too can be an important means of self-realisation, and Arneson pointed out that people might viably choose to do less rewarding work, if it means more leisure time. After all, as we have seen in this book, to gain entry and to sustain one's position in forms of rewarding and meaningful work will often involve considerable effort and determination. This does not mean that we should reject all forms of paternalism, whereby democratic decisions are made that lots of people do not like. But a position that 'recognizes many goods to be equally suitable as dominant aims for a person's life will not recommend state policies that pre-empt individual choice among these aims' (Arneson 1987: 527). Instead, Arneson claimed, the best way to ensure the best balance of equality, freedom and efficiency would be the general redistribution of resources so that people could satisfy their own individual preferences, using a basic guaranteed income for all. This is a serious proposal, widely debated by those who are concerned with the problem of work in modern societies. The French social theorist André Gorz has argued powerfully for such a proposal on the grounds that it is the most appropriate arrangement in a situation where technology drives production and in which actual direct working time is less important than producing and reproducing workforce skills and knowledge (Gorz 1999: 87). But this is based on a problematic assessment of the state of technology, which assumes that the burdens of work necessary to maintain and achieve a decent quality of life across the world are diminishing. A guaranteed basic income cannot be dismissed as naive utopianism, but it is not at all clear that is practicable or desirable.[5]

Nevertheless, Arneson was surely right to point to the problem of human diversity, and to wonder whether the introduction of measures to spread meaningful work might actually diminish people's overall good. But might there be ways in which we might begin to think about *adjustments* to the social division of labour short of imagining that it can somehow be eradicated, or its injustices resolved through the basic guaranteed income?

---

5 For a sophisticated consideration of the basic guaranteed income, see Parijs (1997).

Andrew Sayer (2009: 10) has addressed a number of possible objections to 'the idea of sharing tasks of different qualities instead of allocating complex and routine tasks to different workers'. This usefully moves the debate about division of labour on from the hope of eradicating the division between manual and mental labour that concerns utopians such as Schwartz (as well as Marxist utopians, see for example Badiou 2008: 98). Sayer deals with three objections to such adjustments: that they would be inefficient and costly; that they would be unfeasible; and that the unequal social division of labour reflects the different abilities and capacities of workers. He argues that the inefficiency objection has been partly undermined by the failures of Taylorist practices and the (partial) success of some experiments where routine and complex work is more evenly shared. It is also partly undermined by the fact that the unequal social division of labour often reflects the hoarding of privileges rather than the pursuit of efficiency (c.f. Tilly 1998). Sayer concedes the feasibility argument when it comes to the most skilled kinds of work, but he asks whether the routine aspects of skilled work really need to be devolved to others, given that this is likely to be less rewarding for the 'assistant', for whom the job is not part of a complete job, than for the skilled person. What is more, for skilled people to do occasional routine work (say, a group of musicians cleaning up the studio after they have used it) might 'prevent them becoming arrogant and unappreciative of the privilege of being allowed to be excused the greater part of the routine work' (Sayer 2009: 10). Finally, the unequal abilities objection 'reflects a naive conception of the origin of differences in abilities' (Sayer 2009: 11). Sayer uses Adam Smith's remarks on the stupefying effects of the division of labour, and educational research to show that 'abilities are largely a product of socialisation and activities' (citing Gomberg 2007). As well as these factors undermining objections to reforming the social division of labour, Sayer outlines some consequences of the present social division of labour that may override them.

> Is it 'efficient' – or socially just – to restrict the development of large numbers of individuals' skills by confining them to routine work? Is it 'efficient' or just to deny them the recognition that complex work can bring and the self-esteem that tends to follow from that?
>
> (Sayer 2009: 12)

The relevance of all this to creative labour is two-fold. First, as we have seen, in spite of the difficult conditions faced by many creative workers, many of them gain considerable rewards from the recognition that this work allows. But who gets these jobs? Creative workers tend to be highly educated, to come from middle-class backgrounds, and it has been difficult for non-white workers and women to gain access to the most prestigious sectors of the cultural industries. This depends on wider patterns of inequality, including the general social division of labour, and the distribution of routine and complex tasks across different social groups. Those concerned with equality and social justice need to consider ways in which access to the means of cultural production might be broadened in order to make these aspects of good work more widely available to other sectors of the population.

Second, within the cultural industries themselves, there is a division of labour, with some people taking on more of the creative, demanding, challenging but also rewarding work, especially that around symbol-making and craft skills, and others involved in 'humdrum' (Caves 2000) routine tasks. To repeat the earlier example, someone has to clear up after musicians and producers have used a recording studio. We may not want to argue for government regulations that require people to clean up after themselves, even though many people living with lazy individuals, and many parents of teenage children, would happily vote for such a measure in a referendum. But we may want to advocate a shift in social conventions whereby it would be considered a matter of social shame to leave mess for the less privileged to tidy up. And of course cleaning here stands for a whole set of routine tasks that are generally granted little esteem in modern societies. Here the broader question of the gender division of labour is, as in many other cases regarding work, absolutely crucial (see Ehrenreich 2001).

We have been using Sayer's arguments to claim that an adjustment in the social division of labour in the interests of spreading good and bad work is feasible and may well be desirable. Returning to Arneson's objections, another strategy we might adopt to move beyond 'perfectionism' is to look at which political-economic and cultural systems produce good working experiences and products. Russell Keat (2009) has argued that Arneson's market socialist perspective may be too reliant on a neo-classical conception of the market. An important aspect of Arneson's argument is that states ought to be neutral regarding different conceptions of good work. Keat uses comparative political economy to show that, even under contemporary conditions, as opposed to some projected better economic system, there are different varieties of capitalism with different institutional characters, and these varieties differ in the degree to which they can offer 'good work'. Keat cites Hall and Soskice (2001) to claim that 'co-ordinated market economies' such as Germany have been able to offer, to a greater degree than the Anglo-American liberal market model, workplaces with 'autonomy from close monitoring', 'opportunities to influence the decisions of the firm', a high level and range of skills and so on – all features of good and meaningful work, according to a wide range of definitions. This means that there are political choices to be made about which institutional arrangements are most likely to encourage fairness and at what cost, and this cannot simply be left to some monolithic entity known as the market. This undermines Arneson's preference for welfarism and his critique of perfectionism, and suggests the desirability of an approach that requires political debate to take into account ethical questions regarding notions of the human good, and how they might be realised through work.

In this book, we have focused on experiences of creative work, but have framed this within an analysis of what structures and determines those experiences. We have seen that the cultural industries provide some great jobs as well as some awful jobs. In our view, the most pressing issue for a political understanding of creative labour becomes not how to boost the creative or media sector as a whole, which is the fundamental aim of creative industries policy (see Banks and Hesmondhalgh 2009), but how to incorporate creative labour into consideration of the distribution of good and bad work across societies as a whole. Good and bad media work is as much a matter of social justice as it is of individual experience. But both experience and justice are crucial aspects of political struggle.

Appendix
The interviews

Table A.1

Interview No.	Pseudonym	Job title	Industry	Genre	Date
1	Leon	Producer/ film-maker	Television	Documentary	10/03/06
2	Niamh	Musician	Music	Rock/pop	14/03/06
3	Robert	Musician	Music	Rock/pop	14/03/06
4	Giles	Freelance writer	Magazine	Music	28/03/06
5	Wayne	Editor	Magazine	Music	08/05/06
6	Martha	Commissioning editor	Television	Documentary	11/05/06
7	Ellen	Marketer	Magazine	Music	17/05/06
8	Ryan	Artist manager	Music	Rock/pop	24/05/06
9	Larry	Features editor/ writer	Magazine	Men's	20/06/06
10	Annette	Musician	Music	Jazz	23/06/06
11	Ingrid	Managing director	Television	Factual	23/06/06
12	William	Junior writer	Magazine	Men's	30/06/06
13	Matthew	Art director	Magazine	Men's	30/06/06
14	Shaun	Freelance editor	Television	Factual	07/07/06
15	Nell	Assistant producer	Television	Documentary	07/07/06
16	Bob	Actor	Television	Drama/comedy	08/07/06
17	Niall	Music industry analyst	Music	–	11/07/07
18	Aggie	Features editor/ writer	Magazine	Building/ construction	03/08/06
19	Mark	Artist manager	Music	Rock/pop	14/08/06
20	Kieran	Executive producer	Television	Factual	16/08/06
21	Samuel	Freelance producer	Television	Factual	31/08/06
22	Alana	Marketing executive	Music	Rock/pop	05/09/06
23	Lachlan	Freelance sound recordist	Television	Documentary	12/09/06

Table A.1 (continued)

Interview No.	Pseudonym	Job title	Industry	Genre	Date
24	Gary	Freelance director	Television	Documentary	15/09/06
25	Lorne	Freelance camera operator	Television	Factual	18/09/06
26	Katie	Production manager	Television	Factual	18/09/06
27	Adele	Freelance producer	Television	Factual	22/09/06
28	Erik	Freelance writer	Magazine	Men's	05/10/06
29	Simon	Freelance camera operator	Television	Factual	06/10/06
30	Elizabeth	Reviews editor/ writer	Magazine	Music	13/10/06
31	Yasmin	Assistant producer	Television	Factual	31/10/06
32	Thomas	Freelance writer	Magazine	Men's	01/11/06
33	Nigel	Freelance camera operator	Television	Documentary	06/11/06
34	Elliot	Musician	Music	Jazz	23/11/06
35	Margie	Junior researcher	Television	Factual/ entertainment	24/11/06
36	Lyndon	Freelance writer	Magazine	Music	27/11/06
37	Malcolm	Executive producer/film-maker	Television	Documentary	29/11/06
38	Emily	Features editor/ writer	Magazine	Building/ construction	30/11/06
39	Ray	Record company manager	Music	Electronic/hip hop	01/12/06
40	Esther	Head of production	Television	Documentary	05/12/06
41	Lakshman	Freelance writer	Magazine	Music	06/12/06
42	Hannah	Artist manager	Music	Rock/pop	06/12/06
43	Lilith	Producer/ production manager	Television	Documentary	07/12/06
44	Irene	Reporter	Magazine	Building/ construction	08/12/06
45	Lionel	Label owner	Music	Hip hop	13/12/06
46	Norman	Freelance writer	Magazine	Music	14/12/06
47	Neville	Marketer	Magazine	Men's	15/12/06
48	Nathan	Marketing director	Music	Rock/pop	21/02/07
49	Izzy	Marketing manager	Music	Rock/pop	27/02/07
50	Reggie	Editor	Magazine	Building/ construction	02/03/07
51	Sophus	Marketing manager	Magazine	Building/ construction	08/03/07

Table A.1 (continued)

Interview No.	Pseudonym	Job title	Industry	Genre	Date
52	Harry	Series producer	Television	Entertainment	30/03/07
53	Nell	Production manager	Television	Entertainment	30/03/07
54	Jerry	PR company director	Music	Rock/pop/ electronic	25/06/07
55	Marcus	Executive producer	Television	Entertainment	10/07/07
56	Dennis	Managing director	Television	Entertainment	10/07/07
57	Iris	Commissioning editor	Television	Entertainment	30/07/07
58	Eli	Label manager	Music	Hip hop	13/02/07
59	Ally	Producer	Television	Drama	05/03/07
60	Lloyd	Head of A&R	Music	–	06/02/07
61	Tim	Musician	Music	Jazz	15/03/07
62	Keith	Musician	Music	Jazz	27/03/07
63	Ernie	Artist manager	Music	Hip hop	21/12/06

References

Adorno, T. and Horkheimer, M. (1979/1947) 'The culture industry: enlightenment as mass deception', in J. Curran, M. Gurevitch and J. Wollacott (eds) *Mass Communication and Society*, London: Edward Arnold, pp. 349–83.

Aghion, P., Howitt, P., Brant-Collett, M., and García-Peñalosa, C. (1998) *Endogenous Growth Theory*, Cambridge, MA: The MIT Press.

Aldridge, M. and Evetts, J. (2003) 'Rethinking the concept of professionalism: the case of journalism', *British Journal of Sociology*, 54(4): 547–64.

Alford, R. (1998) *The Craft of Inquiry*, Oxford: Oxford University Press.

Amabile, T. (1996) *Creativity in Context: Update to the Social Psychology of Creativity*, Boulder, CO: Westview Press.

Archer, M. (1995) *Realist Social Theory: The Morphogenetic Approach*, Cambridge: Cambridge University Press.

Arneson, R.J. (1987) 'Meaningful work and market socialism', *Ethics*, 97(3): 517–45.

——(1992) 'Is socialism dead? A comment on market socialism and basic income capitalism', *Ethics*, 102(3): 485–511.

Arthur, M.B. and Rousseau, D.M. (eds) (1996) *The Boundaryless Career: A New Employment Principle for a New Organizational Era*, Oxford: Oxford University Press.

Badiou, A. (2008) *The Meaning of Sarkozy*, London: Verso.

Banks, M. (2007) *The Politics of Cultural Work*, Basingstoke: Palgrave.

Banks, M. and Hesmondhalgh, D. (2009) 'Looking for work in creative industries policy', *International Journal of Cultural Policy*, 15(4): 1–16.

Baran, P.A. and Sweezy, P.M. (1966) *Monopoly Capital*, Harmondsworth: Penguin.

Bashford, S. (2006) 'Lifestyle survey 2006: part two', *Broadcast*, 17 November, pp. 18–20.

Bauman, Z. (1987) *Legislators and Interpreters: On Modernity, Post-Modernity and Intellectuals*, Cambridge: Polity.

——(2000) *Liquid Modernity*, Cambridge: Polity.

Beck, U. (1992) *Risk Society: Towards a New Modernity*, London: Sage.

——(2000) *The Brave New World of Work*, Cambridge: Polity.

Beck, U. and Beck-Gernsheim, E. (2002) *Individualization*, London: Sage.

Becker, H. (1951) 'The professional dance musician and his audience', *American Journal of Sociology*, 57(2): 136–44.

——(1982) *Art Worlds*, Berkeley: University of California Press.

BECTU (2009) Freelance rate-card for factual TV programmes, April 2009.Online. Available HTTP: <http://www.bectu.org.uk/filegrab/ratecard.factualtv.apr09[1].pdf> (accessed 5 January 2010).

Bell, D. (1956) *Work and its Discontents*, Boston, MA: Beacon Press.
——(1973) *The Coming of Post-Industrial Society*, New York: Basic Books.
Bellah, R., Madsen, R., Sullivan, W.M., Swidler, A. and Tipton, S.M. (2008/1985) *Habits of the Heart: Individualism and Commitment in American Life*, Berkeley: University of California Press.
Benkler, Y. (2006) *The Wealth of Networks: How Social Production Transforms Markets and Freedom*, New Haven, CT: Yale University Press.
Bennett, J.T. and Kaufman, B.E. (2007) *What Do Unions Do? A Twenty-Year Perspective*, New Brunswick, NJ: Transaction Books.
Bennett, T. (1998) *Culture: A Reformer's Science*, London: Sage.
Benson, R. and Neveu, E. (eds) (2005) *Bourdieu and the Journalistic Field*, Malden, MA: Polity.
Blair, H. (2001) ' "You're only as good as your last job": the labour process and labour market in the British film industry', *Work, Employment & Society*, 15(1): 149–69.
——(2003) 'Winning and losing in flexible labour markets: the formation and operation of networks of interdependence in the UK film industry', *Sociology*, 37(4): 677–94.
Blair, H., Grey, S. and Randle, K. (2001) 'Working in film: employment in a project based industry', *Personnel Review*, 30(2): 170–85.
Blauner, R. (1964) *Alienation and Freedom: The Factory Worker and His Industry*, Chicago, IL: University of Chicago Press.
Boltanksi, L. and Chiapello, E. (2005/1999) *The New Spirit of Capitalism*, London: Verso.
Bolton, S. (2005) *Emotion Management in the Workplace*, Basingstoke: Palgrave Macmillan.
Born, G. (2000) 'Inside television: television research and the sociology of culture', *Screen*, 41(4): 68–96.
——(2002) 'Reflexivity and ambivalence: culture, creativity and government in the BBC', *Cultural Values: Journal of Cultural Research*, 6(1–2): 65–90.
——(2004) *Uncertain Vision: Birt, Dyke and the Reinvention of the BBC*, London: Vintage.
——(2008) 'The social and the aesthetic: methodological principles in the study of cultural production', in J. Alexander and I. Reed (eds) *Meaning and Method: The Cultural Approach to Sociology*, Boulder, CO: Paradigm.
Bourdieu, P. (1984) *Distinction*, London: Routledge and Kegan Paul.
——(1993) *The Field of Cultural Production*, Cambridge: Polity.
——(1996) *The Rules of Art*, Cambridge: Polity.
——(1998) *Acts of Resistance: Against the New Myths of Our Time*, Oxford: Polity.
Bowie, A. (2003) *Aesthetics and Subjectivity*, 2nd edn, Manchester: Manchester University Press.
Braverman, H. (1974) *Labor and Monopoly Capital: The Degradation of Work in the Twentieth Century*, New York: Monthly Review Press.
Breen, G. (2007) 'Work and emancipatory practice: towards a recovery of human beings' productive capacities', *Res Publica*, 13: 381–414.
Briggs, A. (1995) *The History of Broadcasting in the United Kingdom*, vol. 5, Oxford: Oxford University Press.
Broadcast (2007) 'Indies 2007: the annual survey of the UK's independent TV producers', *Broadcast* supplement, 9 March.

Brook, P. (2009) 'In critical defence of "emotional labour": refuting Bolton's critique of Hochschild's concept', *Work, Employment & Society*, 23(3): 531–48.

Brooker, C. (2006) 'Charlie Brooker's screen burn', *The Guardian*, 9 September.

Brophy, E. and de Peuter, G. (2007) 'Immaterial labor, precarity and recomposition', in C. McKerchner and V. Mosco (eds) *Knowledge Workers in the Information Society*, Lanham, MD: Lexington.

Bruns, A. (2008) *Blogs, Wikipedia, Second Life and Beyond*, New York: Peter Lang.

Bryman, A. (2004) *Social Research Methods*, 2nd edn, Oxford: Oxford University Press.

Bunting, M. (2005) *Willing Slaves: How the Overwork Culture is Ruling Our Lives*, London: Harper Perennial.

Burawoy, M. (1979) *Manufacturing Consent*, Chicago, IL: University of Chicago Press.

Caffentzis, G. (1998) 'The end of work or the renaissance of slavery? A critique of Negri and Rifkin'. Online. Available HTTP: <http://info.interactivist.net/node/1287> (accessed 17 June 2008).

Caldwell, J.T. (2008) *Production Culture: Industrial Reflexivity and Critical Practice in Film/Television*, Durham, NC: Duke University Press.

Cantor, M. (1971) *The Hollywood Television Producer*, New York: Basic Books.

Carlyon, L. (2006) 'The issue that won't go away', *Broadcast*, 11 August: 22–23.

Castells, M. (1996) *The Rise of the Network Society*, Oxford: Blackwell.

Caves, R. (2000) *Creative Industries: Contracts between Art and Commerce*, Cambridge: Harvard University Press.

Chrisman, J. (2009) 'Autonomy in moral and political philosophy', *Stanford Encylopedia of Philosophy*. Online. Available HTTP: <http://plato.stanford.edu/entries/autonomy-moral> (accessed 18 August 2009).

Christopherson, S. (2006) 'Behind the scenes: how transnational firms are constructing a new international division of labor in media work', *Geoforum*, 37(5): 739–51.

——(2008) 'Beyond the self-expressive creative worker: an industry perspective on entertainment media', *Theory, Culture & Society*, 25: 73–95.

Christopherson, S. and van Jaarsveld, D. (2005) 'New media after the Dot.com bust', *International Journal of Cultural Policy*, 11: 77–93.

Clegg, S. and Dunkerley, D. (1980) *Organisation, Class and Control*, London: Routledge and Kegan Paul.

Clegg, S., Kornberger, M. and Pitsis, T. (2005) *Managing and Organizations: An Introduction to Theory and Practice*, Los Angeles and London: Sage.

Clough, P.T. (2008) 'The affective turn: political economy, biomedia and bodies', *Theory, Culture & Society*, 25(1): 1–22.

Cockburn, C. (1983) *Brothers: Male Dominance and Technological Change*, London: Pluto.

Coffield, F. (1999) 'Breaking the consensus: lifelong learning as social control', *British Educational Research Journal*, 25(4): 479–99.

Cohen, G.A. (1982) *History, Labour and Freedom*, Oxford: Clarendon Press.

——(1995) *Self-Ownership, Freedom and Equality*, Cambridge: Cambridge University Press.

Cohn, N. (2006) *Triksta: Life and Death and New Orleans Rap*, London: Vintage.

Couldry, N. (2000) *The Place of Media Power*, London: Routledge.

Couldry, N. and Littler, J. (2010) 'Work, power and performance: analysing the "reality" game of *The Apprentice*', *Cultural Sociology*.

Cox, G. (2005) *Cox Review of Creativity in Business: Building on the UK's Strengths,* London: Her Majesty's Stationery Office.

Creative and Cultural Skills (2004) *Britain's Creativity Challenge.* Online. Available HTTP: <http://www.creative-choices.co.uk/upload/pdf/Creativity_Challenge.pdf> (accessed 10 October 2009)

Crompton, R. (2007) 'Gender inequality and the gendered division of labour', in J. Browne (ed.), *The Future of Gender,* Cambridge: Cambridge University Press, pp. 228–49.

Csikszentmihalyi, M. (1990) *Flow: The Psychology of Optimal Experience,* New York: Harper and Row.

——(1997) *Finding Flow,* New York: Basic Books.

Cunningham, S. (2004) 'The creative industries after cultural policy: a genealogy and some preferred futures', *International Journal of Cultural Studies,* 7(1): 105–15.

Davis, H. and Scase, R. (2000) *Managing Creativity,* Buckingham: Open University Press.

DCMS (Department of Culture, Media and Sport) (1998 and 2001) *Creative Industries Mapping Document,* London: DCMS.

——(2007) *Creative Industries Economic Estimates Statistical Bulletin,* London: DCMS.

——(2008) *Creative Britain: New Talents for the New Economy,* London: DCMS.

DeFillippi, R., Grabher, G. and Jones, C. (2007) 'Introduction to paradoxes of creativity: managerial and organizational challenges in the cultural economy', *Journal of Organizational Behavior,* 28(5): 511–21.

Denning, M. (1997) *The Cultural Front,* New York and London: Verso.

——(2004) *Culture in the Age of Three Worlds,* New York and London: Verso.

Deuze, M. (2007) *Media Work,* Cambridge: Polity.

Dewey, John (1980/1934) *Art as Experience,* New York: Perigree.

Dex, S., Willis, J., Paterson, R. and Sheppard, E. (2000) 'Freelance workers and contract uncertainty: the effects of contractual changes in the television industry', *Work, Employment & Society,* 14: 283–305.

DiMaggio, P. (1977) 'Market structure, the creative process and popular culture: towards an organizational reinterpretation of mass-culture theory', *Journal of Popular Culture,* 11: 436–52.

Donald, J. (2004) 'What's new? A letter to Terry Flew', *Continuum,* 18(2): 235–46.

Donzelot, J. (1991) 'Pleasure in work', in G. Burchell, C. Gordon and P. Miller (eds) *The Foucault Effect: Studies in Governmentality,* London: Harvester.

Dowling, E. (2007) 'Producing the dining experience: measure, subjectivity and the affective worker', *Ephemera,* 7(1): 117–32.

Downey, J. (2008) 'Recognition and the renewal of ideology critique', in D. Hesmondhalgh and J. Toynbee (eds), *The Media and Social Theory,* Abingdon: Routledge, pp. 59–74.

Drucker, P. (1959) *Landmarks of Tomorrow: A Report on the New 'Post-Modern' World,* New York: Harper.

Du Gay, P. (1997) 'Introduction', in P. du Gay (ed.) *Production of Culture/Cultures of Production,* London: Sage.

Du Gay, P. and Pryke, M. (2002) 'Cultural economy: an introduction', in P. du Gay and M. Pryke (eds) *Cultural Economy,* London: Sage.

Dyer-Witheford, N. (2005) 'Cyber-Negri: general intellect and immaterial labour', in T. S. Murphy and A. Mustapha (eds) *The Philosophy of Antonio Negri: Resistance in Practice,* London: Pluto.

Edley, N. (2001) 'Analysing masculinity: interpretative repertoires, ideological dilemmas and subject positions', in M. Wetherell, S. Taylor and S.J. Yates (eds) *Discourse as Data: A Guide for Analysis*, London: Sage.

Edwards, P. and Wajcman, J. (2005) *The Politics of Working Life*, Oxford: Oxford University Press.

Ehrenreich, B. (2001) *Nickel and Dimed: On (Not) Getting By in America*, New York: Owl Books.

Eikhof, D. and Haunschild, A. (2007) 'For art's sake! Artistic and economic logics in creative production', *Journal of Organizational Behaviour*, 28: 523–38.

Ekinsmyth, C. (2002) 'Project organization, embeddedness and risk in magazine publishing', *Regional Studies*, 36(3): 229–43.

Ellerman, D. (1992) *Property and Contract in Economics*, Cambridge, MA: Blackwell.

Elliott, P. (1972) *The Making of a Television Series*, London: Sage.

——(1977) 'Media organizations and occupations: an overview', in J. Curran and M. Gurevitch (eds) *Mass Communications and Society*, London: Edward Arnold.

Elster, J. (1985) *Making Sense of Marx*, Cambridge: Cambridge University Press.

——(1986) 'Self-realization in work and politics', *Social Philosophy and Politics*, 3(2): 97–126.

Erikson, K. (1990) 'On work and alienation', in K. Erikson and S.P. Vallas (eds) *The Nature of Work*, New Haven, CT: Yale University Press.

Ezzy, D. (1997) 'Subjectivity and the labour process: conceptualising "good work"', *Sociology*, 31: 427–44.

Faulkner, R. and Anderson, A. (1987) 'Short term projects and emergent careers: evidence from Hollywood', *American Journal of Sociology*, 92: 879–909.

Faulkner, S., Leaver, A., Vis, F. and Williams, K. (2008) 'Art for art's sake or selling up?', *European Journal of Communication*, 23(3): 295–317.

Fenwick, T. (2006) 'Control, contradiction and ambivalence: skill initiatives in Canada', in L. English and J. Groen (eds) *Proceedings of the 25th Conference of the Canadian Association for the Study of Adult Education*, Toronto: York University.

Fineman, S. (1993) *Emotion in Organizations*, London: Sage.

Flew, T. (2004) 'Creativity, the "new humanism" and cultural studies', *Continuum*, 18(2): 161–78.

Florida, R. (2002) *The Rise of the Creative Class*, New York: Basic Books.

Foucault, M. (1973) *The Order of Things: An Archaeology of the Human Sciences*, New York: Vintage.

Frank, R.H. and Cook, P.J. (1996) *The Winner-Take-All Society*, London: Penguin.

Fraser, N. (1989) *Unruly Practices: Power, Discourse and Gender in Contemporary Social Theory*, Minneapolis: University of Minnesota Press.

——(1997) *Justice Interruptus: Critical Reflections on the 'Postsocialist' Condition*, New York: Routledge.

Fraser, N. and Honneth, A. (2003) *Redistribution or Recognition?* London: Verso.

Freeman, R. and Medoff, J. (1985) *What Do Unions Do?* New York: Basic Books.

Friedman, A. (1977) *Industry and Labour: Class Struggle at Work and Monopoly Capitalism*, London: Macmillan.

Frith, S. (1981) *Sound Effects: Youth, Leisure and the Politics of Rock'n'Roll*, London: Pantheon Books.

——(1996) *Performing Rites*, Oxford: Oxford University Press.

Frith, S. and Horne, H. (1987) *Art Into Pop*, London: Methuen.

Froebel, F., Heinrichs, J. and Kreye, O. (1980) *The New International Division of Labour*, Cambridge: Cambridge University Press.

Frow, J. (1995) *Cultural Studies and Cultural Value*, New York: Oxford University Press.

——(1996) *Time and Commodity Culture*, New York: Oxford University Press.

Gall, G. (1997) 'The changing relations of production; union derecognition in the UK magazine industry', *Industrial Relations Journal*, 29: 151–62.

Gans, H. (1980) *Deciding What's News*, New York: Vintage Press.

Gardner, H., Csikszentmihalyi, M. and Damon, W. (2001) *Good Work. When Excellence and Ethics Meet*, New York: Basic Books.

Garnham, N. (1990) *Capitalism and Communication*, London: Sage.

——(2000a) 'Afterword: the cultural commodity and cultural policy', in S. Selwood (ed.) *The UK Cultural Sector*, London: Policy Studies Institute.

——(2000b) *Emancipation, the Media, and Modernity*, Oxford: Oxford University Press.

——(2005) 'From cultural to creative industries: an analysis of the implications of the "creative industries" approach to arts and media policy making in the United Kingdom', *International Journal of Cultural Policy*, 11(1): 15–29.

Gibson, C. (2003) 'Cultures at work: why "culture" matters in research on the "cultural" industries', *Social & Cultural Geography*, 4(2): 201–15.

Giddens, A. (1984) *The Constitution of Society*, Cambridge: Polity.

Gill, R. (2002) 'Cool, creative and egalitarian? Exploring gender in project-based new media work in Europe', *Information, Communication & Society*, 5(1): 70–89.

——(2007) Technobohemians or the New Cybertariat? Amsterdam, Institute of Network Cultures.

Gill, R. and Pratt, A. (2008) 'In the social factory? Immaterial labour, precariousness and cultural work', *Theory, Culture & Society*, 25(7–8): 1–30.

Gitlin, T. (1983) *Inside Prime Time*, New York: Basic Books.

——(1994) *Inside Prime Time*, London: Routledge.

Golding, P. and Murdock, G. (2005) 'Culture, communications and political economy', in J. Curran and M. Gurevitch (eds) *Mass Media and Society*, 4th edn, London: Arnold.

Goldman, W. (1983) *Adventures in the Screen Trade*, New York: Warner Books.

Gomberg, P. (2007) *How To Make Opportunity Equal: Race and Contributive Justice*, Malden, MA: Blackwell.

Gorz, A. (1999) *Reclaiming Work*, Cambridge: Polity.

Gouldner, A.W. (1979) *The Future of Intellectuals and the Rise of the New Class*, New York: Seabury Press.

Gramsci, A. (1971) *Selections from the Prison Notebooks*, London: Laurence and Wishart.

Gray, L.S. and Seeber, R.L. (eds) (1996) *Under the Stars: Essays on Labor Relations in Arts and Entertainment*, Ithaca, NY: ILR Press.

Green, F. (2006) *Demanding Work: The Paradox of Job Quality in the Affluent Economy*. Princeton, NJ: Princeton University Press.

Gregg, M. (2010) 'On Friday night drinks: workplace affect in the age of the cubicle', in M. Gregg and G.J. Seigworth (eds) *The Affect Theory Reader*, Durham, NC: Duke University Press.

Grindstaff, L. (2002) *The Money Shot: Trash, Class, and the Making of TV Talk Shows*, Chicago, IL: University of Chicago Press.

Guardian (2009) 'The BBC's top 50 highest-paid senior managers', 29 October, guardian.co.uk. Online. Available HTTP: <http://www.guardian.co.uk/media/table/2009/oct/29/bbc-senior-managers-pay> (accessed 9 December 2009).

Guilford, J.P. (1950) 'Creativity', *American Psychologist*, 5: 444–54.

Hall, P. and Soskice, F. (eds) (2001) *Varieties of Capitalism*, Oxford: Oxford University Press.

Hallin, D.C. and Mancini, P. (2004) *Comparing Media Systems: Three Models of Media and Politics*, Cambridge: Cambridge University Press.

Hardt, M. and Negri, A. (2000) *Empire*, Cambridge: Harvard University Press.

Harré, R. (1979) *Social Being*, Oxford: Blackwell.

Hartley, J. (ed.) (2005) *Creative Industries*, Oxford: Blackwell.

Harvey, D. (1989) *The Condition of Postmodernity*, Oxford: Blackwell.

——(2003) *The New Imperialism*, New York: Oxford University Press.

Hauser, A. (1999) *The Social History of Art*, London: Routledge and Kegan Paul.

Heelas, P. (2002) 'Work ethics, soft capitalism and the "Turn to Life" ', in P. du Gay and M. Pryke (eds) *Cultural Economy*, London: Sage.

Hemmings, C. (2005) 'Cultural theory and the ontological turn', *Cultural Studies*, 19(5): 548–67.

Hesmondhalgh, D. (2006) 'Bourdieu, the media and cultural production', *Media, Culture & Society*, 28: 211–32.

——(2007) *The Cultural Industries*, 2nd edn, London: Sage.

——(2008) 'Cultural and creative industries', in T. Bennett and J. Frow (eds) *The Sage Handbook of Cultural Analysis*, London: Sage.

——(2009) 'Digitalisation, music and copyright', in P. Jeffcut and A.C. Pratt (eds) *Creativity and Innovation in the Cultural Economy*, Abingdon and New York: Routledge.

——(2010a) 'Normativity and social justice in the analysis of creative labour', *Journal of Cultural Research*, 14(2).

——(2010b) 'Media industry studies, media production studies', in J. Curran (ed.) *The Media and Society*, London: Bloomsbury.

Hesmondhalgh, D. and Baker, S. (2008) 'Creative work and emotional labour in the television industry', *Theory, Culture & Society*, 25(7–8): 97–118.

Hesmondhalgh, D. and Toynbee, J. (eds) (2008) *The Media and Social Theory*, Abingdon: Routledge.

Hess, J. (1999) *Reconstituting the Body Politic: Enlightenment, Public Culture and the Invention of Aesthetic Autonomy*, Detroit, MI: Wayne State University Press.

Hirsch, P.M. (1972) 'Processing fads and fashions: an organization-set analysis of cultural industry systems', *American Journal of Sociology*, 77: 639–59.

Hochschild, A.R. (1983) *The Managed Heart: Commercialization of Human Feeling*, Berkeley: University of California Press.

——(1989) 'Reply to Cas Wouters's review essay on *The Managed Heart*', *Theory, Culture & Society*, 6: 439–45.

——(1997) *The Time Bind: When Work Becomes Home and Home Becomes Work*, New York: Metropolitan Books.

——(2003) *The Commercialization of Intimate Life: Notes from Home and Work*, Berkeley: University of California Press.

——(2008) 'Feeling around the world', *Contexts*, 7(2): 80.

Hodson, R. (2001) *Dignity at Work*, Cambridge: Cambridge University Press.

Holmes, B. (2004) 'Artistic autonomy and the communication society', *Third Text*, 18(6): 547–55.

Holt, J. and Perren, A. (2009) *Media Industries: History, Theory and Method*, Oxford: Wiley Blackwell.

Honneth, A. (2004) 'Organized self-realization: some paradoxes of individualization', *European Journal of Social Theory*, 7(4): 463–78.

Howkins, J. (2001) *The Creative Economy*, London: Allen Lane.

Hughes, E. (2003) 'Careers', in D. Harper and H.M. Lawson (eds) *The Cultural Study of Work*, New York: Rowman & Littlefield.

Huws, U. (2006–7) 'The spark in the engine: creative workers in a global economy', *Work Organisation, Labour & Globalisation*, 1: 1–12.

Illouz, E. (2007) *Cold Intimacies: The Making of Emotional Capitalism*, Cambridge: Polity.

Jenkins, H. (2006) *Convergence Culture*, New York: New York University Press.

Jensen, R. (1999) *The Dream Society – How the Coming Shift from Information to Imagination Will Transform Your Business*, New York: McGraw Hill.

Jones, C. (1996) 'Careers in project networks: the case of the film industry', in M.B. Arthur and D.M. Rousseau (eds) *The Boundaryless Career: A New Employment Principle for a New Organizational Era*, Oxford: Oxford University Press.

Jones, J. (2008) 'The art market according to Damien Hirst'. Online. Available HTTP: <http://www.guardian.co.uk/artanddesign/jonathanjonesblog/2008/oct/28/damien-hirst> (accessed 30 December 2008).

Jones, P. (2004) *Raymond Williams's Sociology of Culture*, Basingstoke: Palgrave Macmillan.

Kamenka, E. (1972) *The Ethical Foundations of Marxism*, London and Boston: Routledge and Kegan Paul.

Keat, R. (2000) *Cultural Goods and the Limits of the Market*, London and New York: Routledge.

——(2009) 'Antiperfectionism, market economies and the right to meaningful work', *Analyse und Kritik*, 31(1): 121–38.

Kellaway, L. (2008) 'No way to manage a bleating luvvie', *Financial Times*, January 20. Online. Available HTTP: <http://www.ft.com/cms/s/0/14f63d30-c5d9–11dc-8378-0000779fd2ac.html?nclick_check=1> (accessed 24 February 2008).

Kennedy, H. (2010) 'Net work: the professionalization of web design', *Media, Culture & Society*, 32: 187–203.

Knights, D. (2000) 'Autonomy retentiveness! Problems and prospects for a post-humanist feminism', *Journal of Management Inquiry*, 9(2): 173–85.

Knights, D. and McCabe, D. (2003) 'Governing through teamwork: reconstituting subjectivity in a call centre', *Journal of Management Studies*, 40: 1587–1619.

Knights, D. and Willmott, H. (1989) 'Power and subjectivity at work: from degredation to subjugation in social relations', *Sociology*, 23: 535–58.

Koestler, A. (1964) *The Act of Creation*, Oxford, Macmillan.

Korczynski, M. (2002) *Human Resource Management in Service Work*, Houndmills: Palgrave.

Kunda, G. (1992) *Engineering Culture*, Philadelphia, PA: Temple University Press.

——(1995) 'Engineering culture: control and commitment in a high-tech corporation', *Organization Science*, 6(2): 228–30.

Laing, D. (2003) 'Musicians' unions', in J. Shepherd, D. Horn, D. Laing, P. Oliver and P. Wicke (eds) *Continuum Encyclopedia of Popular Music of the World*, London and New York: Continuum.

Lampel, J., Lant, T. and Shamsie, J. (2000) 'Balancing act: learning from organizing practices in cultural industries', *Organization Science*, 11(3): 263–9.

Lampel, J., Shamsie, J. and Lant, T. (2006) 'Towards a deeper understanding of cultural industries', in J. Lampel, J. Shamsie and T. Lant (eds), *The Business of Culture: Strategic Perspectives on Entertainment and Media*, Mahwah, NJ: Lawrence Erlbaum, pp. 3–14.

Landry, C. and Bianchini, F. (1995) *The Creative City*, London: Demos.

Larson, M.S. (1977) *The Rise of the Professions*, Berkeley, CA: University of California Press.

Lasch, C. (1980) *The Culture of Narcissism*, London: Abacus.

Lash, S. and Urry, J. (1994) *Economies of Signs and Space*, London: Sage.

Layder, D. (1997) *Modern Social Theory: Key Debates and New Directions*, London: UCL Press.

Lazzarato, M. (1996) 'Immaterial labor', in P. Virno and M. Hardt (eds) *Radical Thought in Italy*, Minneapolis: University of Minnesota Press.

Leadbeater, C. and Oakley, K. (1999) *The Independents*, London: Demos.

Leitch, S. (2006) *Prosperity for All in the Global Economy – World Class Skills*, London: Her Majesty's Stationery Office.

Lewis, S. (2003) 'The integration of paid work and the rest of life: is post-industrial work the new leisure?', *Leisure Studies*, 22: 343–55.

Lloyd, R. (2006) *Neo-Bohemia: Art and Commerce in the Post-Industrial City*, London: Routledge.

Löfgren, O. (2003) 'The new economy: a cultural history', *Global Networks*, 3(3): 239–54.

McChesney, R.W. (1999) *Rich Media, Poor Democracy*, Urbana and Chicago: University of Illinois Press.

MacDonald, I. (2003) *The People's Music*, London: Pimlico.

McGregor, D. (1960) *The Human Side of Enterprise*, New York: McGraw-Hill.

MacIntyre, A. (1981) *After Virtue: A Study in Moral Theory*, London: Duckworth.

——(1984) *After Virtue: A Study in Moral Theory*, 2nd edn, Notre Dame, IN: Notre Dame University Press.

McKercher, C. and Mosco, V. (eds) (2007a) *Knowledge Workers in the Information Society*, Lanham, MD: Lexington Books.

——(2007b) 'Introduction', in C. McKercher and V. Mosco (eds) *Knowledge Workers in the Information Society*, Lanham, MD: Lexington Books.

McKinlay, A. and Quinn, B. (2007) 'Remaking work, management and industrial relations, c.1979–2000', *Historical Studies in Industrial Relations*, 23(4): 155–80.

McKinlay, A. and Smith, C. (eds) (2009) *Creative Labour: Working in the Creative Industries*, Basingstoke: Palgrave Macmillan.

McMaster, B. (2008) *Supporting Excellence in the Arts: From Measurement to Judgement*, London: DCMS.

McRobbie, A. (1998) *British Fashion Design: Rag Trade or Image Industry?* London: Routledge.

——(2002a) 'Clubs to companies: notes on the decline of political culture in speeded up creative worlds', *Cultural Studies*, 16: 516–31.

——(2002b) 'From Holloway to Hollywood: happiness at work in the new cultural economy?', in P. du Gay and M. Pryke (eds) *Cultural Economy*, London: Sage.

Marx, K. (1959/1844) *Economic and Philosophic Manuscripts of 1844*. Online. Available HTTP: <http://www.marxists.org/archive/marx/works/download/pdf/Economic-Philosophic-Manuscripts-1844.pdf> (accessed 10 January 2010).

——(1990/1867) *Capital*, vol. 1, London: Penguin.

Marx, K. and Engels, F. (1974/1845) *The German Ideology: Including Theses on Feuerbach and Introduction to the Critique of Political Economy*, London: Lawrence and Wishart.

Maslow, A. (1987/1954) *Motivation and Personality*, 3rd edn, New York: Harper and Row.

Maxwell, R. (2001) 'Why culture works', in R. Maxwell (ed.) *Culture Works*, Minneapolis: University of Minnesota Press.

Mayer, V., Banks, M.J. and Caldwell, J. (eds) (2009) *Production Studies: Cultural Studies of Media Industries*, Abingdon: Routledge.

Menger, P.M. (1999) 'Artistic labour markets and careers', *Annual Review of Sociology*, 25: 541–74.

——(2002) *Portrait de l'artiste en travailleur: métamorphoses du capitalisme*, Paris: Seuil.

——(2006) 'Artistic labour markets: contingent work, excess supply and occupational risk management', in V.A. Ginsburgh and D. Throsby (eds) *Handbook of the Economics of Art and Culture*, Amsterdam: Elsevier.

Merton, R.K. and Kendall, P.L. (1946) 'The focused interview', *American Journal of Sociology*, 51: 541–57.

Miège, B. (1989) *The Capitalization of Cultural Production*, New York: International General.

——(2000) *Les industries du contenu face a l'ordre informationnel*, Grenoble: Presses universitaires de Grenoble.

Miller, A. (1976/1949) *Death of a Salesman*, New York: Viking-Penguin.

Miller, T. (2009) 'Can natural Luddites make things explode or travel faster? The new humanities, cultural policy studies, and creative industries', in J. Holt and A. Perren (eds) *Media Industries: History, Theory and Method*, Oxford: Wiley Blackwell.

Miller, T., Govil, N., McMurria, J., et al. (2005) *Global Hollywood 2*, London: British Film Institute.

Mills, C.W. (1951) *White Collar: The American Middle Classes*, Oxford: Oxford University Press.

Morini, C. (2007) 'The feminization of labour in cognitive capitalism', *Feminist Review*, 87(1): 40–59.

Mosco, V. (1989) 'Déjà vu all over again?', *Society*, 26(5): 31–8.

——(1996) *The Political Economy of Communication*, London: Sage.

Mosco, V. and McKercher, C. (2008) *The Laboring of Communication: Will Knowledge Workers of the World Unite?* Lanham, MD: Lexington Books.

Mosco, V. and Wasko, J. (eds) (1983) *The Critical Communications Review: Volume I: Labor, the Working Class and the Media*, Norwood, NJ: Ablex Publishing.

Muirhead, R. (2004) *Just Work*, Cambridge: Harvard University Press.

Murdock, G. (2000) 'Reconstructing the ruined tower: contemporary communications and questions of class', in J. Curran and M. Gurevitch (eds) *Mass Media and Society*, London: Arnold.

——(2003) 'Back to work: cultural labor in altered times', in A. Beck (ed.) *Cultural Work: Understanding the Cultural Industries*, London: Routledge.

Murdock, G. and Golding, P. (1977) 'Capitalism, communication and class relations', in J. Curran, M. Gurevitch and J. Woollacott (eds) *Mass Communication and Society*, London: Edward Arnold.

Murdock, G. and Golding, P. (2005) 'Culture, communications and political economy', in J. Curran and M. Gurevitch (eds) *Mass Media and Society*, 4th edn, London: Arnold.

Murphy, James B. (1993) *The Moral Economy of Labor: Aristotelian Themes in Economic Theory*, New Haven, CT, and London: Yale University Press.

Neale, S. (1990) 'Questions of genre', *Screen*, 31(1): 45–66.

Neff, G., Wissinger, E. and Zukin, S. (2005) 'Entrepreneurial labor among cultural producers: "cool" jobs in "hot" industries', *Social Semiotics*, 15: 307–34.

Negus, K. (1992) *Producing Pop*, London: Edward Arnold.

——(1999) *Music Genres and Corporate Cultures*, London: Routledge.

Negus, K. and Pickering, M. (2004) *Creativity, Communication and Cultural Value*, London: Sage.

Neilson, B. and Rossiter, N. (2005) 'From precarity to precariousness and back again: labour, life and unstable networks', *Fibreculture*, 5. Online. Available HTTP: <http://journal.fibreculture.org/issue5/neilson_rossiter.html> (accessed 10 May 2006).

NESTA (2008) *Beyond the Creative Industries: Mapping the Creative Economy in the United Kingdom*, London: NESTA.

Nixon, S. (2003) *Advertising Cultures*, London: Sage.

Nixon, S. and Crewe, B. (2004) 'Pleasure at work? Gender, consumption and work-based identities in the creative industries', *Consumption, Markets and Culture*, 7(2): 129–47.

Nozick, R. (1974) *Anarchy, State and Utopia*, New York: Basic Books.

Nussbaum, M. and Sen, A. (eds) (1993) *The Quality of Life*, Oxford: Oxford University Press.

O'Connor, J. (2007) *The Creative and Cultural Industries: A Review of the Literature*, London: Creative Partnerships.

O'Doherty, D. and Willmott, H. (2001) 'Debating labour process theory: the issue of subjectivity and the relevance of poststructuralism', *Sociology*, 35(2): 457–76.

Palmer, G. (ed.) (2008) *Exposing Lifestyle Television: The Big Reveal*, Aldershot: Ashgate.

Parijs, P.V. (1997) *Real Freedom for All: What (If Anything) Can Justify Capitalism?* Oxford: Oxford University Press.

Pateman, C. (1988) *The Sexual Contract*, Stanford, CA: Stanford University Press.

Paterson, R. (2001) 'Work histories in television', *Media, Culture & Society*, 23: 495–520.

Peiperl, M., Arthur, M. and Anand, N. (eds) (2002) *Career Creativity: Explorations in the Remaking of Work*, Oxford: Oxford University Press.

Peters, T. (1997) *The Circle of Innovation*, New York: Random House.

Peterson, R.A. and Anand, N. (2004) 'The production of culture perspective', *Annual Review of Sociology*, 30: 311–34.

Pratt, A.C. (2000) 'The cultural industries: a cross national comparison of employment in Great Britain and Japan', in K. Kawasaki (ed.) *Cultural Globalisation and the Cultural Industries: Experiences in the UK and Japan*, Tokyo: Ministry of Education, Science and Culture.

Prichard, C. (2002) 'Creative selves? Critically reading creativity in management discourse', *Creativity and Innovation Management*, 11(4): 265–76.

Purnell, J. (2005) 'Making Britain the world's creative hub', keynote speech presented to the Institute of Public Policy Research, London, June. Online. Available HTTP: <http://theideafeed.com/bookreviews/?p=31> (accessed 10 October 2009).

Rawls, J. (1971) *A Theory of Justice*, Cambridge, MA: Harvard University Press.

Ray, L. and Sayer, A. (1999) 'Introduction', in L. Ray and A. Sayer (eds) *Culture and Economy After the Cultural Turn*, London: Sage.

Read, J. (2003) *The Micro-Politcs of Capital*, Albany: SUNY Press.

Reed, M. (2000) 'The limits of discourse analysis in organizational analysis', *Organization*, 7(3): 524–30.

Regev, M. (2002) 'The "pop-rockization" of popular music', in D. Hesmondhalgh and K. Negus (eds) *Popular Music Studies*, London: Arnold.

Reich, R. (1991) *The Work of Nations*, London: Simon & Schuster.

Research Centre for Television and Interactivity (2003) *Inside the Commissioners: The Culture and Practice of Commissioning at UK Broadcasters – Executive Summary*, Glasgow: Research Centre for Television and Interactivity.

Ritzer, G. (1994) *The McDonaldization of Society*, Thousand Oaks, CA: Pine Forge Press.

Robbins, A. (1992) *Awaken the Giant Within*, New York: Free Press.

Rogers, C.R. (1954) 'Toward a theory of creativity', *ETC: A Review of General Semantics*, 11: 249–60.

Rose, N. (1999) *Powers of Freedom: Reframing Political Thought*, Cambridge: Cambridge University Press.

Ross, A. (2000) 'The mental labour problem', *Social Text*, 18: 1–32.

——(2003) *No-Collar: The Humane Workplace and its Hidden Costs*, New York: Basic Books.

——(2008) 'The new geography of work: power to the precarious?', *Theory, Culture & Society*, 25: 31–49.

——(2009) *Nice Work If You Can Get It: Life and Labor in Precarious Times*, New York: New York University Press.

Rössler, B. (2007) 'Work, recognition, emancipation', in B. Van Den Brink and D. Owen (eds) *Recognition and Power: Axel Honneth and the Tradition of Critical Social Theory*, Cambridge: Cambridge University Press, pp. 135–61.

Ryan, B. (1992) *Making Capital from Culture*, Berlin/New York: Walter de Gruyter.

Rycroft, C. (1995) *A Critical Dictionary of Psychoanalysis*, 2nd edn, London: Penguin.

Said, E. (1994) *Representations of the Intellectual*, London: Vintage Books.

Saundry, R., Antcliff, V. and Stuart, M. (2006) ' "It's more than who you know" – networks and trade unions in the audio-visual industries', *Human Resource Management Journal* 16(4): 376–92.

Saundry, R., Stuart, M. and Antcliff, V. (2007) 'Broadcasting discontent – freelancers, trade unions and the Internet', *New Technology, Work & Employment*, 22: 178–91.

Sayer, A. (1992) *Method in Social Science*, 2nd edn, London and New York: Routledge.

——(1995) *Radical Political Economy: A Critique*, Oxford: Blackwell.

——(2000) *Realism and Social Science*, London: Sage.

——(2005) *The Moral Significance of Class*, Cambridge: Cambridge University Press.

——(2007) 'Dignity at work: broadening the agenda', *Organization*, 14(4): 565–81.

——(2009) 'Contributive justice and meaningful work', *Res Publica* 15:1–16.

Schatzki, T.R. (1996) *Social Practices*, Cambridge: Cambridge University Press.

Schlesinger, P. (1978) *Putting Reality Together*, London: Routledge.

——(2007) 'Creativity: from discourse to doctrine', *Screen*, 48(3): 377–87.

——(2009) 'Creativity and the experts: New Labour, think tanks and the policy process', *International Journal of Press/Politics*, 14(3): 3–20.

Schor, J.B. (1992) *The Overworked American: The Unexpected Decline of Leisure*, New York: Basic Books.

Schumpeter, J.A. (1994/1943) *Capitalism, Socialism and Democracy*, London: Routledge.

Schwartz, A. (1982) 'Meaningful work', *Ethics*, 92: 634–46.

Scott, A. (2005) *On Hollywood: The Place, The Industry*, Princeton, NJ: Princeton University Press.

Sennett, R. (1998) *The Corrosion of Character: The Personal Consequences of Work in the New Capitalism*, New York: Norton.

——(2008) *The Craftsman*, London: Allen Lane.

Sharma, U. and Black, P. (2001) 'Look good, feel better: beauty therapy as emotional labour', *Sociology*, 35(4): 913–31.

Shaw, P. (2004) 'Researching artists' working lives', *Arts Research Digest*, 30, special research feature lift-out.

Shorthose, J. and Strange, G. (2004) 'A more critical view of the creative industries: production, consumption and resistance', *Capital and Class*, 84: 1–7.

Sibeon, R. (2004) *Rethinking Social Theory*, London: Sage.

Sillitoe, A. (1994/1959) *Saturday Night and Sunday Morning*, London: Flamingo.

Simpson, D. (2009) 'After the goldrush', *The Guardian*, G2 section, 16 October, p. 11.

Skillset (2006) *Employment Census 2006: The Results of the Sixth Census of the Audio Visual Industries*, London: Skillset.

——(2009) *Profile of the Publishing Sector*, London: Skillset.

Slater, D. and Tonkiss, F. (2001) *Market Society*, Cambridge: Polity.

Smith, C. (1998) *Creative Britain*, London: Faber and Faber.

Snowdon, G. (2009) 'How work changed in the noughties', *The Guardian, Work* supplement, 19 December, p. 3.

Sohn-Rethel, A. (1978) *Intellectual and Manual Labour*, London: Macmillan.

Sosteric, M. (1996) 'Subjectivity and the labour process: a case study in the restaurant industry', *Work, Employment & Society*, 10(2): 297–318.

Stahl, M. (2006a) 'Reinventing certainties', unpublished thesis, University of California, San Diego.

——(2006b) 'Non-proprietary authorship and the uses of autonomy: artistic labor in American film animation, 1900–2004', *Labor: Studies in Working Class History of the Americas*, 2(4): 87–105.

——(2008) 'Sex and drugs and bait and switch: rockumentary and the new model worker', in D. Hesmondhalgh and J. Toynbee (eds) *The Media and Social Theory*, Abingdon: Routledge.

Steinberg, R.L. and Figart, D.M. (1999) 'Emotional labor since "The Managed Heart"', *Annals of the American Academy of Political and Social Science*, 561: 8–26.

Stinchcombe, A. (1959) 'Bureaucratic and craft administration of production', *Administrative Science Quarterly*, 4: 168–87.

Sussman, G. and Lent, J. (eds) (1998) *Global Productions: Labor in the Making of the "Information Society"*, Cresskill, NJ: Hampton.

Swift, A. (2001) *Political Philosophy*, Cambridge: Polity.

Taylor, P., Mulvey, G., Hyman, J. and Bain, P. (2002) 'Work organisation, control and the experience of work in call centres', *Work, Employment & Society*, 16(1): 133–50.

Taylor, R. (2001) 'The future of employment relations', Swindon: Economic and Social Research Council.

Taylor, S. (2001) 'Locating and conducting discourse analytic research', in M. Wetherell, S. Taylor and S.J. Yates (eds) *Discourse as Data: A Guide for Analysis*, London: Sage.

Terranova, T. (2000) 'Free labor: producing culture for the digital economy', *Social Text*, 63: 33–50.

——(2004) *Network Culture: Politics for the Information Age*, London: Pluto Press.

Thompson, J.B. (1990) *Ideology and Modern Culture*, Cambridge, Polity.

——(1995) *The Media and Modernity*, Cambridge: Polity.

Thompson, P. and McHugh, D. (2009) *Work Organisations: A Critical Approach*, 4th edn, Basingstoke: Palgrave Macmillan.

Throsby, D. (2008) 'The concentric circles model of the cultural industries', *Cultural Trends*, 17(3): 147–64.

Tilgher, A. (1931) *Work, What It Has Meant to Men Through the Ages*, London: G.G. Harrap.

Tilly, C. (1998) *Durable Inequality*, Berkeley: University of California Press.

Towse, R. (1992) 'The labour market for artists', *Richerce Economiche*, 46: 55–74.

Toynbee, J. (2000) *Making Popular Music: Musicians, Creativity and Institutions*, London: Arnold.

——(2001) 'Creating problems: social authorship, copyright and the production of culture', *Pavis Papers in Social and Cultural Research 3*, Milton Keynes: Open University Press.

Tuchman, G. (1978) *Making News*, New York: Free Press.

Tunstall, J. (1993) *Television Producers*, Abingdon: Routledge.

——(ed.) (2001) *Media Occupations and Professions: A Reader*, Oxford: Oxford University Press.

Ursell, G. (2000) 'Television production: issues of exploitation, commodification and subjectivity in UK television labour markets', *Media, Culture & Society*, 22(6): 805–25.

——(2006) 'Working in the media', in D. Hesmondhalgh (ed.) *Media Production*, Maidenhead: Open University Press/The Open University.

Warde, A. (2002) 'Production, consumption and cultural economy', in P. du Gay and M. Pryke (eds) *Cultural Economy*, London: Sage, pp. 185–200.

——(2005) 'Consumption and the theory of practice', *Journal of Consumer Culture*, 5(2): 131–54.

Wasko, J. (1994) *Hollywood in the Information Age*, Cambridge: Polity.

Weber, M. (1930/1903) *The Protestant Ethic and the Spirit of Capitalism*, translated by Talcott Parsons, London: Allen & Unwin.

——(1978/1900) 'Bureaucracy', in M. Weber, *Economy and Society*, Berkeley: University of California Press, pp. 956–1005.

Webster, F. (2005) *Theories of the Information Society*, 2nd edn, London: Routledge.

Weeks, K. (2007) 'Life within and against work', *Ephemera*, 7(1): 233–49.

Weil, S. (1974/1951) *La condition ouvriere*, Paris: Gallimard.

Wetherell, M., Taylor, S. and Yates, S.J. (2001) *Discourse Theory and Practice: A Reader*, London: Sage.

Whyte, W. (1956) *The Organization Man*, New York: Simon and Schuster.

Williams, R. (1965/1958) *Culture and Society*, London: Chatto & Windus.
——(1965/1961) *The Long Revolution*, Harmondsworth: Penguin.
——(1981) *Culture*, London: Fontana.
——(1989) *What I Came to Say*, London: Hutchinson Radius.
Willis, J. and Dex, S. (2003) 'Mothers returning to television production work in a changing environment', in A. Beck (ed.) *Cultural Work: Understanding the Cultural Industries*, London: Routledge.
Willmott, H. and Knights, D. (1989) 'Power and subjectivity at work: from degradation to subjugation in social relations', *Sociology*, 23(4): 535–58.
Wilson, S. (2002/1955) *The Man in the Gray Flannel Suit*, New York: Four Walls Eight Windows.
Winnicott, D.W. (1982) *Play and Reality*, London: Routledge.
Wittel, A. (2001) 'Toward a network sociality', *Theory, Culture & Society*, 18(6): 51–76.
——(2004) 'Culture, labour and subjectivity: for a political economy from below', *Capital & Class*, 84: 11–29.
Witz, A., Warhurst, C. and Nickson, D. (2003) 'The labour of aesthetics and the aesthetics of organization', *Organization*, 10(1): 33–54.
Wolff, J. (1987) 'The ideology of autonomous art', in R. Leppert and S. McClary (eds) *Music and Society*, Minneapolis: University of Minnesota Press.
——(1993) *The Social Production of Art*, 2nd edn, Basingstoke: Macmillan.
Woodmansee, M. (1994) *The Author, Art and the Market: Re-reading the History of Aesthetics*, New York: Columbia University Press.
Work Foundation (2007) *Staying Ahead: The Economic Performance of the UK's Creative Industries*, London: Work Foundation.
Wouters, C. (1989) 'The sociology of emotions and flight attendants: Hochschild's *The Managed Heart*', *Theory, Culture & Society*, 6: 95–123.
Wray, R. and Gibson, O. (2008) 'Leave talent spotting to the suits, says EMI boss'. *Guardian Unlimited*, 28 February. Online. Available HTTP: < http://music.guardian.co.uk/news/story/0,2260355,00.html > (accessed 10 October 2009).
Wright, E.O. (1997) *Class Counts: Comparative Studies in Class Analysis*, Cambridge: University of Cambridge Press.
Zaretsky, E. (1976) *Capitalism: The Family and Personal Life*, New York: Harper and Row.
——(2005) *Secrets of the Soul: A Social and Cultural History of Psychoanalysis*, New York: Vintage.
Zoellner, A. (2009) 'Professional ideology and programme conventions: documentary development in independent British television production', *Mass Communication & Society*, 12(4): 503–36.

Index

Page numbers in *Italics* represent tables; page numbers in **Bold** represent figures.